The Loves

of

George Bernard Shaw

✤✤✤✤✤✤✤✤✤✤

C. G. L. Du Cann

✤✤✤✤✤✤✤✤✤✤

ARTHUR BARKER LIMITED

20 NEW BOND STREET LONDON WI

PRINTED IN GREAT BRITAIN
BY EBENEZER BAYLIS AND SON, LTD.
THE TRINITY PRESS, WORCESTER, AND LONDON

'The best in this kind are but shadows, and the worst are no worse if imagination amend them.'

Shakespeare: A Midsummer Night's Dream

'To one biographer I am a Saint and an Idealist; to another a Don Juan with a woman in every theatre . . . My life has been a hell, but because I have kept the lid on, nobody has peeped into it . . . My trifling, and lying, and ingrained treachery and levity with women. . . .'

Shaw: On Himself

'Women have been a ghastly nuisance in my life. Do you think impotent people as we are called, are sexless? We fall for women more passionately than the so-called normal creatures. Nature can be very cruel . . . I was inadequately equipped for love.'

G.B.S. at 90: Conversation with Stephen Winsten

'If you have any doubts as to my normal virility dismiss them from your mind. I was not impotent; I was not sterile; I was not homosexual; and I was extremely though not promiscuously susceptible. I never associated sexual intercourse with delinquency. I associated it always with delight.'

G.B.S. at 74: Letter to Frank Harris

'It was one of the wittiest knaues that euer God made . . . His pen was sharp-pointed lyke a poinyard; no leafe he wrote on but was lyke a burning glasse to set on fire all his readers . . . No houre but hee sent a whole legion of deuils into some heard of swine or other; nere a line of his but was able to make a man dronken with admiration. His sight pearst like lightning into the entrailes of all abuses.'

Thos. Nasshe on Aretino

Acknowledgement

The extracts from Mrs Bernard Shaw's letter to
T. E. Lawrence on pages 173–177 are reproduced
by permission of the Trustees of the Will of Mrs
Bernard Shaw

CONTENTS

7

LIST OF ILLUSTRATIONS

9   A*

PREFACE

AN OLD proverb declares that good wine needs no bush, or as modern people would say, no boost. Upon that analogy, it may be thought that a good book needs no preface.

But good wine, like anything else that is good, certainly does need recommendations, because mere merit, as we all know from personal experience, gets nothing and no one anywhere in this world. The brightest star cannot shine in a sky thickly clothed in black nimbus clouds. Shaw himself firmly believed in the necessity for prefaces; and unlike his biographers he never wasted them in mere compliments or civilities or advertisements of his sources as though readers were suspicious Scotland Yard detectives demanding: 'But where did you get this, and that, from?'

A preface to the point: that is to say, one having something to say and plainly saying it, is the best of the prefatory kind. In my particular case, I have to appear for the defence.

A GRAVE INDISCRETION

That is necessary because when in 1961 I published a series of ten articles, originally christened by their onlie begetter, The Love-Lives of G.B.S., in a number of newspapers such as the *Evening Standard* (London), *The Irish Times*, the *Glasgow Citizen*, the *Liverpool Post*, and fifteen others abroad, a cry of despair rent the welkin. (Incidentally, if *The Star* had not been murdered for money the series would have appeared there, where G.B.S. began his journalistic career, for that very lively paper was then being edited by that most enterprising and prescient of editors, Mr. Ralph McCarthy, then setting the pace in London evening-journalism.)

That cry of despair came from a fanatical fringe of Shavians whom Bernard Shaw would have contemptuously dismissed as he dismissed Shakespeare-fanatics as Bardolators. Their bleatings were understandable even by me. My children had been re-baptized and re-clothed in sensational headlines, introductions, and cross-headings so that they looked like juvenile delinquents instead of my respectable, young persons.

In cold fact, these articles were neither sensational nor shocking, except to prudes and prigs of the last generation; and insofar as they might seem to be either, not I, but G.B.S. was responsible. If the great man had been alive, I am confident that he would have approved them as strictly accurate, and not going beyond his own admissions and confessions. Far from pleading 'Guilty' to any charge of scandal, Shaw—who declared himself no Shavian as Marx declared himself no Marxist—would have pleaded not even 'Guilty' but certainly 'More Guilty'. Using a favourite retort, he would have said to me exactly what he said of a much earlier writing of mine, Mr. Shaw as Shakespeare-Thief in J. T. Grein's *Arts Gazette*: namely, that I was merely deducing eggs from seeing bits and pieces of egg-shell scattered about.

But bits and pieces scattered about in various places over a long period are one thing. Those same bits and pieces snapped up and stuck together by an Autolycus are no longer that same thing. There is a sense in which, as we know, the whole is much greater—and much more impressive—than its once-scattered parts. So it was in this case. What the outraged Shaw-worshippers could easily swallow as small unconsidered trifles, taken as a presented whole at one gulp, stuck in their gullets and nearly choked them.

To an extent, my sympathies were with my critics. They urged what was incontestible: that there were other and nicer, nobler Shaws: Shaw the playwright, Shaw the humorist, Shaw the humanist, Shaw the economist, Shaw the Fabian and Shaw the this-that-and-the-other. (But who's a-denying of it, Betsy Prig?) They said that to take one side only of him, and that the least respect-worthy, was to distort and to falsify. They added that my heterodoxy was particularly distressing and unfortunate because I had managed to gain a wide audience, most of whom might not know the saintlier sides of the Master and would conclude from my articles that he was a bad lot, like myself.

Useless for me to retort that anyone reading my work with attention, could not possibly arrive at this dreadful conclusion. I was given firmly to understand that it would have been all right if I had written on my subject in a learned review of limited high-brow circulation; or if I had lectured upon it to the elect to the number of fourteen or so who regularly attend meetings of The Shaw Society. But owing to my invincible stupidity and intractable obstinacy this point failed to penetrate at all.

THE OLD SHAVIAN AND YOUNG SHAVIENNE

Amongst my censurers was a distinguished and close friend of Shaw: a bedridden old gentleman of ninety-odd who begged me to visit him. I went. After a light tea and heavy rebuke, he emphasized the latter by telling me how strongly a woman-relative of Shaw's disapproved of my behaviour. I said how sorry I was to hurt anybody's feelings; but remembering Shaw's eggs, I remarked platitudinously but consolingly that one could not make an omelette without breaking those frail objects. Moreover, could I be expected to be more tender of Shavian family susceptibilities than the great man had shown himself? When I began further justification, my auditor reminded me of his great age and of many other matters claiming his limited time, so I humbly took my leave. And there an end.

Next, a perspicacious young Shavienne, while admitting that her hero, not I, was the chief culprit and saying she would not accept Shaw upon himself except in his unpublished diaries (on which I had and have drawn), still reproached me. She declared that there were 'only two love-affairs in any true sense'. She informed me that Shaw 'actually gave up all sexual relations for the last fifty-four years of his life'. She added sapiently enough: 'When one aspect of a person is dealt with in isolation the average reader does not make allowance for the inevitable distortion.' Her final blow was: 'I have heard many references to Shaw as an old rake since your articles appeared.'

As to these accusations, I do not myself see that *l'amitié amoureuse* is not as truly a love-affair as any physical sex-congress. Next, it was the first fifty-four years rather than the last fifty-four, which were most in question. As to distortions: they have their uses and values. Does anyone complain of an El Greco distortion; or a Daumier or a Forain? Or of Shakespeare's timeless distortion of the well-behaved historical Macbeth? Or of Charles Dickens's distortion of the esteemed Yorkshire schoolmaster Shaw into Mr. Wackford Squeers? The distortion of the caricature may serve the cause of truth better than the exact likeness of the camera.

Further, no author can be held responsible for the erratic movement of his readers' various minds: it is enough burden to be responsible for his own mind. And I should have thought that in his incessant and incorrigible philanderings, having regard to their period, Shaw would be better described as an ever-young rake rather than an old one.

A JUSTIFIED SINNER

Sensible persons will dismiss these seemingly-serious and solemnly-made objections by idolators as essentially frivolous and foolish. For my part—and this is justification enough—I preferred to write about what had not been explored before: about Shaw the male coquette, Shaw the actress-exploiter, Shaw the lover, Shaw who was Joey the Clown, Shaw the sinner and Shaw the Private Self. Enough—and more than enough—has been written about Shaw the Graven Image, Shaw the Public Figure, Shaw the Writer, and Shaw The Great.

To understand Shaw as he really was, not as he is fabled to be by the Shaw Personality Cult (of which he was the first and most distinguished member) you cannot leave out of account the failings, the foibles, the follies and the faults of this great, unusual man. The surviving letters to Alice Lockett, his first love, here reviewed for the first time, throw a flood of light on the mentality

14

of Shaw in his twenties, and upon that young Shaw as a lover. They are a rich mine to be quarried for the student of psychology —especially the psychology of a young male intellectual fighting an early sex-battle, and they are reminiscent, as I show, of the youthful Charles Dickens in like case.

More: these Lockett letters shed illumination upon Shaw's love-affairs; notably upon the horrid Jenny Patterson sex-story, of which—unfortunately—we never hear the woman's side. They may persuade us that she was not the only quarrelsome and difficult party in the ding-dong battle that raged so long and painfully between Shaw and his Jenny.

Here is, too, new unpublished material upon Charlotte, his wife, calculated to give us a better understanding of why 'she was always discontented' as her husband complained, though she had no less reason to be, than Carlyle's wife. Again, it is high time that more credit was given to such figures in Shaw's womanizing as Florence Farr, Annie Besant, and Mrs. Patrick Campbell than either Shaw or his biographers-to-date have been willing to concede.

'ALL HAVE SINNED—'

Yet again, if I have sinned in the past or continue to sin in the present, and hope not to repent in the future, I sin in the company of the more orthodox, the authorized and conventional biographers. Indeed for readers to ask for, and to expect, 'the truth, the whole truth and nothing but the truth' is manifestly absurd. None can tell the whole truth about anything or anyone though it has been suggested that truth, like murder, will out—even in an affidavit duly sworn or in the witness-box with the Almighty and a kissed Bible lending combined assistance. But even then, there are those who suspect that it emerges imperfectly. All men are liars said the Psalmist, thereby getting nearer to the whole truth in that burst of candour than anyone else before or since; and if he had added the qualifying phrase 'more or less' he would have got still nearer. He made no exceptions for biographers, not even his own.

As to the standard Shaw-biographers: what can be falser, as

contrasted with so much of the whole truth as is positively known, than the authorized, justly-esteemed monumental works of the American professor, Archibald Henderson? In one, you find Alice Lockett, Jenny Patterson, Erica Cotterill and other sirens conspicuous by their entire absence; May Morris is merely mentioned; Florence Farr is summarily dismissed in a footnote paragraph and her relations with Shaw disguised in the vague, ambiguous phrase 'an intimate friend'.

Or take Frank Harris's work, sponsored by Shaw himself. The North Pole and the Equator are not more different nor further apart than Henderson and Harris. But what need is there of further instances? All are true, and all are false, like almost all human utterance. Of all these so-different portraits of Shaw, including mine, the last word is with Shakespeare: 'The best in this kind are but shadows and the worst are no worse if imagination amend them.' Indeed, his readers' imagination is the writer's best friend.

HORRORS OF OLD AGE

In old age Shaw, deafish and slightly dotty as he described both himself and his Charlotte, was a decaying Dr. Samuel Johnson surrounded by half-Boswells who mercilessly recorded the last maggot-infested, half-rotted fruits that fell from the ancient tree. Drivelling and doting, he was a living refutation of his own Man and Superman where, for the Ancients of Days, as the years lengthened the intellects strengthened. Nothing so heart-rending as that outworn Shaw machine breaking down has been known since a similar such spectacle imperishably recorded:

'From Marlborough's eyes, the tears of dotage flow,
And Swift expires—a driveller and a show.'

Unfortunately this was Shaw's fate. As an old man, having no future but the hope of posthumous fame (which is never enough) inevitably he meandered about his past, like a phantom wandering in a wilderness of tombs. Anxious to justify himself in the eyes of posterity and to protect his reputation from his own follies now that there was no Charlotte to do it as she used to do, the aged Shaw repeated and contradicted himself; took pains to destroy evidence; made mistakes as well as deliberate distortions; and at times was like Shadwell as seen by Dryden, seldom deviating into sense. It is a sad spectacle of fallen intellectual greatness on which there is no need to dwell. Yet it is necessary to warn the reader not to treat all of Shaw's later, and often contradictory and inaccurate, accounts of himself and his women-acquaintances as reliable. But in his last *Will and Testament*, reverting to his truer and former self, he declared that his conduct and character need not be whitewashed.

QUEEN JEZEBEL'S DOGS

Hence no need of whitewash here. This book is not intended merely for the coterie of Shavians, though they will certainly devour it eagerly—even if the fiercer critics amongst them do that only in the spirit of the dogs that ate Queen Jezebel by the walls of Jezreel. It is primarily for a much wider audience, namely, the general public. That audience is concerned not with reading for specialist-study but with reading for pleasure, incidentally picking up painlessly such information as goes joyously hand-in-hand with that continuous interest which creates pleasure.

Like all other artists, authors excrete their work essentially—though not purely—for the pleasure of themselves and such audiences as they may attract. They live to please; therefore they must please to live. They can only do that by being interesting; interest is the one paramount quality, unlike literary style, narrative skill, characterization and other subsidiaries. Upon that point, I sustain myself by the reflection that the sex-adventures of G.B.S. (for sex-adventures they are, even when sublimated from physical congress to the intellectual sphere) are, in themselves, intrinsically interesting. For if any story be really a good one, it may be marred, but cannot be ruined, by lack of skill in the narrator. It can stand up by itself on its merits.

Therefore I leave this book now to do just that. Of its success or failure in that regard, I must, like all my tribe of Naphtali whose mission in life it is 'to give goodly words' and whose badge like Shylock's is sufferance, leave the world to judge either by reading it with pleasure or flinging it aside in disgust.

C. Du C.

I

YOUNG IRISH IMMIGRANT

'I have a mother; I haven't seen her for years; and I don't much care if I never see her. It was through her that I came to be what I am'

—'Cashel Byron's Profession': Chap. IV, 65

I

FEW HUMAN situations are more grievously pathetic than the plight of a poverty-depressed adolescent, conscious of crudity, ignorance and inexperience, contemplating his future life and livelihood through the Iron Curtain of doubt and uncertainty.

Faith and hope may whisper at times. But he knows, only too well, that like the rude forefathers of the hamlet in Gray's immortal *Elegy*, his opportunities are circumscribed by his obscurity and impecuniosity. More fortunate contemporaries have been to public schools or universities or both. Money and influence are shaping their careers. The path to honour, wealth and success has been smoothed for them. But, lacking that friend useful above all other friends, namely hard cash—even the resilient young Disraeli lamented the lack of 'a few rascal counters'—he, ill-taught and debarred from prospects of further education, sees himself in evil case indeed.

Such was the plight of a young Irishman named George Bernard

Shaw in the year 1876, when, despairing of any worthwhile future in his native Dublin, he decided to emigrate to England.

II

Aged twenty, he was younger than his years. Nor was he at this period of life personally prepossessing. Tall, thin almost to emaciation, with flaming red hair, and a pallid complexion, awkward in manner, abnormally shy, nervous and uncertain of himself in company, he was decidedly unattractive to the stranger observing him. Even in this Victorian age, when in general, and not least in their home circles, males were regarded as the more important sex by their female relations, his mother and two sisters had very little regard or affection for him. As the son—in fact the only son—of his father, George Carr Shaw, a failure in life whom the family had deserted, this is perhaps not surprising.

His mother, born Lucinda Elizabeth Gurly, an Irish gentlewoman, might well rue the misalliance which had produced him and his sisters. She had sacrificed her home and her very real prospects of comfort and luxury for life by her marriage to a weakling and drunkard nearly twice her age. A woman of character and resolution and a talented musician, she had deliberately deserted the husband she had vowed to love, honour and obey, and whom she had taken for better for worse, for richer for poorer till death did them part. She had put the Irish Sea between him and her, taking their two daughters Agnes and Lucy with her to London from Dublin.

At that time the boy 'Sonny', as he (later to be world-famous by both his initials and his full name of George Bernard Shaw) was called, had been left behind in Dublin with his father. Over four years elapsed before he copied his mother's and sisters' example by deserting his father and Dublin.

Why he remained behind so long, and why he ultimately took this plunge, is not clear. Shaw who has told us so much of himself and his family with apparent candour, relating discreditable facts with seeming gusto, does not really tell us why he left as, and when, he did leave. There is no story of any quarrel with his father. No reason is given why he did not go with his mother and sisters upon their departure. He was no 'mother's boy' although an only son. There is no evidence that the mother wished for his presence nor that he longed for hers; rather the contrary may be pretty safely presumed.

Conforming to the Irish convention, as powerful with young Irish men and women today as then, the convention of deserting their country for personal advantage, in later life Shaw rationalized his action by denigrating Ireland in general and Dublin in particular:

'My business in life could not be transacted in Dublin out of an experience confined to Ireland. I had to go to London . . . London was the literary centre for the English language and for such artistic culture as the realm of the English language (in which I proposed to be King) could afford. Every Irishman who felt that his business in life was on the higher planes of the cultural professions . . . felt that his first business was to get out of Ireland. I had the same feeling.'

And worse:

'A certain flippant futile derision and belittlement that confuses the noble and serious with the base and ludicrous seems to be peculiar to Dublin.'

He tells us that failure, poverty, obscurity and the ostracism and contempt arising from these misfortunes were all that Dublin offered 'to the enormity of my unconscious ambition'.

It is impossible to accept these high-faluting alleged reasons because we know—also from himself—that he had not yet discovered 'his business in life', and had no idea that his destiny was literature. When he left Dublin in his twentieth year, he had neither found himself nor his work in life, and was only too miserably conscious of his inability to see his way either in life or livelihood.

Just before he came to England—the very day his Dublin employment ended—his elder sister Agnes had died at Ventnor, in the Isle of Wight, of tuberculosis. It may be—though he does not say so—that the loss of this burden upon his mother's straitened resources influenced her to receive him. To do that, he gave up his clerical post in a Dublin estate agency where he had, like Dickens before him, started livelihood as an office-boy—a status disguised by the name of junior clerk. He had begun at eighteen shillings a month—the standard rate of that day—and risen by competence, assiduity and attention to his work to the post of cashier and a salary of £84. This was, so far as it went, success.

Outwardly, he was a humdrum competent clerk-cashier, destined to mediocrity in life and livelihood. Inwardly, outside office life, he was, as will later be seen, very different.

Quite suddenly he gave his firm of Uniacke Townshend & Co. a month's notice. In return, they gave him a testimonial which, so different a picture does it draw of him from his later life, is worth quoting. So, too, in his letter of resignation, the immediate cause for which appears to have been that he had taken offence at his employer Townshend placing his nephew in authority over him. His letter of resignation is extant. It runs:

'Dear Sir—I beg to give you notice that at the end of the month I shall leave your office. My reason is that I object to receive a salary for which I give no adequate value. Not having enough to do, it follows that the little I have done is not well done: when I ceased to act as Cashier I anticipated this and have since become satisfied that I was right. Under these circumstances I prefer to discontinue my service and remain,

Very truly yours,

G. B. Shaw.'

It is the priggish letter of a hurt and offended hobble-de-hoy adopting an attitude of pride and independence which in reality he could ill-afford. Plainly it is a counter-offensive. It is said that the employer offered him an increased salary to remain—which seems highly unlikely if he was really under-employed as he averred. However, the testimonial given to him later by the firm is generous and highly creditable to both sides. It is as follows:

'Mr. George Shaw served in our office from 1st November 1871 to 31st March 1876 when he left at his own desire. He entered as a youth and left us having attained the position of Cashier. He is a young man of great business capacity, strict accuracy, and was thoroughly reliable and trustworthy. We parted from him with regrets and shall always be glad to hear of his welfare,

Uniacke Townshend & Co.,
Land Agents.'

Could any employer—in days before trade-unions, too—say more?

At the time, the young Shaw was proud of, and flattered by, this testimonial, for which his father had asked. But, later in life, he sneered at his 'attempt to earn an honest living' as that 'sin against my nature'. The office-desk had become for him 'the doom of shabby gentility', not a step towards power and wealth; and he emphatically declared in his play *Misalliance* after a long and bitter passage upon a cashier's work: 'Of all the damnable waste of human life that ever was invented, clerking is the very worst.'

Unfortunately for the truth of this strong-sounding exaggeration, one can do nothing with human life except spend it perforce, and it is mere matter of opinion as to whether any particular activity or passivity is 'waste' of it. Shaw, in some ways, benefited from this early contact with business realities: he learned to work hard and regularly at a routine; he learned, too, something of the value and care of money. These are two important mental acquisitions, which the best public schools and universities often fail to teach.

At all events, he was now free. Leaving his father, whom Shaw's young friend Edward McNaulty visited and found at this time 'a lonely sad little man ready to chat at length about his lost family', he left Dublin for London. Arrived there he went straight from Euston in a four-wheeler cab to Chelsea, where his mother and sister lived. The large house in which they probably only had rooms was No. 13 Victoria (now Netherton) Grove.

If you endeavour to find No. 13 in that road today, as Shavian pilgrims sometimes do try to find Shaw's first home in England, you will be defeated. There is no No. 13 today; and it is pretty certain that the ugly brick building of St. Stephen's Hospital (formerly a Poor-Law Institution) occupies its site. But from the pleasant (and large) Victorian houses still existing opposite, one can form a very good idea of the architecture and pleasantness of the old No. 13, surrounded as the neighbourhood was by nurseries and market-gardens.

Incidentally, Arnold Bennett lived in that same road when he arrived in London from Staffordshire—a curious coincidence—and it figures in his novel of 1911, noticed by Shaw in his preface to his *Immaturity*. Bennett's novel is *A Great Man*; he, Bennett, called the road Alexandra Grove and he lived with his friends the Marriotts at No. 6.

Arrived at his mother's home it is said that Shaw was received without enthusiasm. That may be believed. The mother was a disappointed, disillusioned woman who felt bitterly about the boy's father and had just buried her elder daughter. Neither she nor Lucy had seen 'Sonny' for five years, nor had they corresponded, and the boy had become a gawkily provincial youth on the threshold of manhood. To them, undomesticated as both of them were, for both were totally immersed in the musical world, and essaying to make their livings therefrom, the advent of this male must have been a disturbing problem.

What fresh demands would not his presence in the home make upon them? What would he do to help or hinder?

There was little enough money at command to keep up pretensions of gentility to which both women were accustomed, and in which both believed. The deserted father and husband was regularly sending over to London a pound a week. Mrs. Carr Shaw as she called herself always, though cut out of her Aunt Ellen's will because of her disapproved marriage, had received from another member of the family a legacy of £4,000—a substantial sum in those days. Then there were the exiguous and precarious earnings of herself as a music-teacher, and her daughter as an occasional musical performer upon the stage.

It was not as if either mother or sister were fond, or proud, of this young man. 'My mother and I lived together but there was hardly a word between us' says Shaw. She was indeed, as he said, a disillusioned woman. As to sister Lucy: she published later in life some disagreeable booklets of the advice-to-the-young order which show her in no amiable light. Supposed to be the most promising and brilliant one of the family, her marital and musical careers alike ended in failure and frustration.

But what manner of young man was this who had so suddenly and unpredictably invaded London and his mother's home?

III

Like all of us, he was the predetermined product of his heredity and environment, and as yet had not had the chance to modify their effects—so far as this can be done—by the exercise of conscious will-power.

On both sides he had highly-respectable forbears; in the Shaw family there was even a living baronet—Sir Robert Shaw! But his father had notably failed in life. One of fifteen children, at first he had been provided for by a clerkship in the Dublin Courts of Justice. When the post was abolished, he commuted his pension and purchased a partnership in a wholesale corn-merchant's business.

On the strength of this he proposed marriage to Miss Lucinda Elizabeth Gurly, a girl whose 'expectations' came chiefly from her Aunt Ellen, who was bringing her up to make a good marriage with the utmost strictness and in entire ignorance of anything but the 'accomplishments' of a gentlewoman. Tired of home-discipline, this girl seems to have jumped at the Shaw marriage offer in spite of the disparity in years and the fact that he had a squint.

Aunt Ellen was furious. Lucinda was warned that her suitor was unsuitable, and in particular that George 'drank'. She taxed her lover with this aspersion: he reassured her by saying that he had a horror of drink (which was true) and that he was a teetotaller (which was false).

She married him—and forfeited her expectations. They spent their honeymoon at Liverpool (of all unromantic places), and there disillusion began. The bride found in their bedroom a whole army of empty bottles in a cupboard. Horrified, she promptly bolted.

But she, as quickly, returned. For, accosted by men at the docks, this outside world of which she knew nothing intimidated her. They went back to Dublin to live, and there—within four years—their three children, Lucinda Frances Carr (invariably called Lucy); Elinor Agnes (otherwise Yuppy); and George Bernard (Sonny) were born.

'Technically speaking,' the son wrote of his mother, 'I should say she was the worst mother conceivable;' but he admitted that she was incapable of unkindness to any person whatsoever. It would be true to say that she had no taste or talent for wifehood or motherhood or even home-making. Hers was a loveless marriage and an unloving home—a harsh environment indeed for an acutely sensitive and abnormal child.

Once G.B.S. went much further in dishonouring his parents. He asserted that he had been begotten after a brawl when his father was fuddled with drink. Whether that was true or untrue, a son should never have said that, for what good could this black-guarding of his parents do?

The household might be poor and graceless, but it could afford sluts and slatterns as servants—the poorer class of servants—costing in Ireland then only three shillings a week with board and bed. The children were abandoned entirely to the servants, 'utterly unfit to be trusted with three cats much less three children', says Shaw. But for a time there was a visiting governess, Miss Caroline Hill, who was paid by the hour and who taught him well.

Later in life he confided to the famous actress Ellen Terry—of whom more hereafter—this cry of anguish: 'Oh, a devil of a child-hood, Ellen, rich only in dreams, frightful and loveless in realities.'

No wonder he became his self-sufficient and self-reliant self. No wonder that he regarded the mother-child relationship with an entire absence of sentimentality in later years.

The day came when the furtive drinking habits of the father became obvious to the very young child. Walking together, George Carr Shaw jocosely threatened to throw the boy into the adjacent canal. His mind stimulated by fear, the child regarded his father with newly-opened eyes and on returning home he went to his mother.

'Mamma,' he said awed and troubled, 'I think papa is drunk.'

Impatiently the wife and mother turned away from her child exclaiming:

'When is he ever anything else?'

That drunkenness, secret and shameful, affected the child for the rest of his life, making him a fanatical total abstainer.

'My mother was embittered because she expected money to be left to her and it didn't happen, and we all suffered for it,' wrote her son in after-life.

But she might have been much less bitter had her marriage been a happy one and her choice a man whom she could respect, even if she could not love him. In the most vital decision of her life the proud, cold, hard woman had made a grievous mistake. Her aunt had proved right and herself wrong; and her humiliation must have been gall and wormwood to her. Perhaps she might have been more domesticated and given her children a happy home with regular well-cooked meals if the man of the family had been different.

Meanwhile the drinking habits of Shaw the elder caused his family to be ostracized by their numerous relations. Social life was at an end so far as they were concerned. But Shaw was not merely a drunkard; he was an incompetent man of business with a business that rapidly went downhill.

In these circumstances it is not surprising that the boy's education should be sacrificed. To supplement Miss Hill's tuition the boy's clerical uncle, Mr. Carroll, taught him Latin, which proved useless. Then at the age of ten or so he was sent as a day boy to the Wesley Connexional School in Dublin, where he was usually at or near the bottom of the class in spite of his brains.

IV

But change is the first law of life. Suddenly the futile, incompetent father was redeemed from his drinking habits. When he fell down in a fit on his own doorstep, he was so alarmed by the occurrence and by what his doctor told him that he reformed at once. He never relapsed.

It was a remarkable cure. For George Carr Shaw had little will-power, and terror of death seldom lasts long. In this case it lasted for the rest of his life.

A revolution about the same time also happened to the mother as well as the father. Suddenly she found her *métier* in life in music. A strange Dublin character, George John Vandaleur Lee, leader of a Dublin orchestra and a teacher of music and voice-production by unorthodox methods of his own invention, discovered that she possessed a mezzo-soprano voice of pure quality. He set himself to bring her out by teaching her 'The Method'; taught her to sing, and gave her parts to play locally in opera. Rehearsals were held in the Shaw home and soon young Sonny, though he had no executive gift, whistled and sang from morning to night picking up the musical classics by ear.

The musical partnership between Lee and Mrs. Shaw prospered from every point of view. Soon Lee, whose invalid brother died, proposed that he and the Shaws should share a house in a more select street. This was agreed. The *maison à trois* worked well, and no scandal arose. At times, when he was not at sea, Dr. Walter Gurly, Mrs. Shaw's brother and a ship's doctor, joined the household.

A Rabelaisian, irreverent sceptic, this uncle's conversation and anecdotes did a great deal to kill the boy's instinctive reverence. By now his mother was professing a vague temporary atheism, and young Shaw, who had suffered much from enforced churchgoing, left off the detested habit at ten years of age. The father declared the Bible to be 'the damnedest parcel of lies' to the boy himself.

His mother's passionate absorption in her music left young George Bernard more to himself than ever. He got into the habit of visiting the National Gallery in Dublin, until he knew all the pictures intimately. Meanwhile he was devouring books: Scott, Dickens, the *Arabian Nights* and many others.

His clergyman uncle having complained that the boy was learning nothing at the Wesleyan School and had forgotten the Latin he had been taught, Lee—not the boy's father—took the matter in hand. At his suggestion the youngster was sent instead to the Central Model School.

This angered young Shaw deeply. For this was a Roman Catholic School, and Catholics were considered, by the then Protestant ascendancy, low-class at that date in Ireland. The Shaws were Protestants and gentlepeople. Young Shaw at this date was an arrant snob, and he was mortified and resentful as all children are when they feel de-classed. In about seven months he was in open rebellion and had to be taken away.

Even as a man, he could not refrain from showing his humiliation in his *Sixteen Self-Sketches.*

From the Catholic School he was sent to the English Scientific and Commercial Day School until, at between fourteen and fifteen, he went to work in the land-estate office as an office-boy.

And that was the whole of George Bernard Shaw's formal academic education, except for some slight attendance in the holidays at a 'very private school' near Dalkey, kept by the Halpens. What he did there is unknown. This small amount of formal education—by most standards utterly inadequate, and far less than the average for a lad of his station and family—bears a remarkable resemblance to that of Charles Dickens.

But if his formal education was poor indeed, his informal education, again like Dickens's, was the very reverse. He had picked up a most remarkable knowledge of what genuinely appealed to him: music, art and literature. Shaw's father might truthfully have said what John Dickens, Charles's Micawber and prodigal father, said of his son when a person asked where that great genius had been educated:

'Why, sir—ha, ha!—he may be said to have educated himself.'

Is it any wonder that in later life Bernard Shaw, contrasting himself and his achievements with those of his public school and University competitors, was contemptuous of academic education? Perhaps at first the grapes were sour, but later he realized that the seeds within those grapes were often unproductive, especially in the arts.

The close correspondence of his early upbringing with that of Dickens is remarkable. Just having finished my book *The Love Lives of Charles Dickens*, I could not help noticing a number of these striking similarities. Shaw was absolutely Dickens-saturated from childhood. (As a schoolboy he invented tales of an imaginary friend Lobjoit whose unusual name he had got out of some obscure Dickens piece, though I knew a Sir William Lobjoit as a former 'Controller of Horticulture' at the Ministry of Agriculture and told him his title was a blasphemous one, and I felt certain Shaw must have realized the close correspondence with Dickens himself.) Later I found that he had; in *A Secret Kept for 80 Years*.

Of that 'secret' he writes: 'It was to me what the blacking warehouse was to Dickens.' And out-Dickensing Dickens, who could not bear to reveal that heart-rending and snobbish secret of his for fifty years even to his wife, Shaw avers that he could not mention his for eighty years, not even to *his* wife. And what was that unmentionable secret?

Merely that himself, the 'son of a Protestant merchant-gentleman and feudal "downstart"', should go to school with hosts of lower-class Catholic children; sons of petty shopkeepers and tradesmen; which was "inconceivable from the Shaw point of view" '.

He lost caste by going there. His father, he tells us, was as much ashamed of it as he was, and was anxious—even at the cost of £4 a quarter school fees—that he should be restored to Protestant gentility at the 'Scientific and Commercial'. George Bernard remained at this next school less than two years, leaving at fifteen to start work. There his aristocratic pretensions received a further blow. As an office-boy he could call himself a junior clerk, as office-boys invariably do, just as girl-typists always call themselves 'secretaries'. But at the office he was always called 'Shaw', *tout court*, though the young articled, fee-paying gentlemen around him had to be addressed as 'Mister'.

But it was not only in having a disgraceful prodigal father, an unloved and unloving mother, and a long-cherished guilty snobbish boy-secret that Shaw resembled his great predecessor in English literature. There was yet another, perhaps more important, if less picturesque and striking parallel. The university of Dickens, where he read avidly in youth, was the Library of the British Museum, and the same place came in due course to stand in the same relation to Bernard Shaw.

Both, of course, were ardent social reformers in the extremest degree. Dickens would have killed the poor with kindness; Shaw would have exterminated their poverty with socialistic and communistic legislation. Dickens was the forerunner of Shaw, much in the same way that John the Baptist was the forerunner of Jesus Christ.

V

It is a thousand pities that Shaw never wrote his autobiography. He would have produced a masterpiece, and we have too few masterpieces in that particular line of literature. Not that we lack autobiographic material about him, for this colossal egoist was always writing about himself, both in fact and in fiction, for understandably he was more interested in himself than in anybody else— except twice in his life when he fell passionately in love, and once when he married.

Fortunately, however, we are not entirely dependent upon his biographers. Oscar Wilde said that, of a man's disciples, it was always Judas Iscariot who wrote his biography; but on the whole Shaw was fortunate in his three or four biographers. They wrote from affection and admiration though not as yes-men. And they were fortunate in their subject, for, without writing his autobiography, Shaw supplied—indeed, was always supplying—a tremendous amount of biographical material.

But it took provocation to get it out of him. His cast of mind was controversial, and by habit it became more so in later life. When, therefore, such well-known writers as Winston Churchill, and Frank Harris, and obscurities such as Professor Bolger, wrote about Shaw himself, he instantly rose to the bait, and poured out contradictions, explanations, additions and every possible flood of biographical material that he could recall that was to the point.

Almost, I think, it would be possible to write a biography of Shaw out of his own revelations, so profuse are they.

It is from his self-sketches that we are enabled to realize what happened when his father stopped drinking and his mother took up with Lee. It was neither what cynics nor what sentimentalists would expect, for she neither (according to her son) committed adultery with Lee nor became reconciled with her husband.

Lee, it is said, was more enamoured of Lucy than of her mother, but except as an aid to becoming a *prima donna* Lucy Shaw disliked Lee. The boy did not altogether like him either; he did not readily forgive the influence that had sent him to the wrong school. And we may hazard a guess that George Carr Shaw tolerated this paying cuckoo in the nest, because he was too futile and too little regarded to count in the matter.

Frank Harris, the friend, critic, and later biographer of Shaw, as one would suspect from his full-blooded temperament, strongly suspected that Lee and Mrs. Shaw were lovers. So did Archibald Henderson, Shaw's first full-scale biographer. So did Professor Bolger, to whom Shaw wrote a good deal of his family history. But Shaw dealt trenchantly with this idea.

Lee, he declared, was not a scoundrel who seduced Mrs. Shaw. 'A man who could have done that could have seduced the wooden Virgin at Nuremburg,' declared G.B.S. 'My mother could have boarded and lodged the Three Musketeers and D'Artagnan for twenty years without discovering their sex, and they would no more have obtruded it upon her than they would have ventured to smoke in her drawing-room.'

Less convincingly, St. John Ervine, one of Shaw's best biographers, in supporting this hyperbole, declared that Lee's love was the larynx. No doubt; but a man may have more loves than one. However, one feels that if he had the slightest belief in the truth of his mother's adultery, Shaw would have coolly proclaimed it as emphatically as he denied it. In the pursuit of objective truth Shaw was not restrained by considerations of good taste, and he never spared either father or mother in his latter-day criticisms of their dead selves. Nor did he always spare himself—to do him justice.

It is impossible not to see Lee otherwise than as a benefactor to the Shaw family, a benefactor who received little gratitude from any of them. G.B.S. acknowledged that Lee gave his mother in his 'Method' a Cause and a Creed to live for—a gift, indeed. Lee bought a cottage at Dalkey in Dublin and presented it to her in the days of his Irish prosperity. That cottage with its view (which Shaw eulogized as incomparable to the end of his life) did much to awaken the boy's aesthetic sense so far as natural beauty was concerned. Financially, and in all other ways, Lee was a god-send to the Shaws in Dublin.

But his influence and his advanced heteredox views aroused the boy's curiosity. G.B.S. got from him his habit of sleeping with open windows, eating brown bread, and disbelieving in doctors. He learned to speak in public by using Lee's method of voice-production.

The *maison-à-trois* did not last. Lee became convinced that his destiny of fame and fortune in the musical world lay in London; well as he was doing in Dublin, he would do still better there. He went; and soon was living in Park Lane; a short-lived success.

Mrs. Shaw followed, if not him, at any rate, his example. She, too, left for London to follow the profession of music, and to make Lucy an operatic success. Shaw says the father was left by his family 'for the very solid reason that he could not support them, and that life with him had absolutely no prospects for them. In doing so they took off his shoulders a burden he was unable to bear and glad to discard'.

He had changed. Cured of drink, he was now 'the most inoffensive of mortals'.

Shaw's excuse for the desertion does not altogether convince.

As he sent part-maintenance of £1 a week, a part-burden (for which he received nothing) remained. There are more things in a shared life than 'prospects'. And it was the earners who deserted as their earning-powers promised increase. And George Carr Shaw's age was over sixty-two when his son left him.

Shaw believes—or affects to believe—that being without his family was the happiest time in his father's life: 'no more Lee, no more wife, no more grown-up children'. He lived in respectable Dublin lodgings, died there and was buried in Mount Jerome cemetery. When his younger daughter Agnes died, he did not—perhaps he could not afford to—attend her funeral. The family—including his only son—do not seem to have attended his.

His death indeed (like Lee's), according to their son, 'did not disturb her (the wife and mother) one jot', though her daughter Agnes's had done so. A fine wife for any man!

'She had no respect for him in the common sense of the word as he could do nothing dramatically interesting or effective,' says the son. 'And she took him as he was in the kindly Irish fashion . . . she was not in the least bitter.'

She also left him as he was, in an unkindly un-Irish fashion. He had disappointed her expectations, and, as her son explains, she did not forgive. . . .

It is a miserable story. But its special importance is that it illustrates a dreadful and cardinal defect in the emotional make-up of the son, which was probably inherited from his shrewd granite-hard mother. Neither could be cruel; both could be kind; but in the intimate relations they both could be blind and indifferent to others, to a quite incredible extent.

George Bernard Shaw, in later years, was to provide some startling examples of this in his relations with various women.

He was hardly able to do anything else but defend his mother's desertion. For after all he copied the bad example—and profited in the long run by doing so. So did the world. And success and profit justify all otherwise questionable actions.

VI

What did the young Irish emigrant look like physically, at this period of his leaving his country for not his country's good but his own?

There is a photograph of his head and shoulders taken at this period, and he (or another?) wrote underneath it 'G.B.S., newly translated from Dublin to London: Immature and apparently an arrant prig.' The hair of the head is long, parted in the middle and plastered down on both sides; the eyes look a trifle unlike each other in shape; the nose is well-shaped, the mouth neither ascetic nor voluptuous, the ears protuberant, the forehead good. There are the sparse beginnings of a soft beard and moustache of a somewhat undernourished-looking character.

The expression of the face is serious, calm, meditative; perhaps a trifle sad. There is nothing Mephistophelean about it, and nothing of Joey the Clown. It might be the face of a young man contemplating Holy Orders as his career in life; the face of a predestined curate with intellectual leanings.

In the photograph you can neither see that the hair is red nor what the colour of the eyes is. Apparently an arrant prig? Well, perhaps. Immature? Unquestionably.

It is noteworthy, considering after-developments, that this alleged arrant prig is conventionally dressed. The flat collar is starched, the tie correctly knotted in the large fashion of the day, and the braided surtout such as every educated young gentleman of that day wears.

And so—over to London, as a modern Samuel Pepys accustomed to television jargon might say.

But just before we follow him there, it may well be asked: What was the love-life of this young man of twenty before he left Ireland? Few young men indeed reach that age without one or more fallings in love: calf-love is a most frequent circumstance in human life. Shaw seems to have been one of those very few, and that fact needs to be considered. It argues either a deficiency in his make-up or an unusually late development. What! No Juliet? Not

35

even a Rosalind? Shaw himself recognized the lateness of his development.

There was no Maria Beadnell comi-tragedy, out of which Dickens created his Dora of David Copperfield and his Flora of Little Dorrit. Shaw, so loquacious about his Irish days, has no word of any Irish sweetheart. The nearest he gets to it is this artificial unemotional picture:

'Do you remember a dark-eyed girl named Rachel Rosetree? I got up a love-affair with her; and we met one night in the garden and walked about very uncomfortably with our arms round one another and kissed at parting and were most conscientiously romantic. If that love-affair had gone on it would have bored me to death.'

This stinks of acting, and unreal acting at that; Shaw at his least skilful in invention and expression. But one never knows: it may be founded on fact. Certainly Shaw was no Romeo. If there ever was a Rachel Rosetree she counted for nothing in his life. If not, it is significant that he created her 'a dark-eyed' girl, like Shakespeare's 'Dark Lady' Mary Fitton: it was a brunette that genuinely ensnared Shaw later, in what may justly be regarded as the dangerous love of his whole life: his desperate middle-aged passion for the actress who created the heroine of his *Pygmalion*, Mrs. Patrick Campbell.

Perhaps, as he liked to put it flatteringly to himself, the dream-women that he met in music, literature and paintings had spoiled him for 'anything so prosaic as a real woman'. Or more probably there was something wanting in this young man's emotional, or under-emotional, make-up, his excess of intellect being accompanied by a deficiency in feeling. Perhaps he was the son of his mother in this respect, as in some others.

That is a fascinating problem that demands to be explored. The answer to it can only be given upon a review of what Dickens called 'all the lives of mine that Time has in his grip'. Thereby hangs a tale, the remarkable and deeply-significant tale with which this book is concerned.

FIRST LOVE, LOST LOVE:
ALICE LOCKETT

✤✤✤✤✤✤✤✤✤✤✤✤✤✤✤✤✤✤✤✤✤✤✤✤✤✤✤✤✤✤✤✤✤✤✤✤✤

*'Marry Ann; and at the end of a week you'll find no more
inspiration in her than in a plate of muffins'*
       —Man and Superman—Act II

I

IF THE Shavian pilgrim does go to Netherton Grove, motivated
by interest in the first London home of Bernard Shaw in his youth,
he has already been warned that the house is no longer there. But,
as already pointed out, the pilgrimage is not entirely wasted, since
you may deduce with close accuracy the sort of habitation the
three Shaws had at this time, from the existent Victorian houses.

Considering the emphasis—the probable over-emphasis that
Shaw laid upon his hardships and poverty at this period—you will
probably be surprised by the Grove's houses. They were certainly
far above the poverty-line and superior to any house the Shaws
had enjoyed in Dublin.

For the real truth is Mrs. Shaw, for her period and her status
now as a music-mistress, was relatively well off. She had now,
with Agnes dead, only herself and her two other children to keep.
She had, as St. John Ervine points out, an unearned 'income of
£300 a year and may have had more'. Lucy was earning and so

37

was she. The truth is beyond doubt or cavil: the Shaw women were bad managers, uninterested in domestic economy. What other women would have lived on in comfort by ordinary good management the wasteful undomesticated Shaw women found insufficient. In addition to the income stated, Mrs. Shaw was not destitute of capital. Besides the mortgage-interest upon a property in Cork, she had a grandfather's legacy of £4,000. Then there was the 'unearned increment' of the pound a week regularly remitted by her deserted husband. And in purchasing power that money was worth four times what it is today.

II

Did she, at this stage in the family fortunes, hope—or believe—that 'his father's son' would add to the family resources? He might, although he *was* his despised father's son, reasonably enough, be expected to do so. He had earned his living, or at any rate his part-living, in Ireland successfully enough. He might do better, much better for himself and them in England as Irish emigrants commonly did, and do, both in England and America.

He began by taking a three months' holiday, exploring such places as the National Gallery and the British Museum Library, which cost nothing and give so much. He had not yet any set objective in life. His sister Lucy, a girl of character, tiring of his holiday, urged her mother to turn him out of the house unless he got some gainful employment and did something for his board and lodging. Lucy was a girl 'whom everybody loved and who loved nobody'. It was even said that both Oscar and Willie Wilde fell in love with her, which may be doubted. She plumed herself, like Dickens's Ellen Ternan, upon a fancied resemblance to the great actress Ellen Terry, as many young stage-girls of her period did.

Lucy was going to be, everyone agreed, a great success on the concert-hall and on the stage. Already she was getting engagements. No doubt she would make a notable marriage. Why couldn't Sonny work as she was doing? Her great promise had not yet proved delusive, and at this stage it reproached her brother's inactivity.

Spurred by his sister, Bernard sought employment in a bank. He was rejected. He decided to enter the Excise branch of the Civil Service and started to 'cram' for the examinations; but in less than a month he gave it up in disgust. Then Lee—doing well in Park Lane at first—came to his rescue, letting him write as his 'ghost' (i.e. under Lee's name) as the music-critic of an obscure little rag called *The Hornet*. But that paper died.

Lee found other writing for him to do, one piece of which was a pamphlet called *How to Cure Clergyman's Sore Throat*. Once again Lee proved the family benefactor.

But Lee and Mrs. Shaw suddenly quarrelled over his music. Finding that his sacred 'Method', of which Mrs. Shaw was a most devoted follower, did not take on in London, Lee gave up its teaching and professed to teach voice-production in twelve short lessons. Outraged by such treachery, Mrs. Shaw gave Lee up, and still devoted herself to the incomparable 'Method'.

Henceforth Lee went out of the Shaws' life. His prosperity did not endure—perhaps his 'Method' revenged itself. Adversity followed. Suddenly he died of heart disease, virtually bankrupt. Both Mother and Sonny Shaw heard the news of this old friend's death with complete composure. None of the Shaws attended the funeral of this benefactor and former housemate.

Yet he had, according to G.B.S., taught his mother 'to sing by a method that preserved her voice perfectly until her death at over eighty', as well as 'giving her a cause and creed to live for'. And he had also given the two of them Tosca Cottage, which had provided the growing boy with life-long memories of beauty and joy.

This ingratitude has been much (and justly) criticized. It illustrates, surely, in a strong light, the deficiency of feeling that characterized both mother and son; a deficiency that Shaw was to display later on in his love-affairs to a startling degree.

III

Long before John George Vandelcur Lee died, Shaw had decided upon a career as a writer. Two years had been spent, or wasted, in looking for desultory jobs and writing for Lee.

Now, thinking he could do better than George Eliot, he sat down to write his first book, a novel called *Immaturity*, completed in eight months. Publisher after publisher rejected it. The great novelist George Meredith refused it with one word, 'No'; another publisher's reader, believed to be the great statesman and writer John Morley, could not find its purpose in it. However, Morley called it 'undeniably clever but dry, unattractive, and too devoid of any emotion'. Those last words are very significant.

Later Shaw confessed that 'not even the nibbling mice could finish it'. However, he himself had done just that.

At this stage he tells us that 'he was reputed to be as impracticable as another member of the family'—and his mother and sister can hardly be blamed for throwing his feckless father at the head of this parasite on their resources.

Sick, perhaps, of being badgered, he got a post as a telephone engineer with a telephone firm at a salary of £48 a year plus commission. He was now twenty-three. In six months he was promoted and had his salary raised. But within twelve months he capriciously refused further employment—and went back to his writing of novels.

Now, indeed, G.B.S. shows himself a remarkable young man. Every day of his life he sat down and produced five pages of manuscript, namely about 1,500 words daily, day after day, week after week, month after month, year after year, until five books had been produced. It was heavy task-work, but it made a skilled writer of him. Talk about an Israelite's slavery in the days of the Pharaohs, making bricks without straw, grinding those long books out of his imagination in hopeless unsuccessful drudgery!

This lasted five years until he was twenty-eight years old. Balzac alone endured such an unsuccessful novitiate—and went on to immortality in fiction. *Immaturity* was followed by *The Irrational*

Knot, Love Among the Artists, Cashel Byron's Profession and *An Unsocial Socialist*. Not one is a great, or even a really good, novel, but all of them display unusual qualities in their author. Then, realizing after his succession of failures that he could never become a great novelist by long toil and taking thought, and that the root of the matter was not in him, he gave up novel-writing for good.

In nine years this young aspirant with all his cruel industry earned only £6 by his pen—most of it through a patent-medicine advertisement. What a Calvary!

During this period this shy, diffident young recluse, as this solitary sedentary life was making Bernard Shaw, discouraged by his home-circle and the publishing-world alike, had made himself a public speaker. During the writing of *Cashel Byron*, he had also got himself converted to Socialism by attending a meeting at the Memorial Hall in Farringdon Street, which was addressed by Henry George the American single-taxer.

And more seemingly important, he had fallen in love, seriously, as he thought, but in the long run it turned out to be no very serious matter, as such matters go. Certainly it was no Romeo-and-Juliet or Antony-and-Cleopatra or Paolo-and-Francesca affair. Indeed, it proved to be prosaic rather than poetic. Nor did it improve the novel he was writing at the time, so far as its love-passages were concerned, as it ought to have done. That novel was *Cashel Byron's Profession*, and when Shaw was famous it was its prize-fighting scenes that gave it some modicum of acceptance and not its love-passages.

IV

The girl's name was Alice Lockett. She was a music-pupil of his mother's, being taught by the famous Method of Lee. She was also a nurse. Changing her name to Sprockett—a pretty-painful amateurish device—he wrote verses to her of which the following are a specimen:

Love lifted to his lips a chalice
And said, 'My power though many mock it
Hath triumphed through the charms of Alice.
Here's to the health of Alice Sprockett'.

A youth, o'erhearing this, grew jealous;
'Sure as thou hast a head, I'll knock it'
Said he, 'for speaking thus of Alice,
For daring to admire Miss Sprockett.'

Love answered with a smile of malice
'Wretch, hadst thou money in thy pocket
How wouldst thou show thy love for Alice?
What wouldst thou do for Alice Sprockett?'

The youth replied: 'I'd build a palace
And with all rich and rare things stock it
To live for ever there with Alice
To fill my heart with Alice Sprockett.'

Said Love, 'She knows thou art not zealous
And that thy life's light in its socket
Wasting, makes thee unworthy of Alice—
Thou art despised by Alice Sprockett.'

The youth was shamed; but Love was callous
Took wings and vanished like a rocket,
Leaving the swain to mourn for Alice,
To sigh in vain for Alice Sprockett.

This is hardly the language of passion, and if the writer had 'fallen vehemently in love' and 'was always impetuous and importunate in love', as Mr. St. John Ervine tells us, he showed none of those traits in his verses. Algernon Charles Swinburne at the time was electrifying all England with his passionate poems, and Shaw should have sent the girl one of those if he wanted to move her by vehement passion.

Was Alice Lockett the sort of young woman to rouse uncon-

trollable passion, even in a susceptible young man of twenty-six?
A photograph that is extant of her causes the thought: 'Doubtless
a most estimable young person,' but hardly more. She appears no
Faustine nor Dolores, with those lips of which it was written:

> 'Men touch them and leave in a trice
> The lilies and languors of virtue
> For the roses and raptures of vice.'

But, after all, you never know! The camera is a great liar at
times and may have done this young woman a grave injustice. In
his love-letters G.B.S. praises her complexion and good looks. It
was no small feat to rouse the unroused heart of young George
Bernard Shaw, hitherto immune from every Eve except his dream-
women.

At all events, this affair showed one characteristic of true love:
namely, that its course did not run smooth. Though it began in
March 1882 tepidly and only half-seriously, as these weakly
facetious verses seem to show, it later gathered both speed and
momentum, judging by Shaw's love-letters. But if it went fast,
it did not go far.

Some twenty letters from Shaw to Miss Lockett are known to
have survived. They are reviewed and commented on in this book.
Only one of these—the first—has hitherto been published and this
appears in St. John Ervine's biography. Neither Henderson's
monumental tome nor Hesketh Pearson's liveliest of biographies so
much as mentions Alice Lockett, Shaw's first sweetheart. But if
they had known these letters, they certainly would have had much
to say of her.

For the letters are of very great psychological interest, and
highly illustrative not only of Shaw's character and temperament
but also of the way in which literary young men blunder in battling
with the other sex in love. They are extraordinarily like in tone to
the letters extant which the youthful Dickens addressed to Maria
Beadnell—and they make the same youthful mistakes from ignorance of female psychology.

These foolish young lovers, Dickens and Shaw, do not flatter

43

their charmers, although flattery (as Lord Chesterfield could have taught them if their knowledge of human nature did not) is the diet upon which the emotionalism of womanhood most greedily feeds. Instead of praising, lauding and magnifying the beloved one for every virtue, every grace, they give foolish exhibitions of their own self-respect and self-interest. This, of course, is not the way to woo. They parade their own virtues instead of proclaiming hers; they reproach and remonstrate *ad nauseam*; they preach and prate both to her, and at her. Instead of dwelling upon her beauty, her charm, her enchantment, her incomparability, 'making her feel good', they worry her to death with words about themselves, exasperating and bewildering and frightening off the girl by intellectual performances fascinating to themselves but calculated only to make her feel inferior. They have never taken to heart another maxim in Chesterfield's Letters, where he assures his son: that those whom he makes like themselves better will like him very well indeed on that account.

Finally, both these young blunderers attack the reason when they should storm the heart. Quite clearly at this stage of their development both Dickens and Shaw knew women only on paper.

None of Alice Lockett's letters to Shaw has yet come to light, but some of them are said to have been discovered; and if they or any of them are extant they are pretty certain to be published sooner or later. Shaw—again like Dickens—was a great destroyer of other people's private letters to himself. But either Alice returned his letters on parting—a fashion of the day—or he kept copies, which as his letters were hand-written and composed very often in the middle of the night (one is even specified as written at 1.25 a.m.) is very unlikely. But many, many years afterwards, these letters, reviewed in this chapter, were found at the back of a filing cabinet in Shaw's own house.

The finder has told me a startling—almost incredible—thing: that when the letters were found and taken to their author, Shaw could not, at first, either recall the letters, or the young woman to whom he had written them. It is true that at the date of their resurrection he was a very old man: he described himself and his wife as being 'deafish and rather dotty'; but in general upon past events his mind was clear and vigorous still. Alas! for the staying power of sexual love, a love that is not stronger than death or even death-in-life.

All these letters were written from 36 Osnaburgh Street, in North London near Regent's Park, an address to which Mrs. Shaw had moved. It was not such a good neighbourhood in those days as Victoria (now Netherton) Grove; not by any means; but it was much more convenient. The letters begin in September 1883 and end in October 1885. All are signed G.B.S.—itself a standoffish mistake in tactics—one only likely to be committed by a young and inexperienced suitor. In the originals, the arch habit of designating Alice as A and Miss Lockett as Miss L., and the idea of distinguishing between these imaginary 'dual entities', is a favourite pretence. Whether it appealed to Alice Lockett may be questioned; she may well have got sick of its repetition.

There is no reason to suppose that these twenty letters are all that G.B.S. wrote to this girl; probably there were others. But it is time to let the correspondence speak for itself and then to tell how the story ended in a most lame and impotent conclusion.

V

Shaw's correspondence with Alice Lockett seems to have lasted about two years from September 1883 to October 1885. The dates are significant for forming an estimation of the significance of these letters, since they show the youthful writer as very much the child of that conventional and respectable late-Victorian era and very little his later, iconoclastic, Communistic self.

His first letter is a remorseful and disarming plea for forgiveness. He fears that in playing with his own thoughts for the entertainment of this young woman, he struck a note that pained her. He pleads that this was unintentional; and we may well accept that he didn't mean to do it.

In this penitential mood, he adopts a literary device, that he used

45

throughout his writing-career, the rather poor device of emphasizing a word by repeating it several times. Five times—not seventy-times seven as we are bidden in the Gospels—he repeats the key-word 'forgive'. This note played once is well enough, but by constant repetition of the repetition, it later becomes a tiresome and tedious trick, and as such, quite unimpressive.

Another favourite and oft-repeated gambit appears at this time. Shaw always liked to tell young women not to believe him, and sure enough he takes that attitude with Alice; but he frequently and inconsistently tries, again and again, to convince her of the truth of his numerous statements to her. He adopts the Byronic pose, so fascinating at that period, of his wickedness; his tongue is wicked, his pen deadly, his heart cold. When he tells his *inamorata* that he will be angry with himself for writing this letter which asks for forgiveness, he yet realizes that in their next meeting he will give fresh cause for anger.

One can believe that last fear as a likelihood.

The final paragraph of his first letter—if indeed it be his first, for of this one cannot be sure—is faintly amusing.

'Farewell dear Alice. There! is it (the letter) not outrageous? Burn it. Do not read it. Alas! it is too late. You have read it'.

That, if transparent, is at least spontaneous. This letter appears to have no nominative of address at the beginning—a habit of some of the 'advanced' spirits of that day. Nor, apparently, had young Shaw at the beginning of this correspondence yet adopted firmly the use of his second name, rather than his first, or even his famous initials. In one early letter to Alice he alluded to himself as 'George Shaw' twice; at that time he was so called by himself, his family and his friends.

Indeed it is very doubtful if his mother and sister Lucy ever called him by any other name than George. But he grew to dislike this name and to express his contempt for it.

How interested he was in this young Lockett nurse and music-pupil of his mother's is shown by the fact that only three days elapsed before he was writing to her again. Now he adopts a new device which seems to have pleased him greatly: the device of pretending that there are two-persons-in-one of this female deity, namely Alice and Miss Lockett, one beloved the other detested. Literally he loathes the Lockett woman, hating her with deadly hatred because according to his mythology she is a dragon, preying upon Alice whom he will rescue. There were many head-tossing, dignity-seeking, false-speaking Miss Locketts, but only one Alice, 'the sweetest of companions'.

Shaw's picture of himself at this stage of his career and life is an interesting, and apparently sincere, portrait. He calls himself an egotistical George Shaw, such a model of a righteous man. Indeed he does seem to have been, at this time—as so often hereafter—obeying the Biblical injunction to hunger and thirst after righteousness, but perhaps not quite in the Biblical spirit.

He has resolved to be an example to others. He will tread the path of duty. He will respect himself. He intends to walk with the ears of his conscience strained at the alert. He means to do everything as perfectly as it could be done. And finally, he is vowed to improve all those with whom he comes into contact—in short, we may say, not to love, but to improve his neighbour as himself.

Upon this last ideal, 'George Shaw' has the grace to realize that his attitude of being fit and able to improve every person he met is too presumptuous—and he uses his favourite denunciatory word of 'monstrous' to describe it. Apart from this redeeming touch his characterization of himself is that of a smug and egregious young prig.

Yet this side of Shaw was the side which in later life became both saint and sage. But at this period he paints it only to abhor it as the 'measureless conceit and weakness' of one morally in a bad way. Falling in love with Alice he suggests redeemed him from this self-opinionated idea, and made him 'become as a little child' as the New Testament puts it. If it did, such becoming was certainly only a very temporary phenomenon.

We may exempt one part of his programme for himself from all stricture: namely the desire to do everything as perfectly as might be. No doubt this was what made him take so much care and pains and time over his writings. The day was at hand when he would write long hours all day and every day and under any conditions; even under a lamp-post in the street; and when he would not disdain the most modest of reportorial tasks for *The Star* (a side of him which most biographers who paint him as though he were a fully-fledged musical and dramatic critic from his journalistic beginnings ignore). It may be doubted whether Grub Street or Fleet Street ever harboured a more laborious or painstaking writer than Bernard Shaw in his prime and his apprenticeship.

He asks—evidently questioning himself as much if not more than his sweetheart—why he pleases and delights Alice at one moment but stings and mortifies her the next. (The present-day reader will probably answer that he has forgotten his dual-personality ascribed to this young woman. But a moment later he remembers this again.) Alice is not to show his letter to her other self—Miss L—whom it would only enrage.

He writes in great haste after midnight. This, by the way, was far from unusual with him at this period. He had bad writing-habits for which late postal hours and the exigencies of evening-journalism may bear some share of the blame: he would write until 3 or 4 a.m. Nearly all his personal correspondence and much of his professional writing was done at dead of night. Perhaps, too, from inclination he was a night-bird, as town-bred young people usually are.

On another occasion he accuses Alice—a Sunday-school teacher of Walthamstow—of being a typical atheist when they first met. The sole foundation for this provocative suggestion (which any serious young Christian woman must have found positively and grossly offensive in the mental and spiritual climate of 1883) lay in what he called her 'cock-sure' attitude. (Here is the pot calling the kettle black with a vengeance!) Shaw, it seems, had heard a clergyman say of the celebrated Charles Bradlaugh, M.P., the leader of then-militant atheism in England, and a great public figure whom Shaw greatly feared and admired for moral courage and platform-prowess: 'He, a sceptic? Not a bit of it; he is the most cock-sure man in England'.

Ergo: Alice, being cock-sure, was a typical atheist. At this period

48

young Shaw was himself a professed and active unbeliever. To him, atheism was a matter for pride but for Alice it would hardly be anything like that.

Of course, this tactless sort of attack is no way to insinuate one-self into any young woman's good graces. Young Shaw should have studied the art of pleasing instead of the arts of 'showing off'. No wonder that almost the next moment he has to be sorry that he offends her by not being serious, and notices too that he pleases her still less when he is being serious.

Soon he cries out: 'If you have made me feel, have I not made you think?' But made the girl think what? Probably, and im-patiently, only this: that her maladroit suitor was a difficult, or indeed impossible, person to love or to rely upon as a husband in the changes and chances of this perilous mortal life. If he tries to heal her disquiet by describing himself by such adjectives as opinionated, vain, weak, ignorant, lazy and so forth, and confutes himself by saying, 'Dare any man or woman profess themselves impartial, modest, strong, wise and diligent', that would hardly atone for the rest; or make Alice feel anything but additional dis-comfort, one would think.

Equally tactless is what he says to her about another very pretty young lady 'who passes and vanishes', distracting his letter-writing at the B(ritish) Museum. A rival to Alice! He wants Mozart's music and Alice's '*beaux yeux*' to make him happy after a hard day's work at writing. But he spoils this by adding foolishly that he despises happiness and would not really enjoy such a state of things.

Perhaps it is in writing to Alice that he first uses the signature of G.B.S. which quickly became habitual and which he was destined to make first notorious, and later, famous.

One of his letters addresses 'Dear Miss Lockett'. He tells her that Alice had looked so beautiful in spite of fatigue and neuralgia that only his mother's (and Miss Lockett's) presence had prevented him saying a thousand silly things to her. (This is a better note to strike certainly.) He has had a thrill that lasted through a political meeting and four hours of a debate on political economy. Miss

Lockett had been severe with him at tea-time, and he 'took the wicked and forbidden step of writing' to her.

Evidently to the young nurse and Sunday-school teacher the dual-personality of Alice the Good and Miss Lockett the Evil idea was wearing a little thin—as might be expected. Too much repetition stales the best of things, even the vain repetition of prayers, says the Common Prayer Book.

About a fortnight later Shaw writes again, obviously to his Alice rather than to Miss Lockett, although there is no nominative of address beginning the screed to show it. He reproaches Alice bitterly because he got frightfully wet; owing to her zeal to catch a train she would not let him go back for an umbrella. He expected an attack of rheumatic fever as a result. So he called her a wretch and himself a fool. This is a poor, and even dreary, method of courtship it must be admitted.

He would be her slave no longer. She had used him vilely and disappointed him horribly. His 'transparent flatteries' of her were 'monstrous lies'; he recanted every word and pleaded 'temporary insanity' (a *cliché* of the period). He wondered she could have been so credulous as to have believed him. He talked like this to her:

'Must I eternally flatter, flatter, flatter, flatter? When you sit bolt upright opposite me in a railway carriage you look like a Chinese idol. What! I feel like the Chinaman do I? Not in the least, I assure you'.

One can just see the stiff, starchy and conventional 'young person' sitting bolt upright opposite, and not next, to her young Irishman, austerely bent on keeping him in his proper place. However, what can be more wounding than to tell a young girl that all your former praises of her were mere lies and false, insincere flatteries?

Heaven knew when he would recover from this wetting. (Not from the wounds of unrequited love, one notes!)

His last sentence was insensate:

'If ever woman was undeservedly beloved (supposing any man could be found mad enough to love you at little odd moments when your complexion is unusually beautiful) you are she'.

50

He pretentiously signs himself:

'Yours with the most profound Indifference and in the most entire Freedom from any attraction on the part of Any Woman Living, G.B.S.'

That letter stung Alice to an immediate reply—but whatever she said he answered in kind. We can guess something of what she said, and his answer was to call her 'a very silly baby to play with'. She had said that he must not love her for her good looks and complexion but for what she was. His comment on her appearance was: 'Fancy the vanity of a woman praising herself in that fashion! For shame!'

The right comment for the suitor, of course, was 'Who could help loving you for your good looks and complexion when they are so beautiful and lovable like all the rest of you? And I love you for what you are in addition'.

On being loved for what she was, Shaw was equally blunt and trenchant:

'Well, what are you? Come tell me what all these great qualities are for which I am to love you'. And he went through all her qualities of which she had apparently boasted, to deny them: her insight, her superiority to flattery, her true generousness (which he altered to generosity), her scorn of servility, her appearance, her spiritual nature, the nobility of women in general, her heart and fancy; and finally her 'scrupulous justice and gratitude even to such worms as myself'. Such a monstrous outburst of egotism never was penned before, he told her.

As an anti-climax, he sneered at her for not dating her letters, not writing legibly, making spelling mistakes and blemishing the paper 'by vain shows of insincere grief'.

But he could not sustain this denunciation long. Soon he gave up denunciation and became less artificial: 'Alas, dear Alice, all this folly goes against the grain with me tonight. We are . . . petulant children who should be petted and kissed. I am too big to be petted but you are not too big to be kissed'.

As to kissing, he confessed that her beautiful complexion had tempted him often and added:

'Enough. Midnight strikes. My head is in a tumult with matters about which you do not care twopence'.

And he told her he was putting her dual entity into the most sentimental part of his new book. But all this retreat was spoiled because he must needs add a postscript, of which the last sentence was: 'Is it my fault if she does not deserve all the hours I have given to her?'

Following this he wrote another letter which so exasperated the girl that she tore it up and threw the pieces out of the window. The full story of that little tantrum will probably never be known. But G.B.S. wrote a letter to replace the destroyed one—whether the replacement was silly or sensible he felt he could not be sure, but it was a love-letter beginning 'Dearest Alice'—this superlative was a great step forward for he generally eschewed paper-endearment any stronger than 'dear'.

Wishing her good night and begging her forgiveness he told her that she was dancing through his head to a tune that he set out in notation. He was 'full of remorse for saying those things to her' (whatever they may have been). If he had her heart he knew he would break it.

And yet he wished he had it. 'Is not this monstrous?' he asked her. (Monstrous is a word overworked at this period of his life.)

Now he sees a 'dual entity' in himself as he had seen it in her.

He was alone; and yet there was a detestable, hard-headed, heartless, cynical, cool devil seated in his chair telling him that all this is insincere, lying affectation. 'But I defy him—it is he who lies. I have only sold my working hours to him. Hate and mistrust him as much as you will; but believe me too, and help me to snatch a few moments from his withering power'.

Later in this letter he recognizes that the first part of the letter was enough. Calling her 'fatal one', he sends one more good night and becomes incoherent. He concludes: 'I protest that it is all your fault Alice, Alice, Alice, Alice, (17 in all) undeservedly beloved Alice. Am I not a wretched fool?—G.B.S.'

This seems something like genuine feeling. But it did not last long. For within four days in his next epistle 'Dearest Alice' as an invocation has vanished. He is writing 'a brief proper letter—fit for her grandmother to read'. He tells her how he made a hermit's supper for himself out of 'a few nuts and raisins which I found in the cupboard with a cup of cocoa', and fortified by such provender he hopes to finish his work before bed.

He will never talk of love to her again except when she is cross and he sarcastic. He was growing 'too fond of her for such profane stuff'.

A few days later comes a bombshell addressed to 'Dear Miss Lockett'. He suggests their acquaintance 'should cease and for ever'. He despised falsehood and treachery yet he wished her well and forgave her. 'When we next meet let it be as strangers,' he suggests.

What had happened? She had 'outrageously and heartlessly deceived him'—but it is not clear how. Never again would he believe in the professions of people with whom 'religion and an affectation of conscientiousness is only a cloak for the most heartless coquetry'. And very artificially he declared that was an impersonal and general observation and he left its application to her conscience. He continued:

'I relinquish our acquaintance which was never more than the amusement of an idle hour, without regret, save for ever having formed it'. And he signed this offended effusion:

'Yours truly,
    Whom?'

That seems final enough. But there is a continuation for 'dear Alice'. He says both of them are 'too cautious, too calculating, too selfish, too heartless, to venture head over ears in love'. He is writing with an intolerable pen this intolerable letter at an intolerable hour (half-past one in the morning!) In an intolerable mood—to an intolerable coquette, but that last he retracts as false. And he recalls their pleasant and ever-to-be-remembered hours together!

The next epistle is a very brief note, written at 3 a.m. in December 1883. He says he really had important business that night elsewhere but did not tell her because she would rather believe that she was provoking him 'to small spite' than know he was putting business before the pleasure of seeing her. Scrawled across this letter in another handwriting, probably Alice Lockett's one would think: 'Bah! I don't believe a word. I happen to know all about your engagement'.

If Alice wrote like that she must have been something of a spitfire.

Six months elapses before his next letter sending an invitation to tea from his mother. He speaks of her half-facetiously as 'honoured madam' and then as 'dearest ennobler and consoler of my idlest and (without you) darkest hours', signing himself, 'Yours most respectfully, George Mister Shaw'. This mingling of silliness and sincerity must have some special meaning for the persons concerned that altogether evades the reader.

Next time he writes he is like 'a baffled bear' and 'savage beyond measure with you and everyone else'. Why, when he is out of sorts with all his arrangements upset does she become impatient to make everything as difficult and unpleasant as possible? (That is the classic reproach of a husband to wife, by the way.) He had found her odious that evening: she had been a wicked failure and he an ill-used saint.

But in the very next letter he is making excuses for her. Dearest Alice is only an unreasonable child and he is a fool to quarrel with her. To her—the 'infinitely silly one'—he can only take his small troubles—what does she know of his larger needs or how could she sympathize with them?

Then he tells her of a mislaid letter to her with a very pretty beginning which his mother had found, and says it must have amused Mrs. Shaw. He challenges Alice to look his mother in the face at her next (piano) lesson—if she dare!

He tells her an unwanted compliment—that she is the prettiest woman in existence but her handwriting is the vilest. He draws in facsimile her word 'decided'—and it must be agreed that without the context no one could possibly decipher such execrable handwriting. He goes on to specify her handwriting defects in very

54

great detail—but in ending he tells her to take good care of his heart until they meet again.

In another letter he thanks her for flowers in his mother's absence, tells her that he has implicitly followed her instructions about their vase. But cut flowers make him think of children having their heads cut off and being put in vases. Fern leaves sent with the flowers remind him of his boyhood when he 'had a fool's head and a boy's heart' instead of his 'man's head and fool's heart (what there is of it)'. The antithesis is neither brilliant nor convincing. But when she returns he is going to make her fall in love with him just to show how clever he is.

When she tells him later that she has no time for thought his brief comment on that is 'Poor Alice!' Her latest letter to him is described as three sheets of reticencies. For fourteen years he has been writing thousands of letters—perhaps a couple of hundred to women—and what has come of it all? She is a novice at letter writing and an expert at love making; he, the exact opposite. So he tells her to write to him and he will make love to her—'to relieve the enormous solitude I carry about with me'.

There is no known evidence to support young Shaw's charge that Alice Lockett was a love-making expert. It is not very likely that she would be, and what is known of her rather suggests quite the opposite. Certainly no girl would like a young man's suggestion of love-making not for love but merely to relieve a man's loneliness.

Worse candour is to come. He tells her: 'I do not like myself and sometimes I do not like you; but there are moments when our two unfortunate souls seem to cling to the same spar in a gleam of sunshine, free of the other wreckage for a moment.

'Well, let us make the most of the days of our vanity'.

No doubt Shaw was utterly sincere in this last bout of candour. But what impression would the frank confession that he did sometimes dislike her make upon the young girl of her period looking forward to marriage and release from nursing and Sunday-school? She must have regarded Shaw's weathercock courtship of her with considerable doubt and even dismay perhaps. But there is no evidence whatsoever that this young man's intentions were not strictly honourable and his outlook as Puritanical as hers doubtless was.

There is one short note, entirely formal, later on to Dear Miss Lockett apologizing for not sending a magazine. He speaks humorously of the difficulty of getting her address from Alice and 'the impossibility of reading Alice's handwriting' when she did send it. He ends 'Yours fraternally' (the received Socialist ending). Upon that letter has been written in another handwriting, probably Alice Lockett's: 'I have written a curt note of thanks in answer to this, which needs a microscope it is so small.'

It will be realized if this is Alice's comment that the young woman was becoming as critical and acidulated as her opposite number and upon the same point of handwriting too.

More than once Shaw complained to her of waiting unproductively in railway-station waiting-rooms late at night. The waiting-room at Liverpool Street Station he calls 'our' waiting-room. There is a story of a night when he got home at 1 o'clock to meet his questioning mother. 'Where have you been?' asked Mrs. Shaw.

'With Alice.'

'Well, upon my word,' she exclaimed, outraged.

Then after a moment's reflection the mother said resignedly: 'She is old enough to take care of herself.'

Between these two women Shaw protested that he was an ill-used man—though that is not very apparent—being told by one that he was not to be trusted and by the other that it was a shame for him to go on as he did. Moreover, he is kept catching his death in 'unutterably lonely' railway waiting-rooms. Apostrophizing her as 'faithless one' he tells her God will be angry with her for deceiving him (Shaw) and asks if she has no gratitude to God for her good looks.

It is impossible to resist the conclusion that although he indicates that he took much time over this letter-writing, sometimes he said the first thing, of however little worth, that came into his head. Constantly he is self-communing and quite forgetful of his sweetheart. But this excuse must be made for him: that he saw her by snatches and communicated with her late at night when he was tired and depressed, when his life was unhappy and his literary toil—often abortive—was very considerable.

Addressing her as 'Demon! Demon! Demon!' his penultimate letter is, as his letters to her often were, complaining and contradictory of her latest letter. After they had parted for ever, she had insisted on making 'an absolute assignation' with him and parted from him early at 8.32, leaving him 'to absorb a whole railway-stationful of rheumatism' whilst she reached home laughing at him.

He tells her he is furious, but by the end of the letter it is 'Adieu dear demon'. In a post-script he tells her how he nearly put the letter into an envelope to another young woman friend, Elinor Huddart, who had missed an appointment with him and might have taken all the abuse levied at Alice to herself. What effect did he think this revelation would have? (The answer is that he was utterly self-absorbed and regardless of her.)

The latest letter that I have seen, dated October 8th 1885, does not read as though it were the end of their correspondence—and indeed it may not have been. It is characteristically Shavian in the style of his later self; cool, detached, heavily assertive. He cannot see her this week, not even this month, not even until July. He details the work he has to get through, exclaiming to her: 'Avaunt, sorceress!'

He says he can sweeten his pleasure of music, conversation, the grapple of his intelligence with fresher ones, with one kiss. But he cannot saturate and spoil it with fifty thousand. He adds:

'Love-making grows tedious to me—the emotion has evaporated from it. This is your fault.'

She had been lazy and 'unintelligently luxurious' at their last two meetings and he was not spending such evenings again except when he was 'tired and brutish'. He made it plain that he preferred his Fabian associates and his work, where all his sympathies were awake and active.

The authentic later Shaw rings clearly towards the end of this letter. Bluntly he tells her:

'I only value friends for what they can give me: if you can only give me one thing I shall value you only for that. It is useless for you to protest—the matter is not within my will—you will be valued as you deserve, not as you wish to be valued. . . . I want as much as I can get.'

This is harsh doctrine indeed and must have come as a cold douche to the young woman. It may be truth, but if so it is the brutal truth. Or it may be mere attitudinizing. Few young women would find it bracing. His final mock-heroic words to her are:

'Beware, when all the love has gone out of me I am remorseless: I hurl the truth about like destroying lightning.'

Dialectic, however acute and penetrating—particularly egotistical dialectic of this description—is hardly the way to a woman's heart. Besides, it is clear from this last letter that Shaw was rapidly recovering from a romantic infatuation of which his intellect had never approved and which made both parties acutely uncomfortable at times. Intellectually no doubt the young woman was immeasurably Shaw's inferior, and while she must have been intelligent, there is no evidence that she shared in Shaw's political or economic or literary interests at all.

Shaw's own verses aptly sum up the situation. 'She knows thou art not zealous . . . Love took wings and vanished like a rocket.' And perhaps he had Alice in mind when years later he wrote in *Man and Superman*: 'Marry Ann and in a week you'll find no more inspiration in her than in a plate of muffins.' Rather less probably!

It is impossible to avoid the conclusion that marriage with Alice would have been the ghastliest of mistakes—for both. But of these letters, one can say that they are prentice-work, their many surface-faults redeemed by some underlying sincerity and as being preliminary to the Master's work in later correspondence with Ellen Terry and Mrs. Patrick Campbell. They were not mere philandering.

In her way, despite her calling of Victorian nurse and Sunday-school teacher, in addition to Shaw's estimate of her good looks and her complexion, Alice Lockett must have been—in his youthful eyes at least—a fascinating girl.

VI

Was Alice Lockett the original of Henrietta Faustinius in his novel *An Unsocial Socialist*? He told her that her 'dual entity' made 'the foundation for the most sentimental part' of his new book. So she probably was. There may too, have been something of her in Agatha Wylie, another character in that book.

But as the correspondence seems to show, there was little sympathy between Alice and her G.B.S. Shaw lived far more on fellow-intellectual feeling than on sentimental emotion, such as he undoubtedly felt for a time for this young nurse. Besides, by 1884 he was branching out, and greatly enlarging both his circle of men and women acquaintances by joining the Fabian Society, where he instantly began to count.

Nurse Alice Lockett could hardly compete with the highly-intellectual women-Fabians, many of whom were brilliant and some of whom were by no means ill-looking. Could any man of brains prefer the company of Alice to that of Annie Besant, Edith Nesbit, or Beatrice Potter? Besides, what sort of a prospect in husbands was the penniless non-earning writing-failure to a sensible young nurse?

What happened to break the sentimental association, which never seems to have reached the stage of an engagement or understanding, is unknown. It may be that St. John Ervine's conclusion that, after the long and tempestuous correspondence getting nowhere, the affair gradually petered out though it did not entirely end. Neither party can have been altogether satisfied by their association.

But it was not a clean break, as in the case of Dickens and his Maria. Nor was there ever a resuscitation of the old fire twenty years or more after, as in Dickens's case. Nor did Shaw ever succeed in getting such rich 'copy' out of his Alice as Dickens got out of his Flora-Dora.

She remained Mrs. Shaw's music-pupil and met her lover on a friendly basis. At this period he kept fragmentary diaries, none of which has been published, the originals of which are in the custody of the Public Trustee. I have seen copies of them and the entries are brief, dull, commonplace and generally pure matter-of-fact. They are not worth publication, and of course were merely intended as a utilitarian day-to-day record and *aide-memoire*. Rarely does any entry, unless it relates to Mrs. Jenny Patterson, (of whom more later), rise above the level of mere fact-recording.

In these unpublished diaries there are several entries subsequent to the letters to Alice, speaking of her few visits quite unemotionally. But in the diary for May 1887—his diary, not hers as St. John Ervine's book mistakenly states—he writes that he met her unexpectedly as she was leaving his mother's house. He walked with her to the hospital (its name is unspecified) where she worked and says of the encounter:

'We got on the old terms in less than five minutes.'

But nothing came of that. It was evidently a flash in the pan: nothing more. . . .

In due course she married Dr. Salisbury Sharpe and had a number of children. Even then she did not at once pass out of Shaw's life, for she brought her husband to visit Mrs. Shaw socially. On this occasion, she was struck by the fact that G.B.S. looked far from well, as indeed he was not in 1894, for he had been overworking. His sister Agnes's fate was recalled, and it was suggested that he too might be tubercular.

Alice begged her husband to examine him. He willingly did so. But Dr. Sharpe could find nothing wrong with the lungs but one little spot, which he diagnosed as a 'consolidation', perhaps an artery a trifle displaced.

Thereafter Alice Sharpe (*née* Lockett) vanishes out of the Shaw story. Nothing more is seen or heard of this young woman, who for over two years had counted for so much in the early manhood of George Bernard Shaw.

VII

Just as Rosalind disappeared from his existence the moment Romeo met Juliet at the Capulets' ball, so Alice ceased to matter for Shaw when a very different type of woman from this un-sophisticated young nurse, an experienced woman of the world, Mrs. Jenny Patterson, entered the life of G.B.S.

She followed hard on the heels of Alice, in the year 1885. G.B.S. was then twenty-nine years of age and, remarkable to relate, he had never, in Biblical language, carnally known any woman. He attributes his chastity for so long a period past the age of physical puberty for males in general, to two factors; his poverty and his natural fastidiousness. No doubt these may have been influences in the direction of abstinence, but other youngsters who have succumbed to sexual temptation have been quite as poor and quite as little addicted to promiscuity. It is impossible not to think that G.B.S. was less highly-sexed than the average sensual man, and indeed all his relationships with women, taken as a whole throughout a long life, lend support to that theory. Piqued by his friend, Frank Harris, one-time editor, biographer and devotee of sex, in letters and perhaps in life as his pornographic book *My Life and Loves* attests, Shaw wrote a remarkable letter to that fellow-author in 1930 on the subject. Harris had expressed the view that Shaw was under-sexed or physically infirm in some way, and Shaw, who took the view that he was not under- but over-sexed, went into details about himself in this regard, knowing perfectly well that Harris would publish them.

Indeed, the letter copied in its entirety forms the basis of the chapter headed Shaw's Sex Credo in Harris's book about Shaw. In it Shaw trenchantly and frankly says:

'If you have any doubts as to my normal virility dismiss them from your mind. I was not impotent; I was not sterile; I was not homosexual; and I was extremely, though not promiscuously, susceptible.

'Also I was entirely free from the neurosis (as it seems to me) of Original Sin. I never associated sexual intercourse with delin-quency. I associated it always with delight and had no scruples nor remorses nor misgivings of conscience. . . .'

He explained that his sole inhibitions were to protect his women-partners and to respect his husband-friends. He says that after the age of twenty-nine he tried 'all the experiments and learned what there was to be learned from them' (a vague phrase that perhaps ought not to be taken too literally). He avers that after that date he did not need to pursue women. 'I was pursued by them.'

The letter of Shaw's is admittedly genuine. It is necessary to say this because Frank Harris, for the present generation, has an extremely bad reputation, given by such friends as Kingsmill and others, as a liar and falsifier of those contemporaries that he wrote about. That he took liberties with his subjects, especially the dead ones, cannot be denied. He declared that he did it in the interests of art; but it was also in the interest of money, to the lure of which he was even more susceptible than most of us.

Harris also had a bad personal reputation in his own day—though he was also greatly acclaimed for his writings, especially *The Man Shakespeare* and his short story *Montes the Matador*. I knew Harris in my early youth, but not well, and I have nothing but good to say of him. But when the late Arthur Machen, that fine stylist and good man, then writing for the *Evening News*, introduced me to Harris as I had begged him to do he reluctantly did so saying: 'On one condition: You promise me never to lend him any money and also that you will never come back and reproach me for having let you make his acquaintance.'

I readily promised. Neither of these casualties occurred.

But the point here is that Harris is to be trusted in his genuine loyalty to literature. That, with a sentimental attachment to Jesus Christ (as Harris conceived him), was his religion. It follows that he would correctly report Shaw, at any rate while Shaw lived, because he had a genuine appreciation of, and a wholesome respect for, both the man and his achievements, especially in so fundamental a matter as sex. Also Shaw was providing, and likely (out of a tenacious sense of gratitude to his old editor) to go on providing, Harris with lucrative copy when Harris needed money and friendship badly towards the end of his life in Monaco.

The unusual fact that Shaw remained continent until twenty-nine may therefore be accepted. Just as he had been a slow developer in literary expression, so he was a slow developer in sexual expression.

There is no reason, then, to doubt that the Alice Lockett affair was entirely innocent. No doubt if Alice had been an entirely different type of girl: less well-conducted, less self-respecting, respectable and virginal; more ready to take the initiative—for Shaw at this time was abnormally shy, diffident and inexperienced —then both might have given way to the lusts of the flesh. Clearly Alice was not 'that sort of girl'—as the girlish phrase goes—she was conventional and prudish. So, too, at that date was her admirer. Young men, and even not-so-young men, are apt to treat women according to their own valuation of themselves.

Frank Harris, like nearly all of Shaw's biographers, had never heard of Alice. If Shaw at seventy failed to mention her, it is not surprising. She belonged to a period before the dawning of his practical sex-life, and she who in her day mattered so much in his interior life, as his letters to her amply demonstrate, was virtually forgotten amongst the *débris* of his younger days.

But an abortive affair like this one has its influence upon the next. Every Romeo it seems must have his Rosalind as a necessary preliminary to his Juliet: this is not the ideal state of things to romance-lovers, but it conforms to reality; and Shakespeare, in making a Rosalind precede a Juliet, knew very well that he was holding the mirror up to Nature.

III

THAT TEMPESTUOUS PETTICOAT: JENNY PATTERSON

❧❧❧❧❧❧❧❧❧❧❧❧❧❧❧❧❧❧❧❧❧❧❧❧❧❧❧❧❧❧

'Women have been a ghastly nuisance in my life . . . Women tend to regard love as a fusion of body, spirit and mind. It has never been so with me.

'Women have never played an important part in my life. I could always discard them more readily than my friends.'

—G.B.S. to Stephen Winsten

I

THE CONFESSIONS of Bernard Shaw about his love-affairs sometimes make the celebrated confessions of Jean-Jacques Rousseau seem like the shrinking reticence of a Wordsworthian violet by a mossy stone half-hidden from the eye. But since then we have had Somerset Maugham on his dead Syrie!

His candour (if you are disposed to praise him), his lack of delicacy (if you are not), is amazing. Admitting that he is fully entitled to tell the truth, the whole truth and nothing but the truth about himself and about the affair, one still asks: Why was it necessary to make the name of Mrs. Jenny Patterson as notorious as the reputation of Potiphar's wife, when he, G.B.S., was no Joseph in this matter, especially when the poor woman was in her grave?

64

G.B.S. in the prime of
life

The Shavian marriage

The 'tempestuous petticoat' Jenny Patterson

May Morris, daughter of the poet and artist, William Morris

It seems a mean and ungrateful revenge for the affection she showed later on. It certainly was unchivalrous, and not to the credit of a man who prided himself more than once on being a protector of women in sexual affairs.

The year 1885, his twenty-ninth, was an important year in the life of G.B.S. His novel-period of writing over, he was beginning to feel his feet and make headway. He had joined the Fabian Society the year before, and now he was put on its Executive Committee and was lecturing on his newly-found creed of Socialism. Like his mother he had found a Cause and a Creed to live for. Nor was his advocacy of that cause and creed ineffective: that very year, to the surprise and delight of his Fabian associates, he had converted the famous woman-atheist Annie Besant, by one of his speeches, to Fabianism. It was a most notable capture. Also, thanks to William Archer the critic, he had been launched into journalism and was now able to make a living for himself by his pen. That year indeed he made £117 0s. 3d., as one of his unpublished diaries records.

That restoration of his nine years' lost earning-capacity was especially important at this juncture in the affairs of his family. For in April of this year his father had died, thereby depriving the family of his subsidy of a pound a week. But his mother drew a hundred pounds insurance-money upon his father's death; out of this, as again recorded in his diary, he 'ordered clothes at Jaeger's —the first new garments I have had for years'—which cost him a total of some eleven pounds.

In the early part of that year he had become acquainted with another of his mother's music-pupils, a widow named Mrs. Jenny Patterson. She was well-to-do, lived in Brompton Square, and was especially friendly with his mother and sister Lucy. Who and what her deceased husband was, is unknown.

From February on, laconic entries appear in Shaw's unpublished diary for that year, recording various contacts with her. But all his entries are laconic, so nothing is to be deduced from this. In April he tells us she was with his mother and that he 'wasted all the evening'; and on another evening in that month, he cut short his attendance at a concert to go to her house. Finding her alone, he stayed with her until midnight. Clearly the acquaintance was ripening fast. (But, as of equal importance, he records the fact that his dinner that day cost him no less than a shilling and a penny, and the concert half a crown.)

In his curiously meticulous fashion of recording insignificant and unimportant details, he tells himself that on July 4th at 8.20 he called on Mrs. Patterson and found her away from home. Later that same evening he met some unspecified friends, and after an hour or two with them returned to Brompton Square. Mrs. Patterson was at home and he stayed until 1 a.m. Clearly he now was a favoured suitor. On this occasion he relates:

'Vein of conversation distinctly gallant.'

Some days later, he escorted her home from his home by way of the park. He adds:

'Supper, music and curious conversation and a declaration of passion. Left at 3 a.m. *Virgo intacta* still.'

From this date, his current diary shows increased interest in Jenny. On the 17th he relates: 'Mrs. Patterson came, saw her for a few minutes . . . Sat up late to write to Mrs. Patterson.'

On the 18th he again visited her: 'Forced caresses. Thence to Lady Wilde's' (the house of Oscar Wilde's mother in Oakley Street, Chelsea) 'where I met Stuart Glennie, Mrs. Kingsford and others. Called at Brompton Square on my way back, but she had not yet come in and I did not wait.'

On the 19th: 'Went to Brompton Square but was too late to see J.P.' (from this date she is always J.P. and never Jenny, and perhaps this is significant) 'who was going to bed, so walked home. Wrote to her.'

On the 20th: 'Missed again as to J.P. Wrote her a good letter in reply to hers.'

On the 21st: 'Satisfactory letter from J.P.'

Unfortunately, none of his letters to this inamorata nor hers to him is extant. They would undoubtedly illuminate this episode in his emotional life for us. His 'good' letter in reply to hers would undoubtedly be an argumentative and assertive one, for that was his idea of a 'good' letter; probably it would be very like some of those written to Alice Lockett.

Undoubtedly this late beginner was playing with fire. Elsewhere upon this episode he tells us: 'I was an absolute novice. I did not take the initiative.' But by this time he was paying a great deal of attention to women in general, for on the 23rd July he records taking out May Morris, the younger daughter of the famous poet and Socialist leader William Morris, for coffee; and the next day he was busy writing a long letter to Annie Besant, who was now taking more than a little interest in him personally. No longer was he the young literary hermit of Victoria Grove, dedicated simply and solely to his writing-desk.

II

On his twenty-ninth birthday, the 26th July, the culmination came. He spent the evening with Mrs. Patterson, again not leaving her until three o'clock in the morning.

He celebrated that birthday, he records for his own delectation, by 'a new experience'. What had happened? According to his own story, this raw but adult Irishman was 'seduced and raped' (rather a contradiction in terms, for a rape implies the use of force and non-consent, the very opposite of the consent implied in the word seduction) by this Circe in her comfortable lair. Though both Shakespeare-saturated and Dickens-drenched to a quite extraordinary degree, Shaw forgot their advice; notably Tony Weller's advice to his son Sam: 'Be very careful o' widders.'

A sultry, smouldering piece was Shaw's 'J.P.', and fifteen years his senior. According to him she was 'sexually insatiable', which may also mean that he was under-sexed, for the youthful partner of a Delilah does not usually bring such an accusation. Not only was Jenny what the Tudor dramatist Nashe calls 'a gracelesse fornicatress', she also had, as the future was to prove, the very devil of a temper!

This was a very different affair from the tepid and timid calf-love with that rather stuffy young person Alice Lockett, that had led to nowhere. To this experienced and sophisticated temptress, the tall red-haired Irishman succumbed like a rabbit to a rattle-snake.

Of course, being the intellectual he was, he had to rationalize his fall from grace. He could speak like Adam in Genesis: 'The woman tempted me', as the average man in like circumstances would have done; but he could not leave it there. He must explain his yielding to temptation by something more than the instinct innate in every normal man, especially later on when the episode became, in his eyes, nothing better than a squalid debauchery. His self-regard would not allow him to confess that this was nothing more than a belated yielding to temptation and the tyranny of sex.

So he repeated in revised wording what he had said in his letter on sex to Frank Harris in 1930, and in No. 15 of his *Sixteen Self-Sketches* years later. Sexual experience, he told Harris, seemed to him a necessary completion of human growth; he was not attracted by virgins as such, but preferred women who knew what they were doing.

This he alters to: 'Sexual experience seemed a natural appetite and its satisfaction a completion of human experience necessary for fully-qualified authorship.' And the women he prefers become '*fully-matured* women who knew what they were doing'.

He describes the self of the Jenny Patterson period as being 'a continent virgin but an incorrigible philanderer . . . for I wanted to love but not to be appropriated and lose my boundless Uranian liberty . . . Prostitutes, who often accosted me, never attracted me.'

Authors will do much for their craft; but it is difficult to believe that their first fornication is inspired solely by a desire for literary qualification. Nor does Shaw at the time when it happened, speaking to himself in his diary, pretend to have been influenced by any such intellectual considerations.

We can believe him when he tells Harris: 'I liked sexual intercourse because of its amazing power of producing a celestial flood of emotion and exaltation of existence.' But he must add: 'which however momentary gave me a sample of what may one day be the normal state of being for mankind in intellectual ecstasy,' another obvious after-thought. He adds further: 'I always gave the wildest expression to this in a torrent of words' (what a blunder in love-making at a point where silence is more eloquent than speech!) 'partly because I feel it due to the woman to know what I felt in her arms, and partly because I wanted her to share it.'

'But,' he continues, 'except perhaps on one occasion, I never felt quite convinced that I had carried the lady more than half as far as she had carried me.'

'What occasion was that, I wonder?' demands the curious and tantalized reader. Never shall we know. It may (or may not) have been the occasion when he and Jenny Patterson first carnally knew each other.

III

But to return to that momentous birthday and the widow's house in Brompton Square, as important as Rahab's in Jericho to its visitor. After the nocturnal adventure on his birthday, Shaw dallied on the doorstep in farewell to his hostess. Perhaps he talked too much and too loudly, for the parting pair attracted the attention of a neighbour—the last thing, one may be sure, that either of them wished to do.

Watched by this old woman of next door, 'whose evil interpretation of the lateness of my departure alarmed us', says Shaw in his diary, he returned home. There he would face no questionings, for neither his nocturnal nor diurnal comings and goings troubled his mother or sister. His nearest and dearest had let him alone from an early age—a piece of good luck for any intellectual who needs to think and write in solitude.

What the ancient witch said is unknown, but her interpretation was no more evil than what she interpreted. Who she was is also unknown.

Not till the 31st did he write to Jenny before going to bed. On the 3rd August he is giving what his diary calls a full circumstantial account of the affair to MacNaulty. Edward MacNaulty was a youthful friend in Ireland of literary leanings like himself, with whom for many years he exchanged confidences. That same day his now close friend Sidney Webb (afterwards Lord Passfield), the social investigator who married Beatrice Potter and for whose talents Shaw retained unqualified admiration all his life, confided to him a love-disappointment, and the same evening Shaw wrote what he describes as a 'rather fierce' letter to his J.P.

Her reply, which was not delayed, he described as an 'explosion'. Not only was she explosive: she was also jealous and possessive. He became a constant visitor to her house and records the visits, one of which—'to eat and make love until 1.30'—is typical. Again and again, he escorts her home from his mother's home.

On one occasion she put him off, as she was going to Lord Croft to borrow £2,000. What she wanted the money for, and whether she got it, is unknown. He records an angry and plaintive letter from her and the gift of a pair of slippers which she had 'worked' for him.

On the following New Year's Eve, 1886, he went to her house at eleven o'clock, his intention being to see the New Year in with her. But either she was not expecting him or she was offended with him, for he records that his intention was defeated. The lights in her house were out and she had gone to bed. So he stayed at the other side of the Square and watched the Champions and other residents 'come out on their doorsteps to see the New Year in'.

This is futile and uncharacteristic behaviour, but it is much the way ordinary men are apt to behave, in such circumstances as he was then in with this woman. There is a general belief by his biographers that all the concern in this affair was hers. But this New Year misadventure, and the other denial of her presence, do not look as if that were entirely the case all of the time.

At this stage he does not seem to have been happy. He was a late bird, frequently writing until 2 a.m., 3 a.m. and even 4 a.m. (There was a 3 a.m. post for journalistic missives, and he was now contributing to the new evening paper, The Star, of whose assistant editor, H. W. Massingham, he had made a friend, and whose editor, T. P. O'Connor, was a compatriot and well-wisher.) Frequently he castigated himself in his diary for late rising, for inveterate laziness and procrastination, and finds himself afflicted with listlessness, depression and headaches.

Jenny was little, if any, consolation even at her best. At her worst, she was very much the reverse. About a week after New Year's Day he describes a visit to her in a single condemnatory word: Revulsion. Only three days later he finds another man with her—an unnamed visitor—who, according to him (but how did he know?), was 'bent on seduction and we tried which should outstay the other. Eventually he had to go for a train.' He ends the entry with: 'To bed late.'

This horrid competition for the woman finds no place in his published writings, but there it is in his unpublished diary. There is no word of resentment of, or challenge to, Jenny's behaviour. Nothing but the flat record.

But his own 'petticoats' (as Dickens might have called his mother and sister) remained on good terms with Jenny. Indeed, sister Lucy stayed with her in Brompton Square, when she was attacked by pleurisy, and was later taken by her to Broadstairs to convalesce. Did Lucy or his mother know what his relations with Jenny Patterson were? If Lucy had known would she have accepted this hospitality, or Mrs. Shaw have taken the Patterson music-fees?

Soon the diary records violent scenes made by Jenny. After one of these, Shaw wrote to her that their 'future intercourse must be platonic'. She had reason to be jealous, for she had discovered— and read—one of Annie Besant's letters to him, and she had spied on them walking together in the London streets. In reply to his letter she called upon him, distracted by his ultimatum.

There was a patched-up reconciliation which he records:

'Much pathetic kissing and petting after which she went away comparatively happy.'

But that comparative happiness lasted less than three days. Then there was a less troublesome scene, caused by his 'refusing to budge from our new platonic relations'. There was now war declared between them. To carry on her campaign she came to stay with his mother at Fitzroy Square, where the Shaw household was now residing, and constantly interrupted his work when his mother and Lucy were out all day.

'J.P. here made it hard to work. After dinner played Haydn to steady my nerves,' he wrote. Other entries are even more revealing: 'J.P. came, raged, wept, flung a book at my head, etc.' and 'J.P. was here, and though I made a beginning with my article I could not get on, as I felt very tired and good for nothing.'

Even outside the home he could not escape from her. She found him one night in the street 'scribbling and moving about as it was foggy and chilly'. He was writing an article for *The Star*: he had the enviable faculty for an author of being able to write virtually any-where and under all conditions: on a train, on a bus, in the street. 'J.P. . . . came up as I was writing under a lamp-post.' And he did this sort of thing when he dined off bread-and-butter and apples— because he was short of money at the moment and 'Mother was out'.

Yet the affair with Jenny went on and on, in spite of stormy scenes. The weeks passed into months, the months into years, and he could not, or did not, break his bonds. In May, 1890, he visited her, but 'found her so fractious that I presently shook the dust off my feet and went away'. That same month he recorded 'It looks like breaking off'.

IV

The appearance was deceptive. In the autumn of the same year, when he was struggling with his first play, *Widowers' Houses*, at Archer's instigation, and falling genuinely in love with Florence Emery (Florence Farr), his first leading-lady, he has not succeeded in emancipating himself from the toils of Jenny Patterson.

To make bad worse, the two women found out about each other. Florence, a sweet-natured woman, herself inclined to promiscuity and convinced of her charms, took the revelation calmly. Not so Jenny. She was furiously jealous, angry and alarmed. She had taken a holiday in the East, and on her return, finding that her lover had taken advantage of her absence to enter upon relations with her rival, she created hell, of which he wrote:

'Fearful scene about F.E., this being our first meeting since her return from the East. Did not get home until about 3 a.m.'

Nor did it rest there. The very next day the scene was resumed. He confided to Florence the new love his disillusion and fury and repudiation of Jenny the old love and his former relations with her. He wrote a letter in which lust has clearly turned to hatred.* One would have thought that this was the very end. It wasn't.

Less than a fortnight later Jenny is still having scenes with him. One night, getting back from the opera at Covent Garden after midnight, he found her wandering in Fitzroy Square awaiting his return. He could do no less than take her home to Brompton Square in a hansom-cab, long and expensive journey as that would be. He walked home and got to bed after 3 a.m. 'very tired'.

Scene after scene with Mrs. Patterson continued. One wonders how any man on earth could endure such female persecution for so long. The scenes are 'terrific' and 'terrible', 'desperate' and 'very tempestuous'. He could get no work done owing to them, as one can imagine; no wonder he records being 'upset', 'out of sorts', 'revolted by everything'. He had indeed sown the wind and reaped a whirlwind. 'Hell hath no fury like a woman scorned.'

His diary for 1892 has been lost or destroyed. Incredible to relate, the affair with Jenny did not end, during 1892. But on one occasion he had had to escape from her by using brute force, and to enlist the help of his mother in getting her out of the house. The year 1893 dawned; and he was still her property.

But at long last his unbelievable vacillations and inability to rid himself of this fearful incubus came to an end. The virago went too far.

* See Chapter IV, page 85.

V

On February 4th, 1893, the end came. Let his diary tell its own story. It says:

'In the evening I went to F.E. [Florence Emery] and J.P. burst on us very late in the evening. There was a most shocking scene, J.P. being violent and using atrocious language. At last I sent F.E. out of the room, having to restrain J.P. by force from attacking her. I was two hours getting her out of the house and I did not get her home until near 1, nor could I get myself away until 3.

'I was horribly tired and upset but I kept my patience and did not behave badly or ungently. Did not get to bed until 4 and had a disturbed night. I made J.P. write a letter to me expressing her regret and promising not to annoy her again. This was sent to F.E. to reassure her.'

That ugly happening made the break. Firmly and finally at last she was ejected from Shaw's super-strenuous life. Even after that he had to be resolute to avoid her, since her friendship with his mother and sister remained intact. Six months later she was entertaining Mrs. Shaw at Pangbourne. But when Jenny called at Fitzroy Square he kept out of the way, most especially when she called 'ostensibly to cheer up Mother in bed with influenza'.

Thereafter he was taking no chances. No excuse would avail for an interview. Her letters were returned unread and unopened, though they rained upon him for months.

He never saw her again. He had been patient with the patience of Socrates too long; and, unlike the Greek, he was not even married to the wretched termagant. Why should he have tolerated her ungovernable temper and intolerable possessiveness for so long? He should have broken his degrading fetters long ago.

It is a horrid story of slavery to lust and habit. She had money, a fine house in Brompton Square and another in the country. If she had been a poor girl instead of a rich woman, would a man fifteen years her junior have remained in thrall to her and her tantrums? It does not seem likely. Of course, we only have one sad party's side of the story, but it is difficult to see what defence she

74

can have for her conduct, extraordinary in an educated and intelligent woman of some physical attraction.

She held Shaw in his early manhood captive for eight years, a servitude longer than that which the patriarch Jacob endured for either his Leah or his Rachel. It was a feat.

According to Shaw, she never forgave him her repudiation—which was natural enough, having regard to her vindictive and jealous character. In one of his early wills, made before her death, he left her £100 in memory of her kindness (forgetting, or magnanimously ignoring, her unkindness) to him during their period of intimacy. She had been a cheap mistress, but the recompense of £100 will strike some people as an indelicate and parsimonious one. Conceivably she might have regarded it as an insult added to injury, as she was in no need of money.

However, the bequest never took effect, she dying the earlier of the two. Her death-certificate gives her age as eighty but as she died on September 15th, 1924, that would make her only twelve years older than her paramour. However, she told him that she was fifteen years his senior, and a woman with a much younger lover is not likely to maximize the disparity in years between them. Those who knew her gave her more than fifteen years advantage over young Shaw. Probably, like Dickens's Ellen Ternan's, her death-certificate was mistaken—and for the same two reasons, namely, that it was supplied to the registrar by a servant, and it correctly represented a feminine owner's habitual fiction about her age.

How she expended the remainder of her days is unrecorded.

VI

Inevitably Bernard Shaw turned her, and his experience with her, to account in his writings. The strain at the time (as he told his friend in later life, Hesketh Pearson), was unforgettable.

She is Blanche Sartorius in his play *Widowers' Houses*, and Julia Craven in *The Philanderer*. In the latter play, the horribly vulgar scene that took place between Jenny Patterson and her rival

Florence Emery (Farr) is bowdlerized to make the abusive scene between Julia Craven and Grace Tranfield. Did Jenny Patterson ever see the play and recognize herself in Julia? Shaw took this risk, for although the play was never publicly performed until twelve years after it was finished, Mrs. Patterson was still alive. If she saw it she possibly did not recognize herself.

Did Florence Emery see it? If she did she probably did not care: certainly she was not, like her rival, the sort of woman to make a song-and-dance about it. If the piece had been performed at the time when it was written, she might have been asked by the author to play Grace Tranfield. Perhaps he had that casting in mind when he wrote the piece: it can hardly have not crossed his mind.

The Philanderer is by no means one of Shaw's more successful plays. The author too, came to dislike it, and to call it 'a combination of mechanical farce with realistic filth'. There is nothing filthy in the ordinary meaning of that adjective in the play, and Shaw in employing the word was evidently influenced by his memories of the genesis of the scene between the two women.

So far as Blanche Sartorius is concerned, it is exceedingly unlikely that Mrs. Patterson would recognize herself in that character. If she did, she may not have been displeased about it.

But he took a more daring risk with his Jenny than either of these. While he was still under her domination he wrote a short story *Don Giovanni Explains*, in which he is Don Giovanni seduced in his ignorance and inexperience by 'a widow lady'. There seems to be a specially autobiographic touch which we may accept as genuine in the following passage:

'It was my first consummated love affair, and though for nearly two years the lady had no reason to complain of my fidelity, I found the romantic side of our intercourse, which seemed never to pall on her, tedious, unreasonable, and even forced and insincere except at rare moments when the power of love made her beautiful, body and soul.'

This passage is certainly alive, but the reader will ask what manner of man is this Don Giovanni? Shaw has metamorphosed himself into a duellist of the very first water, like the furious Tybalt, sufficiently to cover his tracks. If Mrs. Patterson ever read this story, the probability is that she would not recognize herself in the widow lady of the tale, nor her treacherous much-tried lover in the Don.

Indeed, Shaw told Pearson, with regard to the scene between the women, that to make that scene bearable (which in reality it was not) he had been obliged to reproduce it as a work of art, not as a chronicle.

When Jenny Patterson was dead, Shaw did not spare her reputation—which makes nonsense of his claims, which so many writers have accepted, to be a protector of the women's good names in their associations with himself. It is true he abstained from mentioning her name to Frank Harris. But when he was over ninety—and old enough to know better—he published a photograph of Mrs. Jenny Patterson by name, with the addition of 'My Lady Friend in 1885', in juxtaposition with the revised Frank Harris letter.

One cannot help repeating pertinent questions: Where was the necessity for naming the woman? and Why did he name her? The answer—and it is not a nice answer—seems to be given by himself in words reported by Pearson:

'I can keep my temper under ordinary injuries, though woe betide those who, like Jenny, push the strain too far.'

Woe did betide her, indeed! As long as Shaw's name lasts, she stands in the gaze of posterity marked with Hawthorne's Scarlet Letter. Deservedly, some will say. But should it have been Shaw's hand that marked her pitilessly with the letter of shame? And had this 'sexually insatiable' woman no relatives or friends to be shocked and hurt at her exposure in the pillory?

VII

Life changes us all, even men like Bernard Shaw. Hesketh Pearson records how, when Shaw was eighty-seven, he encountered the 'grand old boy' making a sentimental pilgrimage to the places in London associated with his younger lives. One would never have suspected him of this kind of sentimentality.

He had had a look at Brompton Square amongst other places.

'Why Brompton Square?' demanded Pearson.

'Jenny Patterson lived here,' he answered. 'I have never forgotten how an old woman next door put her head out of the window at three o'clock one morning as Jenny was seeing me off, and made some most objectionable comments at the top of her voice. Neither of us enjoyed the experience, and thereafter I came and went in a less conspicuous manner.'

His memory at that date was beginning to fail. But it is to be hoped and believed that he remembered other things than that old beldame. For example: 'The rare moments when Love made her [his Jenny] beautiful, both body and soul.'

IV

ONE 'BEST AND DEAREST LOVE': FLORENCE FARR

✣✣✣✣✣✣✣✣✣✣✣✣✣✣✣✣✣✣✣✣✣✣✣✣✣✣✣✣✣✣✣✣✣✣✣✣✣

*'Passion served up with cold sauce as in the Shaw-Barker school
of sex, revolts them. Enthusiastic love is the only excuse in their
eyes for going through the rather ungraceful gestures of love'*
—Florence Farr in 'Modern Woman: Her Intentions.'

I

THERE IS an old English proverb to the effect: Take care you
are off with the old love before you are on with the new. It is
sensible advice, and Bernard Shaw in his early manhood paid
heavily for disregarding it.

The jealousy and resentment—cruel as burning coals upon the
flesh—of the old love, Jenny Patterson, when other women
attracted, and were attracted by, Shaw, has already been noticed.
These emotions of hers were fierce and long-lasting, and must
have been severely irksome and embarrassing to their victim.
Shaw, as we have seen, temporized with her again and again, and
seems to have thought that he could keep several women in tow
at the same time. From a shy and shrinking anchorite, he had
developed, by reason of his intrigue with the Patterson widow, into
an inveterate philanderer.

Now it was that there came into his circle of acquaintance a

79

young woman who instantly appealed to his tastes in femininity. Florence Farr appeared to have everything. She was beautiful; she was yielding and sympathetic to the opposite sex; she was refined; she was interested in progressive thought; she was one of the women-of-the-day known as 'The New Woman', inasmuch as she lived a free and independent life apart from any husband or parents. In short, she was a career-woman with a life on the stage.

Career-women, now as common in England as motor-vehicles and television-sets, were then a novelty; and were looked at rather askance. Not, however, in the socialistic circles now frequented by Shaw: there, they were admired and flattered as the most up-to-date development in femininity.

II

Florence Farr was one of the four daughters—not *the* daughter as Shaw's biographers tell us—of Dr. William Farr, himself a person of great eminence in his day, both as a pioneer on sanitary reform and as a statistician second to none in the country. 'But for fate and Lord Beaconsfield, he would have been the Registrar-General,' says a memoir of him. After his day he was quickly forgotten, as medical men are apt to be unless their work is of permanent importance in medical history, linked with some new discovery as Jenner's introduction of vaccination, Lister's of antiseptics, Ehrlich's of salvarsan and Fleming's of penicillin.

Bernard Shaw has a semi-contemptuous reference to him in one of his many prefaces; and one wonders why. Says Shaw: 'He survived his wits before his death in 1883,' and speaks of his losing his fortune by 'senile speculation', although he admits that there was enough left for Florence to live upon without work. It is true that Farr died of a progressively incapacitating paralysis of the brain and bronchitis. But as to his 'senile speculation', he was of humble origin and had nothing but his earnings: indeed, his estate was sworn at only £3,800. In view of his public services, pensions were solicited for his children from the Government of the day; but the Government replied that they had no power to award these but would—and did—contribute £400 to a public testimonial fund. Shaw—though he admits Farr's fame—evidently was ignorant of the full facts, otherwise, holding the principles he professed of service to the State, he would have praised Dr. Farr as his contemporaries' opinion did.

Florence had inherited something of her father's exceptional intellect. She read widely, and was not innocent of authorship (though Shaw and his biographers appear ignorant of that fact) in later life, as we shall see.

However, the stage first attracted her. As she had money, 'resting' (which is the theatrical euphemism for unemployed periods) did not frighten her. She could, to a great extent, choose her parts, though of course no actress, except the very greatest and most successful, can always do that. Her tastes ran to the intellectual drama and serious *rôles*. She held very advanced ideas.

Inevitably this beautiful young actress, leaving home at twenty-three, quickly married. Her husband was an actor called Emery—of the well-known theatrical family of that name, but of whom hardly anything is known. For some suppressed reason, he had found it convenient to disappear to America after four years of marriage. A common enough state of affairs in theatrical circles, then as now, but his wife Florence did not seem to mourn his departure. There was only too plentiful a supply of men ready to take his place, and console the attractive young actress for her marital misfortune—if such it was!

In his socialistic peregrinations, Shaw had become a fairly frequent visitor to the house of William Morris, then one of the foremost men of the day, not merely as a Socialist leader, but as a poet, a medievalist, an aesthete who did not merely talk aesthetics, but who revived the arts and crafts by the work of his own hand and brain. He called himself 'the idle singer of an empty day'. His younger daughter, May, shared her father's activities and beliefs, and she carried his ideas into effect in skilful needlework. Florence Farr was one of May's pupils in embroidery, as a side-line to her stage appearances.

Shaw, despite the charms of Florence, was much attracted by

May, as we shall see in detail later on. This attraction, and even what he called his 'celestial marriage' to May at sight, did not prevent his falling violently in love with Florence. This will strike idealists as impossible or shocking, but he has vouched for it plainly enough. It may be that he met May first. But he was desperately poor at the time, and regarded May as the daughter of a rich and famous man above his pretensions. Perhaps if he had thought there was any hope of winning May, he might have let Florence alone. But May had parents to protect her; Florence had no one.

However, it was not only Florence's independence and availability that made her desirable. In spite of his cold, intellectual nature, in spite of his current *affaire* with Jenny Patterson, Shaw quickly became genuinely and passionately in love with the fair Florence. It made her additionally attractive that he imagined that he saw in her the makings of a very great actress. This especially appealed to him, for he had written part of his first play, and he would need an actress of ability to play in it.

Florence was musical—a further bond between them. By now, Shaw the ex-novelist, had become a contributor of all sorts of bits and pieces to *The Star*, the new Liberal evening paper which from its birth to its second unhappy murder by its owners—'as well kill a man as kill a good book', fiercely said John Milton the poet, and it is equally murder to kill a good newspaper—was always the liveliest and best-written of the London evening papers. From that work, as writer-up of unconsidered trifles, Shaw had graduated to the regular post of musical critic for the paper as 'Corno di Bassetto', which gave him free entry to every good concert in London. What more natural than that he should invite Florence to the concerts and operas and exchange ideas with her upon them? And what can be pleasanter than such exchanges—except more intimate exchanges, to which the music serves as prelude to invitation?

There is no doubt whatever as to the depth and reality of the passion inspired by Florence Farr in Bernard Shaw. Only one other love-affair of his can compare with it at all: the passion inspired in him in his middle-age by another and greater actress, Mrs. Patrick Campbell.

He says himself:

'Only twice in my life have I been sexually infatuated: once as a young man and once in middle life.'

There is no doubt that the words 'once as a young man' refer to his love-affair with Florence Farr. Hear his own eloquent rhapsody written to her:

'This is to certify that—You are my best & dearest love, the regenerator of my heart, the holiest joy of my soul, my treasure, my salvation, my rest, my reward, my darling youngest child, my secret glimpse of Heaven, my Angel of the Annunciation; not yet herself awake, but rousing me from a long sleep with the beat of her unconscious wings and shining upon me with her beautiful eyes that are still blind.'

He added the prosaic anti-climax that he would be free on Wednesday. This is the Bernard Shaw of his early thirties writing to Florence Farr, otherwise Mrs. Emery.

In his early nineties he had forgotten that he had ever written any letter to her at all! He denied it, saying he saw her too often to need to write to her. But she had—understandably—preserved some of his letters, and after her death some few of them were given to the world by Mr. Clifford Bax, the author, to whom she bequeathed them, and who talked to me in Albany about her.

This dithyramb is magnificent in its outpouring. When Shaw buttered the bread of affection—which was seldom—he used no butter-knife, but always a fairly large shovel.

Yet there was much truth in this eulogy of Florence. Her large eyes were beautiful indeed, with crescent eyebrows above them. All her admirers raved of her starry eyes; no one who saw them could forget them, said Clifford Bax. Clever and lovely, it was no wonder that she captured Shaw's heart and was, for a time, veritably his best and dearest love. Whether she was so un-awakened, as her lover said, may well be doubted. She had brains. Mr. Bax, in whose early marital home she often stayed, told me how good, kind and sweet-natured she was. It was never suggested that her actor-husband had left her for any domestic trouble or fault of hers, and she was essentially a gentle complying type of woman. Possibly he had left his wife and his country for the good of both of them.

One can well imagine that from the day Shaw fell in love with Florence, his Jenny would be relegated inevitably to a back seat. Jenny in temper was almost the exact opposite of her rival: Florence was amiable, sweet-natured, incapable of jealousy, desirous of pleasing, being pleased and of giving and receiving pleasure, and certainly not insatiably sexual like the other woman.

Like Jenny, Florence appeared in Shaw's unpublished diaries. The first mention of her is in October 1890, where he records having a long talk with her at a private view of Arts and Crafts. He records nothing of what their talk was about.

Later he records escorting her to a Crystal Palace concert. There it is clear that Jenny somehow learned of the existence of this dangerous rival, and 'J.P. was angry and jealous about F.E., so the day ended unpleasantly!' About a month after their first meeting, he and Florence 'have their first really intimate conversation'.

Soon there are notes about seeing both women. The entries are eloquently antithetical, for example: 'Went over to F.E. in the evening—a happy evening'; and 'J.P. came in the evening & made a scene'. . . .

III

Early in their relationship he confided to Florence his troubles with J.P., though whether he made a clean breast of the affair may be doubted. Nor is it at all clear why he confided this unpleasant and distasteful business (or part of it!) to his new love. It may be that tongues wagged and Florence asked questions. Or it may be that he feared her finding out and took the bull by the horns. Or—equally likely—because her own past was not chaste and her affection was sympathetic, she made his confidences easy and natural. Perhaps it may have been more than one of these alternative motives that actuated him.

Whatever it was, it is quite certain that Florence knew the trial that Jenny was, and also that she was a supplanted rival. For in May 1891 he wrote a letter headed: In the Train (which Florence preserved) in which he let himself go in a way unusual with him about his J.P., as follows:

'I shall go to bed now without staying to discuss that other relation. At this moment I am in a contemptuous fury and vehemently assert that your Christmas estimate of it was the right one.' (Presumably 'it' was his trouble with Jenny.) 'Not for 40,000 such relations will I forego one 40,000th part of my relation with you. Every grain of cement she shakes from it falls like a block of granite on her own flimsy castle in the air, the work of my own imagination. The silly triumph with which she takes with the air of a conqueror, that which I have torn out of my entrails for her, almost brings the lightning down upon her. Imagine being told— what I cannot write. Damnation, triple damnation! You must give me back my peace. If you are disengaged tomorrow afternoon will you come to Prince's Hall (*not* St. James's, mind) on the enclosed ticket. The hart pants for cooling streams.'

A remarkable and revealing outburst, indeed. One would have thought that an end with Jenny was at hand and that this sorely-tried male would endure no more. If Florence had been as jealous and demanding as her rival, no doubt he would have nerved himself to cut the Gordian Knot at a blow. As it was, the persecution went on and on to his infinite discouragement and with serious effects upon his writing.

IV

The consolation that he found in his love for Florence was not merely physical or emotional. It had its intellectual side.

Early in their acquaintance, he, having conceived partly through his friendship with William Archer, a confirmed Ibsenite at first-hand, a great enthusiam for the work of that Norwegian dramatist, then scarcely known in England, directed Florence's mind to Ibsen's plays. In particular, he especially showed her the tragic character, Rebecca West, in *Rosmersholm*. The result was that both of them played the piece together privately in Bloomsbury—believed to be the only time Shaw ever acted on the stage, though he was always acting off it, according to his personal friends and to his wife in later life.

This effort led to what was perhaps the greatest stage triumph that Florence Farr ever achieved. When *Rosmersholm* was publicly produced, her acting as Rebecca created an extraordinary impression upon the intellectual public. She had been most assiduously coached by her lover in the part, and, anxious to please, and not yet wearied, as she afterwards became, of his exigent intellectual demands upon her, she rose nobly to the occasion. Even in these early days Shaw was a confident and tireless teacher of the art of acting to those players who would listen to him.

Florence Farr made another *succès d'estime* in the equally difficult *rôle* of Beatrice Cenci at the Shelley centenary. But what was more important to Shaw was that she was ready to take the leading part of Blanche Sartorious in *Widowers' Houses*, his first play. She played it exceedingly well, but did she know that Jenny Patterson was the model for this heroine? Did Jenny Patterson know that? According to St. John Ervine, Jenny was in the audience.

What a situation! More grimly comic and ironic than the play itself is the fact that one of the author's mistresses was playing the part of the other mistress, while that other mistress sat and watched her rival impersonating her. What an exquisitely contrived revenge by the dramatist for J.P.'s persecution of him!

If the audience had known that . . . If the dramatic critics had known it. . . .

Yet, strangely enough, the irony of the situation has escaped notice, to this day. Shaw himself never called attention to it, but he must have been conscious of it.

Another irony was that William Archer, esteemed as one of the best dramatic critics of his time, and Shaw's close friend and benefactor, seeing this play, pronounced that his friend had no talent for the theatre and advised him strongly to give it up. It reminds one that Ibsen himself and Chekhov were similarly advised in their early days.

V

If Jenny Patterson did know or guess that she was Blanche Sartorious, then she knew from December 9th, 1892, for that was the date of the play. Less than two months later there was a tremendous explosion—probably the most unpleasant experience of Shaw's philandering days.

It was the end of Jenny Patterson so far as Bernard Shaw was concerned, and the painful scene between his J.P. and his F.E. has already been related in his own words in the last chapter. Florence herself has left no account of the scene nor of her reactions to it. It must have been painful for her, to say the least of it, as indeed for Shaw also, but he had deserved it and perhaps she did not.

Shaw used this undignified scene between the two women in his second play, *The Philanderer*, where Julia Craven is again modelled upon his J.P., showing what a deep impression her utterly ungovernable temper expressed in raging scenes had made upon the embryo dramatist. It has been described as Shaw's worst play, and the author himself, as we have seen, has expressed strong disgust for it as a nasty play. Archer thought it an outrage on art and decency; and, produced by the Independent Theatre, it was a failure. Nor has it ever proved even moderately successful. Indeed, the American actor, Richard Mansfield, rejected the offer of it to him in one cabled word: 'Declined.'

Again, what Jenny Patterson or Florence Farr thought of its most famous reproduction of the horrid scene between themselves, or whether, either or both, recognized it or themselves, we do not know. The play quickly fell into obscurity after Florence had taken the principal part of Grace Tranfield.

Certainly Shaw wrote parts in these two earliest of his plays with Florence Farr in mind. There was yet another to come for her. In 1894, Miss Horniman of Manchester, of the much advertised Horniman's tea family, was a wealthy woman with a pronounced penchant for the theatre and a belief in the 'advanced ideas' of the time. Keeping herself in the background because of nonconformist family disapproval, she offered Florence Farr money for a theatrical season of modern intellectual drama in London.

Florence took the then Avenue Theatre (afterwards The Playhouse) near the Thames Embankment in London, and told Shaw of this godsend. Naturally, Shaw saw it as a heaven-sent opportunity; and not content to have *Widowers' Houses* merely revived, rapidly composed a new play to take advantage of so favourable a situation.

This was *Arms and the Man,* in which Florence played Louka. It was preceded as a curtain-raiser by the Irish poet Yeats's *The Land of Heart's Desire,* specially written for Florence also. Few actresses or women can have extorted such a double tribute. The first night was a 'startling' success—the epithet is Shaw's. Of Shaw's play, King Edward the Seventh who enjoyed it said: 'Of course the author's mad.'

Though the play was a popular success in a small-sized theatre and an artistic one in its Press notices, it kept eating up Miss Horniman's money, for the average receipts were only £17. Later on, it was destined to several revivals and to be a financial success. Upon it was founded that popular comic-opera *The Chocolate Soldier,* just as *My Fair Lady* was founded on Shaw's later play *Pygmalion.*

But *Arms and the Man*—his fourth—was the last play of Bernard Shaw's in which Florence played.

VI

The course of Shaw-love, like that other, and opposite, kind of love of which Shakespeare tells us, 'never did run smooth'. The loves of Florence and G.B.S., as he invariably signed himself (even to her), were no exception to this tempestuous rule in spite of Florence's innate kindness and sweetness. So it does look as if Shaw himself may have been the *agent provocateur* of Jenny Patterson's crimes.

What was the matter in Florence's case? In 1891 she was as Shaw proclaimed; 'oh my other self—not, not my other self but my very self'. That was just what she was not. Essentially she was a poetic, romantic, warm-hearted woman, while Shaw was a prosaic, realistic, cold-blooded man. In the first flush of love, his enthusiasm for her could carry her away, and his colder self as well. But just as Shaw could not live in the Patterson tropical climate for ever, or indeed for long, so he could not live in Florence's temperate climate long, but must seek the Arctic wastes congenial to himself.

How Florence felt about his attitude to sex is shown in one revealing sentence in a small book she wrote years after, in 1910, a book unnoticed by Shaw-biographers which deserves attention. This short book of less than a hundred pages, *Modern Woman: Her Intentions* is well-written, and by no means unreadable, or entirely out of date, even today.

Speaking of girls with brains and 'love's rites', i.e. the sexual act, she writes:

'. . . they do not care enough for love to perform its rites unless they are animated with the ardour of love. *Passion served up with cold sauce as in the Shaw-Barker school of sex revolts them.* Enthusiastic love is the only excuse in their eyes for going through the rather ungraceful gestures of love.'

Clearly she had no use for the risk of living with a man whose love had become a mere habit. And of the curious passage cited— which seems to be the only allusion discoverable to her affair with Shaw, made by herself—one may wonder why a woman should need an excuse for the sexual act, which should surely arise naturally and spontaneously? That 'Shaw-Barker school of sex' phrase of hers is barbed, indeed. Did Shaw ever come across it, or read this book of hers? There is no evidence that he did.

However, in their early friendship he—apparently disinterestedly—advised her to divorce her husband. Not, however, in order that he might marry her. As an 'emancipated woman' of her day, who had had quite enough with four years' experience of conventional marriage, she had no further desire for marriage bonds. Moreover, by nature, she was as tranquil and undemanding as her predecessor J.P. had been stormy and demanding.

Indeed, Shaw says he had some difficulty in persuading her to divorce Emery. That is understandable; for she has put on record her dislike of the incidents of the English divorce system which virtually make the divorce, a remedy for marital misfortunes, into a crime. But the argument that persuaded her was Shaw's argument that her actor-husband might return to England and make serious legal claims upon her.

If Shaw was unsatisfactory sexually to her, as the passage from her book seems to show, he had good reason to be similarly dissatisfied. He says that this 'young independent professional woman', enjoying as such 'an exceptional freedom of social intercourse in artistic circles in London', behaved altogether too freely with other men.

He puts it thus: 'As she was clever, good-natured and very good-looking, all her men friends fell in love with her. This had occurred so often that she had lost all patience with the hesitating preliminaries of her less practised adorers. Accordingly when they clearly longed to kiss her, and she did not dislike them sufficiently to make their gratification too great a strain on her excessive good nature, she would seize the stammering suitor firmly by the wrists, bring him into her arms by a smart pull, and saying, "Let's get it over", allow the startled gentleman to have his kiss and then proceed to converse with him at her ease on subjects of more general interest.'

That—on the face of it—is a description by an onlooker, which Shaw can hardly have been. No doubt Florence related to him one such incident, but it can hardly have been the routine procedure that he suggests. It is typical of Shaw's picturesque exaggerations, written with the seeming objectivity of a journalist reporting for a sensational newspaper. He gives no hint of his own feelings or reaction to such a happening (or happenings) at all. A man in love can hardly like such behaviour on the part of the beloved, but Shaw was writing this tale of promiscuity long after the love had died.

There was a time when, in connection with Florence, Shaw did suffer the pangs of despised love. As the French cynic tells us, in any love-affair there is always one who loves and one who accepts and allows the love. Certainly Shaw for a time loved Florence far more than she, with all her natural complaisance, could bring herself to love him.

One love-letter of his, heartrending in its sincerity, makes that abundantly clear. She had forgotten—and therefore failed to keep —an appointment with him and he wrote to reproach her: 'When my need was at its holiest, I found darkness, emptiness, void. How could you do this thing? This was to have been the happiness of all my great happiness, the deepest and restfullest of all my tranquillities, the very best of all my loves and I was robbed of it.'

Calling her a wretch, he casts 'a million reproaches' upon her for ever.

When a woman fails to turn up to a rendezvous with her lover it is plain that her feelings for him must be lukewarm indeed. And in such circumstances what more wounding excuse to his *amour-propre* can be given, than: 'I forgot'?

In his letter Shaw added, more prosaically, that for the purpose of their assignation he had got rid of his mother by sending her to the Opera; made a journalistic colleague break an appointment to release himself; had left one meeting early and given another one the slip: all for Florence and her beloved presence. And then—she did not turn up!

He never—or at any rate in after years—had any illusions as to himself not being her only love. He stated that 'she set no bounds to her relations with men whom she liked and always had a sort of Leporello list of a dozen adventures'. Talking later on to his friend and biographer, Hesketh Pearson, he repeats this picture of her emotional instability. 'She attached no more importance to what you call love-affairs than Casanova or Frank Harris; and she was too good-natured to refuse anything to anyone she really liked. I think she was rather proud of her Leporello list which contained fourteen names in 1894. She herself said that if a man started love-making, she felt at once as if she was on the stage and must act up to his acting.'

It will be observed that with the passage of time, poor Florence's

'Leporello list' has grown. As Shaw told Pearson at the same time flatly: 'I did not write any letters to Florence Farr. I saw her too often.' Pearson firstly points out: 'Shaw's memory is shaky'—which is a kindly understatement. In hard fact, some twenty-five letters of his which Florence preserved have been published, and on these being produced to Shaw by their owner, Mr. Clifford Bax, his comment merely was: 'Where the dickens did you get them?'

Much must be forgiven to the failing recollection of a very old man, but the sin which one must impute to Shaw is deeper than mere failure to recollect accurately.

Although the married Shaw would naturally desire to play down his affair with Florence, yet there can be no question of the strength, depth and reality of his obsession with her at the time. His letters to her attest that.

In one of them, telling her that he was the noblest creature she had yet met 'in the world of monkeys where I found you straying', he adds, 'Some of them thought you a pretty female ape; others thought you a goddess: the first asked you to play with them; the second asked to be allowed to worship you: you could not say No to either. Then came I, the man, and made you my woman, on your stopping me as I wandered lonely through the forest.

'For many years had I wandered alone, sufficient to myself: I will, at a word, wander on again alone. But what will you do? Return to the monkeys? It is not possible; self-sufficient must you also become or else find no less a man than I, to be your mate.'

Contrast the tone of the things Shaw said *to* her with the tone of things he said *about* her after she was dead and unable to answer or defend herself. One is surely driven to the conclusion that never in amatory history were there such discreditable changes. 'At lovers' perjuries they say Jove laughs,' wrote Shakespeare; but not, surely, at such as these in their ignobility. Florence, it is to be feared, had cut his self-esteem to the quick, and it is not in human nature—unless one has the magnanimity of a Marcus Aurelius—to forgive such a wound. But Shaw's sex-accusations against Florence are an outrage and in the most odious taste.

VII

However, it was not only as a mistress—where, from Shaw's expressions, it looks as if the quality he most valued in her was her 'restfulness'—that Florence had her deficiencies. It was as an actress as well.

He had set his heart—and also, more important, his mind—on making her a great actress, the vehicle of the 'New Drama' and his own plays-to-be. He believed that great actresses are not merely born but are made by correct teaching, hard work, and incessant study and practice. Also he held a theory akin to the Miltonic theory that for a man to write a great poem he must live himself as a poem, a model of virtue in thought, word and deed. Shaw thought that to be a great actress the actress must be a great woman, fit mate for a great man.

'Joey the Clown'—as Mrs. Campbell was later on to call Shaw—was intensely solemn and serious upon this subject. It was part of such religion as he then professed. He set himself with all his powers to turn Florence Farr, a good actress, into a really great one, believing—deceived perhaps by his love of the young woman—that she, as people say, 'had it in her'.

He was mistaken, as events proved. She just hadn't got it in her. Nor did she wish to have it in her. In her heart she cared nothing for Shavian ideals; quite opposite ideals in ideas fascinated her. Her mystical, romantic temperament left to itself proved in later life almost the exact opposite of Shaw's, as we shall see.

Meanwhile, G.B.S. worked incessantly to perfect her in acting. The trouble he took, the thought he gave, the adjurations he bestowed upon her are perfectly amazing; his tuition was perpetual and relentless. It was a struggle indeed, for complaisant as she generally was, Florence did not respond to his training.

One letter of this period is enough to show the detached, unwearying pains he took, and his despair that he was not getting the results he wanted.

In this one: She was a 'lost wretch'. In the first scene she was insufferable. She was reproached for tightening her upper lip, bunching-up her back, stiffening her neck, holding on by her elbows, and saying 'suppose-it-is-not-for-one-but-for-another' (as one word) so as to 'strike the house dumb with its utter want of any inflexion or meaning.' She was a 'will-less girl'; a 'miserable ill-starred woman', whose 'bypaths and shortcuts' only led her backward. To be with her was hell; she made him frightfully unhappy; he asked: 'What is "the true relation" between us? The relation of the North Pole to the South . . . you have driven me to utter desperation: I can no longer be satisfied to suffer and shake my fist at the stars.'

If teaching, preaching, scolding and bullying by a Shaw could make a fair actress into a really great one, Florence Farr would have been an Ellen Terry. He laboured incessantly 'to make the most of her'. He wanted his will-less girl to be 'mistress of her art, not the slave of its intoxications and externals'. She must not live 'in and for herself, instead of in and for the world'. How could he endure on Judgement Day to be asked: 'Why did you suffer her to do her work so badly?'

Florence wilted under the Shavian discipline and tuition. Shaw thought her early life had been too easy: she thought he was making her present life too hard. She was both romantic and poetic; and she found her lover deficient in both regards. Very reluctantly, Shaw had to recognize his failure. The capacity for hard stage work, the instinctive technique, above all, the divine fire that is the gift of the gods alone—these were not in Florence Farr. Shavian instruction was no substitute. The truth was that she had not the inborn gift. For that reason it was a case of love's labour lost; and she realized it quicker than he. She said of Shaw: 'He is like New York: it's hell and damnation for him to be doing nothing.'

Certainly Shaw gave her no respite from his teachings and preachings. In the long run he was forced to realize that his 'desperate efforts' only worried and discouraged her.

Inevitably, the end came.

VIII

She left Shaw for the poet and mystic W. B. Yeats, whose *Land of Heart's Desire* was much more to her taste and temperament than any of Shaw's plays or dissertations. Yeats took her in hand very much as Shaw had done, but he was infinitely gentler and more appreciative. There was all the difference in the world between the Irish poet and the Irish playwright. 'Yeats was such a handsome man that I knew I hadn't an earthly,' said Shaw.

But it went deeper than mere looks.

In spite of her desertion of Shaw in his plays, there was neither quarrel nor recrimination between the former lovers. They parted; and, in modern parlance, that was that.

Shaw had lost both his mistress and his leading lady. It did not matter; there were others in the offing. As an actress, Janet Achurch had aroused his enthusiasm to the boredom of his friends. For the rest, he was engaged in philandering with his own 'Leporello list'; names upon which were Annie Besant, May Morris, Edith Bland and others.

Of the ending Shaw says: 'We detached ourselves naturally and painlessly; and presently I got married.' One can believe that it was painless—perhaps even a relief—to Florence. But one can hardly believe that the downfall of his cherished hopes, the flinging away of so much expended care and pains, the defeat of his cherished dream of making a great actress out of Florence Farr, the blow of the public defection of a leading exponent of the New Drama upon the stage was painless to Shaw.

Florence's new *rôle* was that of performing in Yeats's poetic dramas and the like, on the stage, but more often on concert platforms. With a Hibernian lyre and a classical costume, she now appeared before a different and more soulful public than those intellectual worshippers of Ibsen and his school.

Shaw was utterly contemptuous of 'cantillating', which, he said, was no new art, as she thought. Cats did the same thing, serenading each other, Shaw said contemptuously. It was the mere chanting of curates; the intoning of toastmasters; and of public speakers with nothing to say. It was as bad as Bernhardt at her worst. Yeats thought it novel because he never went to church. 'Cantillating' only turned ordinary twaddle into a nerve-destroying crooning that—greatest crime of all—did not convey the meaning and feeling of the author.

But all this denigration was futile. Not by such talk was the enthusiastic Florence to be detached from the 'cantillation' of her Yeats. Shaw says he left Florence to Yeats's mercy. He had no option. Yeats was a far more congenial spirit to her than Shaw.

Though she had been interested in, and deeply concerned with, women's suffrage and advanced femininity, most of the social, political and economic questions that Shaw cared for so deeply, hardly interested her at all. Her own interests lay in occultism, the Hermetic Art and similarly esoteric subjects; and she was capable of searching for the wisdom of the ancient Chaldeans in the Hebrew Alphabet, as a little book of hers ('by F. Farr Emery') in its sixteen pages shows. She also wrote on The Way of Wisdom signing herself S.S.D.D.—denoting the membership of a secret society for the study of mysticism to which she and Yeats adhered.

She also wrote a masque called *The Mystery of Time* and a short story *The Dancing Faun* under her maiden name of Florence Farr. From the fact that none of Shaw's biographers mentions her as an authoress you might conclude that her productions were negligible. They were, however, warmly praised by good judges on their appearance, and, without being important, her writings are talented.

The one of them that perhaps is most impressive is called *A Calendar of Philosophy*. It consists of striking brief excerpts from writers more or less well known, most of whom are not philosophers in the technical sense at all. In this compilation she shows a distinctly individual and unhackneyed taste and remarkably wide reading. What is especially significant is that, although she quotes many contemporary authors, such as Arthur Symons, Cunningham

Mrs. Patrick Campbell

Mrs. Patrick Campbell
as Eliza Doolittle in the
first English production
of *Pygmalion* at His
Majesty's Theatre, 1914

A letter to 'Stella'
(Mrs. Patrick Camp-
bell) on a reconstruc-
tion of her make-up
table at the Royalty
Theatre

Graham, Maeterlinck, Verlaine, William Morris, Ezra Pound—and Yeats, there is not one single extract from Shaw's writings. Yet, it must be said, Shaw is easily one of the most quotable of English authors and a perfect mine of golden phrases.

Why does she quote nothing of G.B.S.? It cannot be believed that one so acutely susceptible to excellence, in thought and expression, as Florence certainly was, was deaf and blind to those merits in her former lover's work. It can only be that she was unwilling to ask his permission to quote from his copyright. No doubt Shaw would, if asked, have willingly granted it, for he was never petty-minded in such matters.

And, however much he may have felt her desertion at the time, he quickly got over it. There is, moreover, uncontestable evidence that he retained to the end a personal concern for her welfare and need. He had her successor in Janet Achurch (an actress more or less happily married to Charles Charrington, an actor of the day) whom, as an actress, Shaw praised in exaggerated terms out of zeal for Ibsen and the new movement in the theatre. In June 1893, Shaw had given this lady a presentation copy of *Widowers' Houses*, inscribed with their names and the following verse:

> This book henceforth belongs to Janet
> The greatest actress on this planet
> 'Twas written by a fond adorer
> Who saw her first as Ibsen's Nora.

Again, G.B.S. was mistaken in his estimate. But soon he was shooting at higher game than Janet Achurch, the actress of a coterie; for he cherished the hope—destined to be elusive—of getting Ellen Terry to act in his newest play, *The Man of Destiny*.

But his hopes of Janet and Ellen did not make Florence Farr lose any sleep, for her hopes were now centred upon another man, and in another direction than Ibsen and the New Drama.

IX

Time passed. The connection between Florence and Yeats 'painlessly' ended, as that other Shaw connection had done. But Yeats's references to her are invariably appreciative of her high quality. Yeats's wife suggests that Florence got bored with her husband, and this may be true.

Her sympathetic nature is well illustrated by Yeats's tribute: 'She was the only person to whom I could tell everything'; and again, in his description of her as 'an almost perfect poetic actress'.

Even at fifty, Florence Farr's beauty was unimpaired, if we may trust the testimony of the rising generation of that time. They said that one of the standing figures in Burne-Jones's admired picture *The Golden Stairs* must have been a portrait of her from the life. Very likely it was; but beyond the likeness there is no record that she sat to the painter.

X

Suddenly the newspaper-reading public (which knew Florence Farr only as an actress attached to certain definite schools of acting) were impressed by the news in 1912 that Florence had left England in order to live in Ceylon permanently.

Her close friends, knowing of her deep and long-standing interest in Oriental thought, were not so surprised. Outside her own circle many questions were asked. For good? Yes, for good! But why? She was in her prime, still lovely and much sought after in 'advanced' circles. People, Shaw amongst them, just could not understand this abrupt and strange departure, without reason or explanation. What on earth would she do in Ceylon?

Her motives and purpose were eagerly canvassed. No. There was no scandal. At last she wrote to her friends from the island where, as a hymn-writer tells English folk, there are spicy breezes and where

'Every prospect pleases
And only man is vile'

a shocking libel on the Ceylonese who are no worse—if no better —than the rest of us.

Florence told her friends that she was translating Tamil poetry, and among other activities 'had a job like Queen Elizabeth'. She was Lady Superintendent of a college in Jaffna. She has 'a really interesting life at last'. (Can life with Shaw or Yeats have been uninteresting?)

Later came news of an operation for cancer. Bernard Shaw, deeply upset by the shocking news, cabled urgently for particulars. Florence had been deeply upset, too, and even indignant, because her malady had been said at first to be a 'nasty boil', after which 'cancer seems decent'. For the first time since babyhood, she was helpless, having to be nursed, but full of courage and spirit.

Then, when she was told of the death of Aubrey Beardsley's sister Mabel, the mystery of her Ceylon journey was solved. 'I am always glad to hear of someone making a good end. I came here to make mine brave,' she wrote back. It is easier to be brave among strangers, than among grieving and helpless friends watching the last agonies.

Bravely she died in April 1917 in a Vedantist seminary, having previously left to her friend Clifford Bax a black box not to be opened until after her death. It contained her love letters from Shaw and Yeats. 'Shaw has been a most faithful friend to me,' was her tribute.

Such is the story of Florence Farr. . . .

To use a vulgar colloquialism, she may have been what is called 'an easy piece', if you accept G.B.S.'s account of her as literally true. But she was very much more: she was sweet, kind, brave and good. Nor was she unintellectual or untalented—far from it, as her career shows. She was a credit to the 'emancipated woman' fetish of her era in England. So far as Shaw was concerned, her sin lay in her inability to use him to the utmost: she made him feel that he and his efforts were thrown away upon her.

'All my love-affairs end tragically because the women can't use me.' 'It is only when I am being used that I can feel my own existence, enjoy my own life. They [the women] lie low and let me imagine things about them but in the end a frightful unhappiness, an unspeakable weariness comes; and the Wandering Jew must go on in search of someone who can use him to the utmost of his capacity. Everything real in life is based on need!' Such was Shaw's verdict.

Yes; but so far as Florence Farr was concerned, Shaw had to be used for his own purposes, not for hers. Those purposes of his were not hers to the limit as he wanted them to be. She needed and wanted to be herself; not the mere incarnation upon the stage of his ideas.

And can you call it a tragic ending when two people part 'naturally and painlessly', to lead their own lives as these twain, thereafter, did? Florence's tragedy lay not in leaving Shaw, but in her self-imposed exile and her premature death from a ghastly and painful disease, far from her home or friends.

But, long before she died, a deeper spiritual tragedy had happened: his holiest joy, his secret glimpse of heaven, his Angel of the Annunciation had declined in Bernard Shaw's mind to a mere good-natured wanton, a Nell Gwynne with a Leporello list. Worse: in his heart she had come to have so small a corner that, in old age, his decayed memory could not remember having written even one of his passionate love-letters to her.

You see . . . there had been so many others since then. . . .

Speaking from the grave, this poor woman said of this former lover nothing but good: 'a most faithful friend'. No doubt she had known many worse men; perhaps, too, she was touched by his cable asking for details of her last malady. Shaw indeed was, in general, a good friend: a far more loyal friend than a lover. But would she have thought him a faithful friend if she had read his callous descriptions of her, given to the public after she was powerless to defend herself? It is time that justice was done to Florence Farr's memory.

Time, the all-conquering, makes short work with Shavian love. It was not of such love that was written the tremendous human battle-cry of defiance: Love is stronger than death. One can only suppose that if this woman of George Bernard Shaw's had been the woman taken in adultery of the Gospel, he, this philanderer, would have accepted the invitation to cast the first stone at her, for is not that, exactly, what he did?

But the wounded name of Florence Farr can be safely left to the compassion and understanding of every generous heart.

V

A PRIVATE MARRIAGE DEED:
ANNIE BESANT

❧❧❧❧❧❧❧❧❧❧❧❧❧❧❧❧❧❧❧❧❧❧❧❧❧❧❧❧❧❧❧

'She was fiercely proud . . . I ought to have done much more for her and she much less for me . . . I do not like the proverb "Love me little, love me long", but whoever invented it had a very narrow escape of finding its true form which is "Love me lightly, love me long." And that is how I loved, and still love, Annie Besant.'
—Shaw in 'Dr. Annie Besant: 50 years in Public Work'

I

NO WOMAN of our time dominates the imagination of Britain as the famous and lovely Annie Besant unmistakably did in late Victorian times. Magnetic, graceful, contralto-voiced, in an age of oratory she was unsurpassed in her ability to move audiences. She also plied a fairly persuasive, if sometimes a somewhat platitudinous, pen.

To this was added the attraction of scandal. A clergyman's wife who had left husband and home to become an atheist, and to join forces with England's most notorious atheist and Radical, Charles Bradlaugh, M.P., who single-handed had defeated both the Government and the House of Commons on the Oaths question, was a portent of changing times indeed.

Annie Besant (*née* Wood, who rhymed her name with 'pleasant') came of good family. One kinsman was Lord Chancellor Hatherley, another Field-Marshal Sir Evelyn Wood, V.C. Her father, William Burton Persse Wood, a City man, dying suddenly left his wife and three children badly off. But Annie's mother, like Annie herself, was a woman of spirit and initiative. She started with the encouragement of Dr. Vaughan, the headmaster of Harrow, a schoolhouse at that school which proved an outstanding success. It enabled her to give her son Henry a public-school and University education, and to provide for herself and her surviving daughter Annie. With her considerable savings entrusted to her solicitor, all seemed well. Unfortunately, the solicitor's defalcations engulfed nearly the whole of Mrs. Besant's money. She sank under this second life-disaster, and died soon after.

In those days, a girl was seldom given an academic education, since her future was thought to lie merely in marriage. Consequently, Annie had nothing like the educational advantages of her brother Henry—a fact which she, a girl of brains, came very much to resent. Largely she was trained by Miss Marryat—sister of the famous Captain Marryat, whose naval fictions for boys enjoyed the widest possible popularity, and are not yet dead.

Miss Marryat, a woman of piety and Evangelistic principles, trained the serious and apparently docile young girl along those lines. But the maiden revolted: the first of many such repudiations in her life, which indeed were so frequent that her latest biographer called his life of her, aptly enough, by the title *The Five Lives of Annie Besant*. This was an under-statement, for this richly-endowed young person, like many of us, had more lives than the proverbial cat with nine.

At that time, the Oxford Movement (not to be confused with our generation's Oxford Group, otherwise Buchmanism) was turning High Church ritualism into later-day Anglo-Catholicism. It was a fashionable and growing movement. The ardent, impulsive, serious-minded young Annie Wood was caught by it. She read widely in the works of the Fathers of the Church; she fasted; she prayed; she even flagellated herself.

All this might have done her no harm. But in this phase of thought and emotion, she had the misfortune, when staying with her grandparents at Clapham, to meet a local young curate. Curates are not dangerous as a rule, except to females, as indeed this particular one was destined to be for the good and lovely Annie.

He was the Reverend Frank Besant, a brother of Sir Walter Besant, the author of some good Victorian novels and the founder of the present-day Society of Authors. Frank was commonplace and conventional; High Church, but not extreme; more interested in parish records and mathematical problems than religion in its real sense. What he lacked, Annie's young and ardent imagination at first endowed him with.

In the result, they were married when the girl was only twenty. It proved a tragedy for them both. Summing it up from Annie's standpoint, the popular journalist, W. T. Stead, who was drowned in the *Titanic* disaster, said of the mistaken marriage: 'She could not be the bride of Heaven and therefore became the bride of Frank Besant who was hardly an adequate substitute.'

Out of his Lord Chancellor's patronage, Lord Hatherley provided for Annie's husband and Annie by giving him the living of Sibsey, a tiny village in Lincolnshire.

II

Annie was as innocent as a flower. Her bridal night came as a horrid shock to her susceptibilities, but she had physical as well as intellectual ardour, and she bore her dull husband two children, a son and a daughter. Annie found that her clerical spouse 'had very high ideas of a husband's authority and a wife's submission'.

Being the Vicar's wife and a mother proved far too little for Annie's active energetic nature. Her brain was busy not with wifehood, motherhood and household affairs alone but with theological problems. Her wide reading and her worrying engendered doubts. She found that her husband could neither understand nor sympathize with her or her doubts. To him, of course, they were sinful in any Churchwoman, but especially reprehensible in the Vicar's wife.

For spiritual counsel in her torturing lack of faith, Annie went to Oxford to see the great Dr. Pusey, a leader of the High Church school of thought. His ghostly counsel did little good.

'It is not your duty to ascertain the truth. It is your duty to believe the truth laid down by the Church,' he said. And when she spoke of leaving the Church, he flatly forbade her 'to lead into your own lost state, souls for whom Christ died'.

Perhaps that spiritual prohibition halted her for a time, but not for long. Back in Sibsey, she told her horrified husband that she would no longer partake of the Holy Communion. She offered to continue her attendance at matins and evensong. There was argument, and he yielded at first. But perturbed by possible parish comment, and even diocesan disapproval, he retracted his surrender and issued an ultimatum.

Either she must receive the sacrament and behave as the parson's wife should, or leave the Vicarage. She left.

Obeying the divine injunction in an opposite sense, she left all to follow where her intellect led her. Whatever one may think of her, she was in deep distress; and it was an act of rare moral courage, when, to the condemnation of her little circle and against all the tenets of her Christian upbringing, she flung herself alone into the deep waters of London life.

To follow whom or what? She only knew: to wherever her belief, or lack of belief, led. This, of course, is the stuff of which martyrs and heroines are made. She had acted exactly as Ibsen's Nora of *A Doll's House* acted in banging the door—though at the time Ibsen and his doll-woman were unknown to her.

III

Her food, clothing and shelter were hardly provided for. It is true that the Reverend Frank made the bolting wife and mother an allowance—what else could he do? But it was a small allowance, insufficient for herself, her still-living, ruined mother and her baby daughter Mabel. Her son Digby was with his father.

She started to earn, and earned very little, for times were hard and woman-labour decried. Then she met the great Charles Bradlaugh who instantly gave her a cause-without-a-creed; the cause of atheism and secularism. This she embraced wholeheartedly.

In former days, in her husband's empty church she had experimented in public speaking and proved to herself (though not to anyone else) that she was an orator by inborn gift. Now she rapidly proved it to all England, and as a consequence, in no time at all, she was co-leader with Bradlaugh of the advanced antireligious propaganda of that day. Those were the days when public-speaking (the platform, as it was called) dominated contemporary thought, even more than the Press which reported it, and even more than television does today.

Very quickly Annie Besant was famous. Nor did she confine herself to oratory. Pamphlets poured from her pen. She began to edit free-thinking periodicals which did rather more than pay their way. She had, in fact, established her name and fame beyond doubt. To her secularist circle and to the general public she was a famous woman, but to professing Christians in general, and Anglicans in particular, she was an infamous phenomenon.

Her fame, or infamy, reached even to remote Sibsey. The concern of the Vicar may be imagined. He came to London to remonstrate and assert his rights. It is said that in his rage and vexation he struck her. The result of the interview was that a formal separation was arranged, herself to have her daughter Mabel, the father to have the son, and she to receive maintenance of £110 a year.

But this arrangement did not last because Bradlaugh and Mrs. Besant, having become interested in birth-control as a solution to the poverty of the poorest, provoked a tempest of fresh denunciation by publishing an opuscule by a Dr. Charles Knowlton called *Facts of Philosophy, or The Private Companion of Young Married People*. It was the forerunner of Dr. Marie Stopes's works upon Birth Control; and it so horrified the authorities that the two atheistical leaders were arrested and sent for trial before the Lord Chief Justice of England, for publishing what in law was described as an obscene libel.

The furore was great. The vilest scandals were disseminated, one of the worst being that Horatio Bottomley, later the M.P. and fraudulent speculator, was the illegitimate son of Bradlaugh and Annie Besant. Though Lord Chief Justice Cockburn summed up in favour of the accused at the trial, the shocked jury convicted. An appeal was lodged. The convictions were quashed.

IV

All England had watched the trial and appeal with bated breath, divided into two camps. Bradlaugh and Annie Besant were now more foully attacked. The Reverend Frank Besant was compelled by the state of public opinion, and his own conception of his duty as a beneficed clergyman and a father, to get both children saved from their mother's immoral non-Christian influence. Legal action followed to deprive her of both children's custody; her allowance was stopped. Jessel, the Master of the Rolls, heard the case and deprived Mrs. Besant of the custody. The decision incited great indignation amongst advanced people and £2,000 was raised by public subscription towards Mrs. Besant's law costs.

Mrs. Besant promptly sued for divorce but failed to get her decree.

It was this state of affairs that brought her into collision with George Bernard Shaw, then one of the rising hopes of the advanced guard both in atheism and socialism. Advanced opinion was, naturally enough, solid for Mrs. Besant and against her deprivation of her own children. One dissentient voice was heard: the voice of young Shaw.

Everyone was citing the case of the poet Shelley, deprived by the Lord Chancellor of his day of his children as an unfit person to have them, on the ground of his atheistical opinions. It was agreed by advanced opinion that Mrs. Besant's case was as monstrously wrong and unjust as Shelley's.

Now Shaw was a great admirer and imitator of Shelley as a genius, a vegetarian, an atheist, and as a courageous thinker in advance of his age. But—paradoxically—he upheld the view that Shelley, having regard to his domestic instability, was the last person to have the care of any child, his own or anyone's. Shaw had no admiration for his own parents' upbringing of himself, as we have seen, or for parents in general as children's caretakers. He quoted the view of William Morris that the last person to have control of a child was its parents. Similarly, Mrs. Besant, who was always immersed in important work entailing much absence from home, ought not to be entrusted with her own children.

There was enough sense and truth in this view to annoy the advanced movement. Naturally, this view of Shaw's was told to Mrs. Besant. Equally naturally, she was incensed by it.

v

The day came when she had an opportunity of dealing with this adversary. She and Bradlaugh were Radicals, and in early 1885 Shaw was to lecture before the Dialectical Society on Socialism. The then young and inexperienced lecturer was warned that the famous and brilliant Mrs. Besant intended to be at the subsequent debate and to make mincemeat of him.

Very nervous, Shaw resigned himself to his fate at the tongue of the redoubtable young woman. She was there in the audience. He put his case—and awaited annihilation. But Mrs. Besant sat silent. Another speaker put the opposite side of the case. Whereupon, to everyone's surprise, Mrs. Besant then rose and demolished the opposition instead of Shaw.

Sensation!

It is sometimes said that the brilliance of Shaw's case converted Annie then and there. Shaw, ready to claim all the credit going, and some more, makes no such claim. But she met him and asked him to nominate her for election to the new socialistic Fabian Society, and to dine with her. Shaw was only too pleased to do both. The Society needed converts of mark, and young Shaw was impecunious enough to need dinner.

A real friendship between the highly-gifted pair quickly developed, with the promise of becoming something much warmer. To date, the adherence of the famous Mrs. Besant was the most important capture of the Fabians; everyone had heard of her; she was a national figure whose gifts were acknowledged even by her bitterest enemies. On the other hand, the Fabian leaders were then obscure nobodies: Sidney Webb, Graham Wallas, Beatrice Potter, Sydney Olivier, Bernard Shaw: not one English man or woman in a thousand had heard of one of these names in the early 1880s. Hubert Bland and his wife, Edith Nesbit, were known for their journalism and authorship but not for Fabianism or politics.

Amongst innumerable activities, Mrs. Besant edited a periodical called *Our Corner* in support of the Secularist Cause. She now promptly gave a corner in it to socialistic propaganda, thereby upsetting her Radical friend Bradlaugh. She did more. Hearing of her new young friend's poverty and his abortive novels, she accepted two of the latter for paid serial publication in this journal. It was no formal acceptance, either. *The Irrational Knot* ran during three years, 1885 to 1887; and *Love Among the Artists* for two years 1887 to 1888. With the expiry of the latter, the journal itself expired.

She also paid for his occasional articles and criticisms. But, when Shaw discovered that she was paying 'her inevitable largesse' not out of the funds of the National Secular Society but out of her own purse, poor as he was he refused the payments.

'An incorrigible benefactress' is Shaw's phrase for her upon this matter. She was, indeed.

They played duets together. Often Shaw escorted her home. They attended meetings and concerts, and were constant companions.

By now, Shaw, after his initiation into gallantry by Mrs. Patterson, was becoming a skilled and incorrigible philanderer. Annie Besant was exposed to the full force of the youthful fascination of this fellow-Fabian and apparently fast friend. They worked tirelessly in the socialistic, trade-union and revolutionary causes, as well as openly spending much of their leisure in each other's company.

But Annie Besant knew nothing of such contemporaneous women-friends of Shaw as Jennie Patterson, Grace Gilchrist, the Spooner girl, or Florence Farr. Jennie Patterson knew of her and was inordinately jealous, miserably following the pair in the street when Shaw escorted her rival home.

She does not seem to have dared, however, to confront this famous woman with her jealousy as she confronted Florence Farr. But as Shaw's unpublished diary records, one Christmas Day she invaded his room, read and stole some of Annie Besant's letters to him. It took him almost the whole day to get them out of her clutches.

Meanwhile, while Shaw's private life was engaged in philandering, the public life of the country was hotting-up. Trade was bad. Unemployment was rife; the masses were discontented and seething with sedition. Meetings and demonstrations, marches and clashes with the police were becoming frequent.

Naturally, Bernard Shaw and Annie Besant as believers in a coming social revolution of the workers in opposition to the 'wicked capitalists'—Shaw had read Karl Marx's classic work *Das Kapital* in French (there was no English edition yet) which temporarily converted him to the extremist revolutionary socialism —were intimately concerned with the economic situation and its possible consequences in revolution.

What is nowadays called 'a showdown', between the authorities responsible for the maintenance of law and order and the insurgent working-classes, was clearly imminent.

VI

On a November day in 1887, known in Trade Union history for many years as 'Bloody Sunday', a vast procession of London's unemployed and their compatriots was led by John Burns and

R. B. Cunningham Graham, M.P., two well-known socialist leaders. These two were a fine contrast: Burns, then a typical working-man, and Graham, in reality and appearance, an aristocrat.

The Commissioner of the Police for the Metropolis, Sir Charles Warren, prohibited a mass meeting in Trafalgar Square from which the procession was to start. Rights of free speech and of congregation in that Square were supposedly infringed by the police prohibition, and both sides prepared for a trial of strength.

The Northern contingent of the demonstrators gathered in force on Clerkenwell Green. Shaw spoke to this multitude, urging resolution and disciplined behaviour on the march. The celebrated William Morris marched at the head, Shaw and Mrs. Besant marched side by side at her special request. Shaw had tried hard to dissuade Annie from taking part on the ground that there might be danger, but she insisted on personally demonstrating and marching to Trafalgar Square.

That contingent reached Bloomsbury safely. But elsewhere disorder had broken out; shops had been attacked and looted and the police had received orders to crush the demonstration. When the Morris-Shaw-Besant contingent reached Bloomsbury, they met whole masses of people in flight, pursued by the police using their truncheons.

'You must get out of this,' Shaw said to Mrs. Besant urgently. She obeyed and ran off. That was the last he saw of her that day. People were being knocked down, and out, all over the street.

One of his followers rushed up to Shaw saying: 'Shaw, give us a lead. What are we to do?'

Paralysed by the dismaying situation, Shaw did not know what to answer. He could only gasp out:

'Nothing. Each of us must get to the Square the best way he can.'

In Trafalgar Square there was panic. Cavalry had arrived to reinforce the police. The horses charged the resisters in the mob. knocking down the sightseers who failed to get out of their way, There was riot and pandemonium.

Burns and Graham were arrested, Graham very much injured. Edward Carpenter was clubbed by what he called 'that crawling thing—a policeman!' Many respectable people were manhandled and hurt, and later there was bitter criticism of the authorities' action. But the mass meeting and the processions were broken up and dispersed. Order was restored.

Smarting under their defeat, Mrs. Besant and some others of advanced opinions reacted swiftly. They urged a mass return to the Square next Sunday in an even greater demonstration of protest. Annie showed amazing energy and resource. Collecting funds, organizing defences for those arrested, agitating, mobilizing the Press, were only a few of her activities.

But Shaw, who had believed in the Shelleyan and socialistic doctrine that 'the People' were invincible: 'Ye are many. They are few', had received a severe mental shock. A physical coward (as he cheerfully admitted), he now perceived the utter folly of expecting an unarmed, undisciplined multitude to prevail by physical force exerted against trained, disciplined soldiers and obedient policemen. That lesson of the experience of 'Bloody Sunday' was not lost upon him. So, when Mrs. Besant, amid wild applause, moved a resolution to repeat the demonstration and fight the authorities, it was her great friend 'Comrade Shaw' who, in a strongly-argumentative speech, seconded the opposition of the editor of the *Freethinker*, the well-known G. W. Foote.

Shaw's most telling point, perhaps, was that at worst the Government, in order to quell riot and incipient revolution, could use the newly-invented machine-gun—the Maxim—to spray the rioters. Against such a weapon what could fists and bodies do? Nor would the police and soldiers side with the populace; they would implicitly obey the orders of their superiors if, and when, ordered to fire on the mob.

That was a douche of cold common-sense upon the heated enthusiasm engendered by Annie Besant's emotional speech. Her resolution so warmly and vigorously applauded was overwhelmingly lost, all her supporters deserting her.

What Annie Besant thought of Shaw's opposition is not recorded, but no one in the Movement thought well of his behaviour on Bloody Sunday. He overheard a critic saying to Cunningham Graham:

'Who is this Bernard Shaw, anyway? What has he done?'

'He was the first man to run away from Trafalgar Square on Bloody Sunday,' answered Graham.

Shaw, who now regarded Graham as a romanticist more ornamental than useful to the Cause (he put this romanticism in his plays), did not shrink from repeating this anecdote, commenting: 'He flattered me. I had not even that much sense.'

Never did Shaw—to do him the justice he deserves—ever pretend to physical courage. He used to explain that when shooting or other violence started, he would be found under the bed, only to come out when all the violence was over and genuine constructive business started. He knew his own strength and weaknesses. His attitude was, in Browning's language, 'No hero, I confess,' but he was not ashamed to be 'no hero'. 'I am a thinker, not a fighter,' he said.

But after all, it is not impossible to be both.

VII

The fiasco of Bloody Sunday and its aftermath, however, certainly shook Shaw. It brought him no credit. One of his followers accosted him, later on, with bitter reproaches for leading poor ignorant men into a disaster, and having no remedy for the defeat they had suffered.

For once, the agile tongue of Shaw had no answer to an accusation. Ever thereafter this bookworm had a more realistic idea of revolutions, which were so different in modern life from the irresponsible talks of them in theoretical propaganda.

Through all these events, before them and after them, his close personal relations with Annie Besant went on. Stephen Winsten, a friend of his in later years, tells how Annie Besant made a present to him of an umbrella. It was so ugly—she was deficient in good taste—that he gave it back to her. She instantly flung it over the fence in Regent's Park where they were walking together at the time.

To tease her—or perhaps also to placate her—he made a drawing showing a lot of little umbrellas coming through the fence. Probably it had no effect, for the great orator had no sense of humour at all.

In spite of their temperamental differences, which were numerous and considerable, their friendship strengthened. They still were constantly together in privacy and publicly. In his unpublished diaries Shaw has many references to Mrs. Besant. It is perhaps significant that he does not refer to her by her initials, as in the cases of J.P. and F.E. Most of these references are trifling enough, relating chiefly to music and escortings. But one or two are significant indeed.

Thus in 1886, he writes how his Fabian activities had 'brought me much into contact with Mrs. Besant'! (It was not only his Fabian activities, as we have seen.) He goes on: 'Towards the end of the year this intimacy became of a very close and personal sort, without however going further than a friendship.' He complains about this time of his inveterate laziness, procrastination, listlessness and depression. His nocturnal habits remained bad; he would write late, even to 2 a.m., and more than once to 4 a.m.

At the beginning of 1887 he is still more uneasy about his relations with Annie. He writes:

'The intimacy with Mrs. Besant alluded to last year reached in January a point at which it threatened to become a vulgar intrigue, chiefly through my fault. But I roused myself in time and avoided this. I however frequently went to her house on Monday evenings and played pianoforte duets, mostly Haydn's symphonies, with her. At Xmas, I returned all her letters and she mine. Reading over my letters before destroying them, rather disgusted me with my trifling of the last two years over women.'

And how did Shaw avoid a vulgar intrigue with Annie Besant? Her priestlike and prophetical character is not the type with whom one associates amorous vulgar intrigues, and it says much for Shaw's fascination and masculinity that he was able to get anywhere near an intrigue with her. It must be true, for he was writing not for publication but for his private and secret self.

Later in life he was to talk of her sexlessness, but that seems contradicted by her wifehood, motherhood and Shaw's own testimony here. Indeed, all through her life Annie showed no lack of feminine susceptibility to the male sex. Bradlaugh would gladly have married her on his wife's death.

The unpublished diaries do not tell the full story of Shaw's break with Mrs. Besant—indeed they never tell the full story about anything, they relate only the briefest factual notes of happenings. But the full story is so extraordinary that it deserves telling in full.

Naturally enough, this serious-minded young woman had been led by her unhappy conjugal experience to make a study of marriage as an institution. Very thoroughly, indeed, had she done this. The result was the production of a cheaply-priced pamphlet entitled: *Marriage—as it was, is and ought to be*. Many of Mrs. Besant's writings, especially of this period, are superficial; her *Thought Power* is a decided exception and so is this pamphlet.

This little work is a painstaking and brilliant exposition of its subject which would have done credit to any divorce-judge, barrister or solicitor. Obviously, Mrs. Besant had read widely, and pondered deeply, on the subject. Also, of course, she had sustained a lacerating personal experience of its problems in real life over her own marriage.

Shaw, on the other hand, had been nothing but a speculator or spectator upon matrimony. He had not yet been married.

Accordingly, to regulate the close and personal intimacy, and to avoid the threatening and vulgar intrigue, it was Mrs. Besant who undertook the task of drawing up a deed, an extra-legal marriage contract, for a marriage between them. Shaw was fond of drafting documents and prided himself (not altogether unjustly) upon his skill in such work. But, in this instance, he very properly left the drafting to her, for had she not the experience of conjugality and cohabitation that he lacked?

Shaw seems to have acquiesced in, if he did not encourage, her enterprise. It will be remembered that her divorce petition had failed and she was still, in law, the legal wife of the Rev. Frank Besant who was still alive: Shaw of course was unmarried, and merely the paramour of Mrs. Jenny Patterson.

Naturally, there would be no marriage ceremony in any religious 'place of worship', or in any registry office. What did that matter to these free spirits contemptuous of man-made laws and ordinances? They could marry themselves without either parson or state official, or even a Scottish declaration in the presence of witnesses.

The amused onlooker may reflect that one, or other, or both of the parties, to the illegal contract must have been moved by a spirit of caution, not to say distrust of the other party. Certainly the comedic side of Bernard Shaw was calculated to rouse some doubt in any solemn woman, contemplating a serious decision.

At last, Mrs. Besant rested from her Chancery-like labours. She brought her carefully-drafted and completed document to Bernard Shaw for his approval and signature.

Unlike most prospective signatories, he did not sign at once on the dotted line at invitation without perusal of the whole document. He read it through. Then he burst out:

'Good God! This is worse than all the vows exacted by all the Churches on earth.'

With that devastating comment, he handed the document back to her, laughing.

She was deeply mortified. But she held to her contract—though it was a useless thing, with no legal validity in it at all, unless Shaw chose to regard his signature to it as morally binding upon him. He was not likely to take that attitude, for the socialist movement of that time held, on the whole, views that were generally called 'free love'—an expression much repeated by its political opponents to damn the whole movement and to prove its wickedness and that of its adherents. On her part, she would neither compromise nor temporize. With her—as on other occasions in her stormy life—it was all or nothing. But Shaw would not sign.

It was agreed that there was nothing more to be done. They could only break the association.

In true conventional Victorian fashion, they agreed that each should return the other's letters. They had indeed exchanged many *billets-doux* and much other correspondence, which both of them had carefully preserved on the understanding that the letters should be destroyed. In this regard both of them faithfully kept their mutual promise over the letters that ended the intimacy, though they remained on distantly friendly terms as workers for The Cause.

Such was the way the intimate part of their association ended; an ending which Shaw describes in his private diary, as though it was his own doing entirely by his 'rousing himself in time' lest worse should happen. It was on Christmas Day that Jenny Patterson had possessed herself of some of this rival's love-letters, and considering that Shaw had not yet broken nor decided to break with his Jenny he may have been glad to have his and Annie Besant's letters destroyed.

Anyhow, destroyed they were. Posterity has been cheated no doubt of much interesting reading-matter, and possibly some new illumination upon the characters of a remarkable man and woman in their early adulthood.

VIII

Shaw, that milk-and-water Casanova, no doubt took the breach coolly enough. There was Jenny in the offing still. Nor did he wish to be bound exclusively to any woman—as young men commonly do not, except in the first fine careless rapture of first love.

He probably feared Annie; besides, the breach was convenient to him. But the breach—as it commonly is—was different for the woman. She cared, perhaps deeply. Hesketh Pearson suggests that her hair turned grey and that she even contemplated suicide. If her hair changed colour, that may have been due to other causes than unrequited love, and I can find no evidence of Annie Besant contemplating suicide at this time.

What is certain is that she flung herself with even more ardour—if that were possible—into her public life. Ceaselessly she propagated her ideas upon socialism, irreligion, politics, economics, and sex-relations. But, for her, Socialism without Shaw was like mustard without beef. She had never cared for the other Fabian leaders; nor they for her. In the world's estimation she was much more than they: in her own estimation she was the superior for she commanded a great public who heard her gladly as a unique figure in the national life. But in the estimation of the leading Fabians, they were intellectually her superiors, and indeed their grasp of theoretical economics and politics was much stronger than hers. Her emotionalism and fervour, which swayed audiences, repelled some Fabians to whom arid and abstract reasoning and statistics were their breath of life.

The loss of her guardian half-lover was not the only blow at this time. Bradlaugh, Foote, and the stalwarts of the National Secular Society were now doubtful and critical of her. *Our Corner*, her magazine, had ended. Her work for socialism and trade-unionism was entirely unpaid. Her income suffered grave diminution.

Shaw realized this situation and tried to put some reviewing of books in her way. He had by now worked up quite a good connection for himself: Massingham, assistant editor of *The Star* for which paper he wrote much more material than the musical articles signed Corno di Bassetto, was his friend and benefactor. The editor, T. P. O'Connor, whilst distrusting his socialism liked him, and was willing to help him. Then, too, W. T. Stead, at that date the most famous journalist of them all, was also his friend. Through these influential channels, Shaw was in a position to help and repay Mrs. Besant for the help she had given to him. No longer was he the needy novelist with no influence in the world.

Whatever may have been his faults and failings as a lover, as we have seen Shaw was always helpful in friendship. He was ready to pay his debt of gratitude to a fellow-worker; far readier, indeed, than in the case of a relative. Out of a mass of books sent to him for review, a lengthy, pretentious tome called *The Secret Doctrine* by a woman lately come into prominence, but regarded by him as an adventuress, charlatan and fraudswoman, Madame H. P. Blavatsky, was given by him to Mrs. Besant for her to review.

From Shaw's standpoint, this well-meaning action proved fatal. She read the book conscientiously; she wrote her review. To Shaw's consternation, the next thing was that all London was buzzing with news of an article in *The Star* by Annie Besant entitled 'Why I became a Theosophist'.

She had met the book's author, Madame Blavatsky, and her book had converted its reviewer.

Shaw rushed to undo the mischief unwittingly done by his gratuitous good deed. He saw her, and gave her convincing evidence, as he thought it, of Blavatsky's frauds. She refused to accept it, adding that even if true it did not disprove the new religion she had found valid for herself.

Shaw reasoned with her in vain. Then he tried charm, offering to be her Mahatma. That was equally in vain. He no longer mattered in comparison with Madame Blavatsky, that masculine and hypnotic Russian whom some of her nearest associates, such as Colonel Olcott, believed to be a man.

In consequence of her new orientation, Annie Besant broke with her immediate past: with Secularism and Socialism both and with her friends in both those spheres. For all effective purposes, she also broke with Shaw.

The rest of this extraordinary woman's life-story belongs not to the story of Shaw but to world-history. Briefly, she rose to be the revered head, the woman-Pope, of Theosophy. Also she became the equally revered protagonist of Indian Home Rule, which eventually broke the British rule over India for ever and lost our country its 'brightest jewel in the Imperial crown': the Indian Empire. Just as the earlier Mrs. Besant had queened it over the tradition-bound, factual English, so the later Mrs. Besant queened it equally well over the subtle, metaphysical Hindu.

Shaw had lost his greatest captive. But he put her into his plays. She was the model for Raina in *Arms and the Man* and for Mrs. Clandon in *You Never Can Tell*.

Mrs. Besant never re-married, although the Rev. Frank, her

husband, died suddenly of heart-failure in 1917. By that time, her great gifts and magnetic personality had made her a world-figuer, revered by millions. She died in 1933 at the age of 85.

IX

Bernard Shaw and Annie Besant went their separate, but not unremembering, ways, and each found secure niches in the hall of Fame.

The story is told of a young Indian called Krishnamurta, the special protégé of Mrs. Annie Besant, coming over to England and meeting Shaw. Krishnamurta was a young man of astonishing physical beauty and of considerable mental gifts. Indeed, even now many people regard him as what is called a 'World-Teacher', and his hortatory books certainly deserve respect from those who are outside his following. But Mrs. Besant had early proclaimed the young boy as a Messiah, or Star rising in the East; a Christ incarnate for the regeneration of a simple world.

The young man gained credit by modestly repudiating this *rôle*, and adopting that of a merely earnest seeker after truth and enlightenment. Shaw, on meeting him, warmly approved of this attitude, and of the young man's conversation; he also thought him the most perfect human being physically that he had ever seen.

He asked Krishnamurta whether he often saw Mrs. Besant, and the young man replied that he did very often, sometimes as often as every day.

'And how is she in health?' Shaw inquired. (Both Shaw and Mrs. Besant were old people by that time.)

'Very well. But at her great age she cannot think consecutively.'

'She never could,' retorted Shaw.

That was a typical, unjust Shavianism. Shaw should have reminded himself of his fears over her debate of so long ago, when he expected his logical case to be demolished, and of her marriage-pamphlet.

VI

THE MYSTICAL MARRIAGE:
MAY MORRIS

✤✤

'. . . *A creator of an atmosphere subtly disintegrative of house-holds. Whenever I think of my behaviour in those days I grow afraid of myself. I don't know why it was but all the women I really cared for were already married.*'

—G.B.S. on Himself

I

IRREVERENT AND scoffing as he might seem to many other people, G.B.S., even as a young man, had his heroes. He was faithful to most of these, throughout his long life: against these few he, who did not spare even his nearest and dearest relatives, never uttered a word of denigration.

One of these whom he regarded as truly great was the atheist leader Charles Bradlaugh, whom he confessed was the only man he feared to meet in debate. For Bradlaugh's personality and strong character, Shaw cherished a profound respect.

Another of his heroes was Sidney Webb, that dull economic and political investigator—whom Shaw regarded as a far greater political theorist than himself, and far better brain. His regard and admiration for Webb never wavered. And when Webb as Lord Passfield died, it was Shaw's strong representation to the Labour

121

Government that secured Webb's burial in Westminster Abbey. Other heroes of Shaw's, as is indeed well known, were Ibsen, the Norwegian playwright and Samuel Butler, of *Erewhon* fame.

Another contemporary to whom Shaw bent the knee in reverent genuflection was the Victorian poet-medievalist and craftsman, William Morris. Morris, the author of *The Earthly Paradise* and *News from Nowhere* had seceded from Hyndman's Social Democratic Federation to lead the Socialist League. It was a great day for young Shaw when he unexpectedly received an invitation to Morris's home at Hammersmith. Up to that date, he had reverenced Morris from afar.

His invitation out of the blue was a by-product of Shaw's own enterprise. Unable to get any publisher to accept his novels, he had suggested to James Leigh Joynes, an ex-Etonian housemaster engaged in socialistic activities, that he, as editor of a Socialist weekly called *Today*, might serialize one of them in his periodical.

Joynes agreed. The one chosen was *An Unsocial Socialist*. It started in January and ran until December, 1884. Though the serialization brought no money to Shaw—the paper weakly (as well as weekly) kept going on free contributions, yet it gave Shaw himself an advertisement.

Morris read the story each week, liked it and decided he must meet its author. Hence the invitation—the first of many.

Now, Morris's invitations to either his town house at Hammersmith or his country house, Kelmscott Manor in Gloucestershire, were esteemed not only by Bernard Shaw but by all sorts and conditions of men and women. Morris was not only famous: he was wealthy; and, extraordinary to relate, in days when wealthy socialists were regarded as a contradiction in terms, he was a Socialist leader. His influence in decoration, art and aesthetics was great, but his influence as a Socialist leader was unreal, for he was neither an orator nor had he anything truly original to contribute to Socialist thought.

Nowadays, rich socialists attached to the Labour Party are like the other devils, legion; but, in his day, Morris being rich and a

Socialist was an eccentric phenomenon. Pauper Socialists buzzed excitedly around him like wasps round a jam-jar.

One of these—and by no means the least vocal—was Bernard Shaw.

Morris had married his model, Jane Bryden of Oxford, and she sat for many other painters, notably Dante Gabriel Rossetti, who has immortalized her.

Neither Mrs. Morris, beautiful and aristocratic to her finger-tips, nor her elder daughter, Jenny, cared for rag-tag and bobtail proletarians. They ignored such visitors. The younger daughter, Mary, whose home name was May, was more tolerant. She was ready to receive her father's revolutionary friends, however unattractive in mind, body or estate.

Born in 1863, she was one heroine of Sir Edward Burne-Jones's then-celebrated picture, *The Golden Stairs*, where she is the attractive descending figure. That led to the legend that she was beautiful. Certainly, she was tall, dark, tastefully attired and striking, but she was not beautiful. There was a decided touch of masculinity about her—the sort of thing which gets accentuated and less attractive with the years. Wholly sympathetic to her father's love of the arts and crafts, she had taken up embroidery and was busily engaged in teaching it to such young women enthusiasts as would come to her for tuition.

One of these pupils was Florence Farr (Mrs. Emery), the actress, who, like so many others of her day and generation, found the Morris family congenial, and their mission to propagate all forms of beauty attractive. It was, in fact, at the Morrises' home that Shaw and Florence Farr first met.

However, the mature Shaw, awakened to sex by his experiences with Jenny Patterson, was no one-woman man.

II

One day, young Bernard Shaw was leaving the Morris home— fabulous for its beauty, luxury and exquisite taste—when he encountered May for the first time. She was coming from the dining-room into the hall. She was dressed *à la* Rossetti; and Shaw, blinded by her appearance and her reputed and legendary beauty, was instantly smitten.

But let him tell his fantastical story in his own words:

'One Sunday evening after lecturing and supping I was on the threshold of the Hammersmith house when I turned to make my farewell, and at this moment she came from the dining-room into the hall. I looked at her, rejoicing in her lovely dress and lovely self; and she looked at me very carefully and quite deliberately made a gesture of assent with her eyes. . . .'

And then?

Shaw goes on: 'I was immediately conscious that a Mystic Betrothal was registered in Heaven, to be fulfilled when all the material obstacles should melt away, and my own position rescued from the squalors of my poverty and unsuccess, for subconsciously I had no doubt that she too knew her own value, a knowledge that involved a knowledge of everyone else. To engage her in any way—to go to Morris her father and announce that I was taking advantage of the access granted to me as a comrade-Communist to commend his daughter to a desperately insolvent marriage did not seem to me as a sociably possible proceeding. It did not occur to me even, that fidelity to the Mystic Betrothal need interfere with the ordinary course of my relations with other women. I made no sign at all: I had no doubt that the thing was written in the skies for both of us.'

III

Now, what could be more delightful and romantic, or less trouble-making than a mystical betrothal with Heaven as its register office?

The Recording Angel, as registrar, charges no fees. No mundane engagement-ring has to be bought. It is cheaper than Woolworth's. No parental consent, or the girl's own family thrust upon you!

It must be heavenly, in a double sense of the word.

But how does a girl make 'a gesture of assent' with her eyes? Did May vulgarly wink? Or merely blink at the dazzling red-headed Irishman?

Even the most constant reader of girls' eyes would be surprised to see them 'gesture', though he may read assent—or dissent—there clearly enough.

On this momentous occasion, neither of the pair uttered a syllable. 'Love is enough,' as one of William Morris's lyrics sings.

'The thing was written in the skies for both of us,' declared Shaw, positively. And it occurred to him that this celestial engagement need not 'interfere with the ordinary course of my relations with other women'. So Jenny Patterson, Florence Farr and the rest could continue being loved by Shaw. What could be more convenient?

Time went by and still Shaw, the suitor in the Jaegar suiting—one of his latest fads—made no sign. He said no word. He still came to the Morris suppers for Socialists. But being a vegetarian and a non-drinker, he was not easy to entertain.

Often, like the Gilbert and Sullivan hero, 'he sipped no sup and he craved no crumb, but he sighed for the love of his lady'. But the lady knew nothing about it.

Now, it is quite useless to sigh for a lady when she does not know what you are doing. The proper place to sigh is in the lady's arms. Otherwise it's a waste of energy and time, as every aspirant knows. Clearly young Shaw was no young Lochinvar; rather was he Lochinvar's opposite, the laggard-in-love.

Turning from Shavian fiction to sober fact, it is quite certain that if Shaw refrained from declaring the honourable intentions of heaven and himself, he did not avoid May. He tried to interest her in his sister Lucy, and gave Miss Morris a sketch of Lucy Shaw that he had made. He introduced his mother to May's father. And when he managed to get May to come with him for a cup of coffee at Ludgate Hill Station—no very heavenly nectar—he proudly recorded the fact in his diary, thus showing the importance he attached to it.

Meanwhile, the other women in their ways had a certain worth for him. His pretensions to May as his celestial Bride did not interfere with his intrigues with other women, as his unpublished diaries plainly show. No doubt that eminent Mormon polygamist, Brigham Young, might have said what Shaw said: that the idea of confining his attentions to one female never even occurred to him. And the 'celestial bride' phrase is horridly reminiscent of the unfrocked Anglican curate Smyth-Piggott in his Abode of Love at Spaxton. He, too, claimed celestial brides.

Shaw professed to believe strongly throughout his long life in equality of marriage-opportunity. He wanted equality of income in order to make equality in marriage, and bitterly denounced class-conscious marriage restricting the choice of life-partners. It seems disingenuous, then, for him to plead that the idea of his marriage with May Morris was 'not a socially possible proceeding'. Nor was he, at this time, hopelessly insolvent; he was in fact doing well, earning over £400 a year as a journalist. That amount would be worth about £2,000 today, and the taxation upon it then was derisory. Moreover, he had prospects, and May would inherit more than enough for two.

Whom did he, a young man of the world by now, imagine May Morris could command as eligible for her hand? For all the great William's fame and imposing personal appearance he came of tradesmen's stock, and he was by no means *persona grata* with Society. The circle of possible suitors was a strictly limited one; and if Shaw had been really serious his cleverness would have seen this, just as any serious suitor would have ceased philandering in other quarters.

IV

Now while this laggard-in-love was dilly-dallying and striking attitudes to an audience of one, and that one not the girl but himself, a young Lochinvar-of-sorts was up and doing. He was another comrade-Communist; he was much poorer than Shaw and had no particular prospects. However, he showed much more courage and initiative than his rival.

For while Shaw hesitated, relying on heaven, a strange reliance for a professing atheist, Henry Halliday Sparling acted. A mere hanger-on of the Morris régime, he promptly proposed marriage to Mary and was accepted.

No doubt the mother of Mary was silent, for Shaw called Mrs. Morris the silentest woman he had ever met. She disliked him, and the only remark that she ever addressed to him was once at pudding-time when she, contemptuous of his food and drink fads, pressed a second helping of pudding upon him with the sensible remark: 'There: that will do you good. There's suet in it,' the suet being the animal food G.B.S. so much avoided. What Morris the father thought of May's choice of Sparling is unrecorded, but he did not actively oppose it. Shaw suspected he was stupefied, as Shaw says he himself was.

St. John Ervine, one of the best of G.B.S.'s biographers, described Sparling as an odd little insignificant fellow who hung about the fringes of adventurous and artistic corners hoping that some day somebody would take some notice of him. He also calls him the slightest-looking man one could meet, seeming as if he were Uriah Heep's grandson, and a little ragbag of a fellow totally unsuited to Mary Morris.

However contemptible Sparling may have been, whatever his merit or discredit, he had at any rate won the prize. He had triumphed over Shaw and the heavenly powers who had registered the Shavian celestial betrothal.

And what did he, the heavenly bridegroom-to-be, do about this vulgar earthly contretemps? Did he point out the just cause and impediment why these two persons, Henry and May, should not be joined together in holy, or even unholy, matrimony? Did he remonstrate with his celestially-affianced to remind her of the heavenly espousal? Did he enter a caveat against the projected misalliance?

He did none of these things. Instead, he did strictly nothing. As though there were no mystic betrothal and the coming ter-restrial marriage were no concern of his!

William Morris found some employment for his prospective

son-in-law in connection with his own Kelmscott Press, for Sparling had some feeble pretensions to being a *littérateur*, an *homme de lettres*.

For his inactivity over his celestial lady-love Shaw found excuses. The marriage was perfectly natural and entirely his own fault for taking the mystical betrothal for granted. Sparling was a convenient Socialist and a regular speaker for the cause and his character was blameless. So, although he was less eligible than Shaw himself, with more limited possibilities of future eminence, Shaw's view was 'there was nothing to be done but accept the situation'.

One can only exclaim in Shakespearian words, 'O most lame and impotent conclusion'. The excuses given are transparently absurd: no man surrenders a woman for such reasons.

'But I regarded it, and still regard it, as the most monstrous breach of faith in the history of romance,' says Shaw. Then why did he not, at the very least, reproach the lady for the monstrous breach of faith, and offer her true spouse as a substitute? He concluded, feasibly enough, that his limitless imagination had deceived him in the matter of the mystic betrothal to May Morris.

And the couple were married with no let or hindrance from anyone, and Shaw was left to such consolations as he could find with his other women. But the heavenly powers—if indeed heavenly powers were involved—had not finished their sport with May Morris (now May Sparling) and Bernard Shaw.

v

For Shaw remained friends with the married pair. Some time later, he was suffering from overwork, much of it due to his socialistic propaganda outbursts; and the newly-married socialistic pair naturally sympathized with Comrade Shaw's grievous plight.

He needed rest and change. By way of supplying both, they hospitably invited G.B.S. to come and stay with them.

Shaw accepted with alacrity. The house had all the Morris charm, for Mrs. Sparling had her father's sense of beauty and something of his decorative faculty; moreover, there was no lack of money to ensure comfort and luxury for any guest. So Shaw found himself blessedly resting and content.

In that *ménage à trois* everything went well for a time, according to Shaw, and no doubt it may have done for a time. That is what usually happens in such cases. Mrs. Sparling was glad to have him, he says without saying why. Mr. Sparling was equally glad because (says Shaw) his presence kept the wife in good humour and producing better meals than when catering for a mere husband. (But why better meals for a vegetarian?)

'It was probably,' Shaw opines, 'the happiest passage in our whole lives.' But the mere earthly husband thought Shaw was betraying him by captivating his wife, and that he himself was the reverse of happy. Perhaps it was a case of some men not knowing when they are well off, but clearly it was an explosive situation. Let Shaw continue the tale as he tells it.

'The violated betrothal was avenging itself . . . When I had quite recovered and there was no longer any excuse for staying unless I proposed to do so permanently and parasitically, her legal marriage dissolved as all illusions do; and the mystic marriage asserted itself irresistibly. I had to consummate it or perish.'

The perspicacious reader will notice, with surprise no doubt, that the mystic betrothal has turned into a mystic marriage without further ceremony. And which of the two alternatives did the heavenly husband select? Let Shaw continue the story, for even at his least convincing, he is always most interesting.

When it became evident that the betrothal would not suffer this (thrice-fold cohabitation) to be an innocent arrangement, the case (he says) became complicated. 'To begin with, the legal husband was a friend whose conduct towards me had always been irreproachable. To be welcomed in his house and then steal his wife was revolting to my sense of honour, and socially inexcusable, for though I was as extreme a freethinker in sexual and religious questions as any human being could be, I was not the dupe of the Bohemian Anarchism that is very common in socialist or literary circles.

'I knew that a scandal would damage both of us and damage the Cause as well. It seems easy, in view of my later position, to have sat down together as three friends and arranged a divorce; but at that time I could not afford to marry and I was by no means sure that he could afford to be divorced. Besides, I hated the idea of a prosaic and even mercenary marriage: that, somehow or other, was not on the plane of the mystic betrothal. The more I reasoned about the situation, the worse it was doomed to appear.

'So I did not agree about it. I vanished.'

This is all very amusing, as it was intended to be to the readers of it, if not to the participants in it, except one. But it is highly disingenuous. The 'irreproachable conduct' of the terrestrial husband, however, consisted in having supplanted the rightful romantic celestial husband. As to stealing a wife: from Shaw's supposed standpoint, he was merely reclaiming his own property wrongly filched from him: he had what lawyers call a claim of right made in good faith (according to himself) and such a claim negatives stealing by virtue of the Larceny Act. Socialist and literary circles of that period recognized 'free love' only too readily.

Shaw could have afforded to marry, as we have seen, as also could the lady. He could have made sure of Sparling's being able to afford a divorce by the simple expedient of asking him; and good evidence arises later on that he could afford it. Besides, May's purse could have come to the rescue if she wished for her celestial bridegroom; and one observes that the poetic and romantic Edenic marriage has metamorphosed into its very opposite, a prosaic and mercenary marriage, on nearer approach to it.

The plain truth is, of course, that Shaw was trifling with what was in reality a horribly serious situation which might have involved him in an action for damages in the courts by a wronged and incensed husband. All this airy-fairy nonsense was concocted to conceal the ugly situation.

Sparling has left on record his view of the matter. That view was the ordinary view of the ordinary husband; he regarded himself as betrayed by a false and treacherous friend and a disloyal wife. He was sore about it, for when Shaw did his vanishing trick he left behind an alienated wife and a wrecked marriage. What avoidance of scandal was there in that painful situation, of which Sparling was not inhibited by love of the Cause from complaining about? He aired his grievance to all those comrades willing to listen; and it stands on record for all time.

VI

Sparling, that man of action, did more than complain. He copied Shaw's example: he deserted, too. After all, he was banished from his wife's affections and might well see no point in remaining a nominal husband. Let us see how Shaw deals with that second vanishing:

'Then the vengeance of the violated betrothal consummated itself in a transport of tragedy and comedy. For the husband vanished, too. The *ménage* which had prospered so pleasantly as a *ménage à trois* proved intolerable as a *ménage à deux*. This marriage, which all the mystic powers had forbidden from the first, went to pieces when the unlucky pair no longer had me between them.

'Of the particulars of the rupture I know nothing, but in the upshot he fled to the Continent and eventually submitted chivalrously to being divorced as the guilty party, though the alternative was technically arranged for him. If I recollect aright, he married again, this time I hope more suitably, and lived as happily as he might until his death, which came sooner than an actuary would have predicted.

'The beautiful one abolished him, root and branch, resuming her famous name. . . .'

But was this horrid culmination of a wrecked home the vengeance of the 'betrothal' or the vengeance of the supplanted-supplanting Bernard Shaw? It is correct that there was a divorce, and Shaw escaped (as no doubt he wished, but which was more than he deserved) the odium of being cited in the Divorce Court as the co-respondent and false friend. Sparling took the blame, as

Shaw admits, thus sheltering both wife and Judas-friend, Judas indeed, for there are more adulteries than physical adulteries, as Jesus Christ taught. Which was magnanimous of Sparling in the circumstances.

Sparling's second marriage to a Scottish woman was a success. But he never forgave Shaw. Probably May Morris never forgave him either, for upon his own showing he had twice let her down.

She is supposed to have been beautiful by the Shaw biographers, such as Ervine and Hesketh Pearson, who mention her in detail. Her reputation is largely due to painters such as Rossetti and Burne-Jones, and to the fact that an eligible girl who dresses exceptionally and is gifted by wealth is always beautiful to masculine hopes. Moreover, everything Morrisian, from his wallpapers to his females, was beautiful *per se*. Mrs. Morris certainly was. Morris could not possibly be guilty of the bad taste of having a daughter who was not beautiful.

Unfortunately, photographs of May Morris are extant, and these speak for themselves. Only partiality could describe her as beautiful as she appears in her photographs. But it may be said, by those who admire swarthy females with a touch of masculinity about them, and liable to become hirsute in later life, that the camera may lie as egregiously almost as any flattering portrait-painter, be he a Sargent or a Lavery.

When it became clear that 'George', as his mother and sister now called Shaw, did not intend to marry May Morris, the incipient friendship between his females and this semi-intended died a natural death. There were no more teas at Fitzroy Square, no more concerts in company, no more Shaw family souvenirs for May.

Indeed, Lucy sneered privately at May's predicament. Pointing May out at the Dolmetch Concerts to a friend she remarked: 'There goes Mrs. Sparling. She's just divorced her husband because she wants to marry George.' Again, to a friend from Margate she loudly said:

'May made a fool of herself over G.B.S., and there is no doubt ruined the whole of the romantic side of her life. I believe her only object in divorcing Sparling was to give G. the chance of marrying her. She obtained her decree absolute the very day he was married.' (1st June, 1898).

'That, and her father's death [he died in 1896, 2 years earlier] turned her into a typical figure of woe. The worst of it was, she always wore her heart on her sleeve, and everyone knew about her madness for G.

'I shall never forget the picture she presented the last time I saw her, in perfectly straight down clinging black garments, her black hair divided in the middle and combed low over her ears; a little flat bonnet that looked as if it had been made out of a triangle of buckram covered with a plain piece of silk; no adornment of any kind; and so flat on her head that you could not tell where the hair ended and the bonnet began, and the extraordinary sadness and gloom of her face, which never was at any time subject to lights and shades of expression, and the listless droop of her carriage; all went to make up a most pitiful personification of grief.

'She used frequently to come to our house, but has never been since G. married. I don't know how she employs her time now. She used to have a school of embroidery . . . her father left her well off which was not the best thing that could happen to her.'

Lucy goes on to speak of a delightful two-hours' talk with her brother, adding: 'He and I are always two thorough blackguards when we get together alone.'

Clearly Lucy Shaw had more than a small share of her brother's literary ability—but she had never seen her brother's story of the May Morris affair, which at first was published only in America. But having that account, one may ask whether, in fact, Mrs. Sparling made a fool of herself, or was made a fool of by Shaw. Shaw is entirely silent about Mrs. Sparling's 'woe' or 'madness'; one can understand his silence on the first topic, though he would certainly have bragged of the second had it existed.

But what could be more ironic than May becoming entirely free on the very day her absconding heavenly bridegroom, having deprived her of her earthly one, made a prosaic mercenary marriage (of the kind he had professed to hate) with a non-mystical other woman!

The censorious may think that Shaw was not only a thorough blackguard when in company with his sister, although his sister spoke in jest, no doubt. But he went further than merely repudiating his celestial bride. Later on, like Dickens over one of his several loves, he turned the episode into literary copy, hard cash, publishing it in America under the title, *What I Knew about William Morris*. Then—temporarily—Shaw devoted himself to more important matters and people.

VII

Whether you call it abandonment or banishment—Shaw uses both these words—the breach between George Bernard Shaw and May Morris lasted long. But he says he knew better than that he was abolished by May.

For forty years later, when Shaw's marriage was beyond disturbance and May's grass-widowhood was in the same condition, for she was destined never to re-marry, there was a sequel. Safe at last, Shaw, an old man accompanied by his elderly wife, motored down to Gloucestershire to revive old associations as elderly authors are fond of doing. May was living in the old Morris country home.

Let Shaw take up his forty-years interrupted tale:

'. . . The spell of Kelmscott Manor came upon me. I turned off the high road from Rochdale to Oxford, and soon found myself in the church with the tempting candle-sticks that nobody ever stole, and at the grave of William and Jane Morris, which I had never seen before. I was soon on the garden flagway to the ancient door of the Manor House.

'It was opened by a young lady whose aspect terrified me. She was obviously strong enough to take me by the scruff of my neck and pitch me neck and crop out of the curtilage; and she looked as if for two pins she would do it as she demanded sternly who I was.

'I named myself apologetically.

'The mystical betrothal, strong as ever, operated at once, though the athletic lady [Miss Lobb] could have known nothing about it. She threw the door wide open as if I belonged to the place and had been away for ten minutes or so; and presently the beautiful daughter and I, now harmless old folks, met again as if nothing had happened.'

Once again Shaw was luckier than he deserved. It would have served the then famous author right if May Morris had refused to receive him and his wife.

Hesketh Pearson asked Shaw later whether at this last meeting, when the fires were out, May Morris referred to the mystic betrothal. 'No, no,' answered Shaw. 'Besides, my wife was present.' From this, it would appear that Shaw in former days had told May his Irish blarney of the mystic betrothal, and perhaps that accounted for those excellent meals he enjoyed in the Sparling home.

Prompted again by his friend Pearson, Shaw remembered that the reputedly lovely May had grown a moustache.

However, he defended the moustache as being neither a Victor Emmanuel nor a Chaplin-Hitler variety one, which, had it not been decorative, the lady would have removed with a razor.

And with this touch of bathos, worthy of his comedian father whom the son always depicted as indulging in the comic anti-climax, Mrs. Patrick Campbell's Joey the Clown finished his clowning with the unfortunate May Morris, guying her relentlessly for a multitude of American readers.

VIII

It may be that May Morris did not know of the American publication when, later on, she was so ill-advised as to ask Shaw for a tribute to her father. (She was erecting a worthy memorial of daughterly piety to the great William in the shape of a sumptuous edition, beautifully printed, of his collected works. The set ran to thirty-six large volumes, and May wanted their old friend to write an introduction to Volume 2 of the series.)

Considering his genuine belief that William Morris was one of the permanent glories of English literature, and considering, too, all that he owed his hero for hospitality and countenance in his needy days of a literary neophyte, Shaw could hardly refuse May's request. He therefore wrote the desired preface, and in it, with a real touch of mischief, he interpolated the fantastical story of the alleged mystic betrothal as told in the American publication.

According to one story, May Morris's reaction was contained in a brief exclamatory ejaculation: 'Really, Shaw!!'

But she wrote to G.B.S. on 23rd April, 1936: 'As to our harmless personal relations, I should have been inclined to let them lie unsung, on the grounds that no one cares a hang about me.' She was then seventy-three.

But upon the practical question of what should be done with the introduction, May Morris sought advice. It was pointed out to her that if she refused to print it, it might be printed elsewhere—as indeed it had been! Or later it might be disinterred or resuscitated in a garbled form by some researcher. Eventually she decided to take the bull by the horns and publish the tale exactly as Shaw had told it.

Which she did. Very wisely she added nothing of her own, either in denial or confirmation of what a professing lover had chosen to give to the world about her and himself.

Pure fantasia as the fictional betrothal is, it illustrates how pseudo-romantic and sentimental Bernard Shaw was at heart, in spite of his public pose of being utterly unromantic and realistic.

Later in life he similarly pretended that Helen Huntingdon, Granville Barker's American second wife, who disliked him intensely as a real or supposedly evil influence on her husband, had bewitched him into ill-health, another fantasia showing that he was a prey to irrational superstitions at which he publicly scoffed. Indeed, the May Morris episode tells us a great deal of his many-sided character, especially perhaps its least admirable sides: his inability to express his beliefs in action coupled with his extraordinary ability to express them in words; his procrastination, of which his mother and his unpublished diaries often complained;

his invincible and repeated endeavour to sublimate his sexual urges into philandering; his bad taste, common to his profession, in being unable to resist using private matters and private persons for copy and cash; and finally his journalistic readiness to sacrifice fact in the interests of a picturesque and piquant fiction, served up for public consumption, with the sauce of identified well-known names.

Just as it needs no ghost to come from the grave to tell us in *Hamlet* what is already guessed, so it does not need myself or the learned four doctors—Dr. Archibald Henderson, Dr. R. F. Rattray, Dr. St. John Ervine, and Dr. H. G. Farmer—who have expatiated so much upon Shaw, to tell ordinary readers what to think of the May Morris story. Yet if readers require their own views to be buttressed by authority, it is enough to quote one sentence from the first of these: the one in which Dr. Henderson says:

'Shaw's principle was comic exaggeration, and by stating things far above the facts he succeeded in falling far below the truth.'

The plight of May Morris in the story, as in hard fact, leaves a wry taste on the palate. Neither saint nor sinner, she is shown as a futile, frustrated female, put in the pillory to be pitied by the kind-hearted or pelted by the scorn of the unfeeling. It was either an act of spite or an act of great insensitiveness by Shaw; one that common gratitude to the dead William Morris might have forbidden.

E*

VII

KARL MARX'S DAUGHTER: ELEANOR MARX-AVELING

❉❉❉❉❉❉❉❉❉❉❉❉❉❉❉❉❉❉❉❉❉❉❉❉❉❉❉❉❉❉❉❉❉❉❉❉❉

'It is extraordinary how a despicable character and a physically repulsive man attracts the loveliest women. Eleanor was extremely attractive and was more of this generation than of the dark age in which I lived. . . . Both of us were rather on the conventional side.'

—G.B.S. on the Marx-Aveling Tragedy

I

NO BOOK ever written—not even that congerie of books the Holy Bible—has been so much talked about, and so little read, as Karl Marx's *Das Kapital*. People speak of Marx as a god or as a devil, like Dryden's Buckingham portrayed as Zimri; but few indeed in England have read a single word of him or know anything of the facts of his life.

This strange state of affairs prevailed just as much in the days of the youthful George Bernard Shaw as today, except that Marx was not then metamorphosed into the Deity of Communism. He was labouring in the British Museum reading-room at the same time as the young Shaw, and Shaw might easily have run into him there. But Shaw never did, in fact. What happened was that Shaw encountered his younger daughter Eleanor there.

138

Before that, Shaw had greatly distinguished himself in the English socialist world by reading Marx's masterpiece, destined to conquer regions that Caesar, Alexander and Napoleon never knew; to precipitate the Russian and Chinese revolutions; and to revolutionize the world of economic and political thought down to our own day. He read it in French, and, what is more, he thoroughly mastered its difficult doctrines and became excited and enthusiastic about them.

Now, English socialists at that date were by no means enthusiastic about Karl Marx or his writings. First, he was a foreigner and an extreme revolutionary. Next, English socialism was divided into warring and discordant sects, only one of which, H. M. Hyndman's Social Democratic Federation (from which William Morris had seceded and formed his Socialist League) professed Marxism; and most of these social-democrats had not read their prophet. Further, English socialism, or most of it, retained a strongly insular tinge and had strong affiliations with Radicalism and even Liberalism. That brand of socialism to which Shaw himself officially belonged, namely Fabianism, believed even then in Sidney Webb's phrase, 'the inevitability of gradualism', and in permeating both Liberal and Tory parties with socialistic ideas. No sharp distinction was drawn between 'Socialism' and 'Communism' by the faithful at large: both these names were mere synonyms for 'the nationalization of all the means of production, distribution and exchange'.

Young G.B.S. was a perfervid Marxian revolutionary, until Philip Wicksteed convinced him that certain of the Marxian economic theories were fundamentally unsound, and until his adventures in the company of Annie Besant on Bloody Sunday convinced him that political revolution by mob-uprising—in England at any rate—was quite impracticable against disciplined and armed police and soldiery. But he never renounced his Marxist faith as a whole, and to the day of his death described himself as a Marxian and Communist. 'Marx made a man of me,' he said, at seventy years of age.

Karl Marx's younger daughter Eleanor loved and reverenced

her father, as well she might, having regard to the painful sacri-
fices she had seen him make for his creed and his disinterested
devotion to the cause he had espoused from youth upwards.
Naturally, the young Shaw and she had a bond of intellectual
sympathy when they met in the reading-room of the British
Museum, where she was doing research-work at the scanty wage
of eighteen pence per hour.

II

But Eleanor Marx had other attractions than intellectual ones
for young G.B.S. in 1882 when he read her father's epoch-making
book and met her in Bloomsbury.

He was twenty-six; she also was twenty-six. 'Tussy', as her
loving father called his youngest, had the black hair and black eyes
of that father whom his devoted family called 'The Moor'. She
also had an exceptionally musical voice, and G.B.S. was susceptible both to brunettes and to musical voices. She was also very
vivacious, sensitive and emotional; keenly interested in politics,
literature and the drama. She had considerable linguistic talent,
enabling her to translate French, German and Italian with
facility at international socialistic Congresses. Nor was that all.
She translated Flaubert's *Madame Bovary* into English, and her
translation is a minor masterpiece in itself.

'Tussy *is* me,' her father Karl Marx used to say.

Striking in appearance and gifted with intellectual distinction,
it is no wonder Eleanor Marx and young Shaw became warm
friends. A description of her by a not favourable observer, Beatrice
Potter, afterwards Mrs. Webb, may be quoted as showing what
she was like at this period. According to this critic she had fine
black eyes, lovely black hair flying in all directions, dressed in a
slovenly picturesque way and led an unhealthy excited life.

However, she was essentially a serious-minded girl, neither
flirtatious nor coquettish in spite of her high spirits and new-
fangled cigarette-smoking, and one not to be caught by mere
philandering. Nor had either she or Shaw at this period any

money; and Shaw, who had vacillated over the wealthy May Morris, was not likely to hurry the capture of Eleanor Marx's heart.

Besides, Eleanor was accustomed to much more adulation than Shaw was accustomed to bestow on any of his women. All her home circle adored her, and looked upon her as a girl of high promise. In fact she was spoiled not only by her father, mother and sisters, but also by the devoted family retainer and servant Lenchen Demuth, whose entirely disinterested love and loyalty to the Marx family in their extreme poverty is quite incredible by the standards of today.

Understandably in this case of poverty, Shaw hesitated. And again, as in the case of May Morris, a bolder Richmond took the field and wooed the girl. This wooer was Dr. Edward Bibbens Aveling, a figure at that date of considerable consequence in advanced circles as a leading atheist, Darwinist and Marxist. He had attained also considerable academic distinction as a scientific teacher, lecturer and author.

Previous to this he had been closely associated—too closely, some thought, in view of his reputation—with the then atheist leader, Annie Besant, who had enrolled herself as one of his science students and who was lyrical in his praises. Aveling, at first regarded as a great acquisition by the secularism and socialism of his time, was soon the subject of very many scandals in connection with his girl-pupils, of whom Shaw was to say that he not only seduced them but also stole their microscopes!

Very suddenly his association with Annie Besant ceased, and although nothing is known as to the cause of the sudden cessation, it may well be that when he transferred his affection from her, Annie Besant discovered his true character, after shutting her eyes and ears to it right up till then. For as long as she could, Annie Besant defended his character. For instance, the following strange notice attacking Eleanor and defending Aveling was written by Mrs. Besant in one of the papers she controlled, *The Reformer*, in December 1883.

'My name is being used by a Miss Eleanor Marx, daughter of the late Karl Marx, to give authority to a gross and scandalous libel on Dr. Edward Aveling. She invented the libel and then promulgated it, giving me as the author of the statement, hoping thereby to create a breach, and to hinder or impede the free-thought case by introducing discord and quarrel amongst co-workers in the ranks. So far, fortunately, the attempt has failed, for Dr. Aveling brought the statement to me when it reached his ears. As, however, it may reach many privately who will not have heard of the private exposure of the lie, I warn all London Free-thinkers and especially those of the N.W. London Branch (of which Aveling was president) against accepting any statement made in my name by Miss Eleanor Marx or by any of her friends.'

This was waspish indeed, not to say possibly libellous in itself. Annie goes on to say that such treacherous strangers as Eleanor creeping into 'our movement' were the most useful 'tools' of the Christian foe. Before this she had published an exasperated view that Aveling in 1882 had taken to reading in the British Museum (just as some take to drinking in public houses) and unfortunately fell into the Bohemian Socialists male *and female* who flourish there. Annie was not yet a socialist.

What the alleged lie and the gross scandalous libel were, is unknown. But it looks as if the Marx–Aveling courtship began with the girl's hostility; and as if Aveling, piqued by it, set himself successfully to break it down and convert it into its exact opposite, like Richard III wooing Anne. Mrs. Besant must have been out-raged by Aveling's making up to the hated Eleanor Marx. By 1885, she, Bradlaugh and the secularist movement had dropped Dr. Aveling, once its darling recruit.

One thing is known. Suddenly that formidable and sincere co-leader of the atheists, Charles Bradlaugh, M.P., appeared at Dr. Aveling's Bloomsbury lodgings armed with authority from Mrs. Besant to demand the return of every one of Mrs. Besant's letters to him. Bradlaugh was a man to be feared, and not one to take any denial. It is not surprising that Aveling yielded up the letters at once. The fact that Bradlaugh took this step in person rather than in writing may shed light on the low regard in which Aveling's honour was held.

III

Karl Marx, in dealing with socialistic comrades, was fully as stark and strong a character as Bradlaugh; but when Aveling pursued his daughter he was no more, having recently died (1883). He had protected her when at sixteen the French revolutionary Lissafarry had flirted with her. It may be, of course, that her father's death made Eleanor emotionally as well as physically more vulnerable. At any rate, succumb to Aveling's wooing she did when she was twenty-eight.

Now Aveling was married already, but living apart from his wife and unable to get a divorce. But Eleanor Marx—while once again G.B.S. was playing his *rôle* of the laggard-in-love—was a girl of moral courage and she had the courage of the 'free love' so much chattered about by the conventionally-married socialists around her. She did not hesitate. She flung in her lot with Aveling, and eloped. Nor did she disguise the position. She made a public pronouncement amongst the 'comrades' that she would openly live with Dr. Aveling, and that her name henceforward would be Mrs. Eleanor Marx-Aveling.

In doing this, she sacrificed more than conventional reputation. She had left the British Museum and had obtained a very well-paid post as a teacher in a better-class school where she was greatly valued for her services as well as for herself. She refused to keep the unconventional and equivocal position secret from the school and notified its principal formally in writing of it. The school felt obliged to dismiss a teacher 'living in sin'. Of course, many other doors were closed to her at once.

In the socialistic circles where the name of Marx was well known and becoming better known every year, especially on the Continent, and where she, herself, was an admired and honoured young figure, the announcement of the Aveling connection made a great and painful sensation. It is one thing for advanced thinkers to utter advanced thoughts and quite another for them to act upon them: it is as strange as if Christians should literally carry out their creed by taking no thought for the morrow, by renouncing parents

143

and spouses, and by their clergy giving up benefices, houses and stipends and following Christ by wandering abroad and living on casual alms. But Eleanor had acted; and while her act caused consternation, many praised her courage and fidelity to her faith and her paramour.

Aveling was universally reprobated. Already regarded as a questionable scoundrel, his villainy was now recognized by the whole movement. Engels, the life-long and loyal friend of Karl Marx, was especially bitter and took steps to get Aveling drummed out of the continental groups. The difficulty was that to lose Aveling meant the loss of Eleanor, and no one wanted that, although the name of Marx was by no means then the magic talisman it has since become.

So the Marx-Avelings remained members of the extreme section of the movement, though there were many individual members who would have nothing to do with the male partner.

Shaw fully shared in the general reprobation of Aveling's conduct and in the general commiseration for Eleanor. A nobody at this period of his life, he was in no position to warn a young woman of his own age of the perils-to-come of her headlong, self-sacrificing course. But he can hardly have been merely uneasy in his mind; owing to Aveling's having included him amongst his victims by borrowing money which he never repaid, he must have also been uneasy in his conscience. For if he had honourably proposed marriage to Eleanor earlier, or even if he had seriously courted her, perhaps her association with Aveling might never have happened.

By braving the censure of the world deliberately, the former Eleanor Marx had certainly burnt her boats and cut off her retreat.

IV

The Marx-Avelings, directly the announcement of their 'free marriage' was made, left London for a cottage at Bole Hill, Wirksworth, in Derbyshire, for a brief escape from the hubbub that their exploit had caused. Perhaps on this brief honeymoon, with the man she had chosen, Eleanor was happy, but to one skilled observer she seemed otherwise, and if so, that idyllic happiness was not of long duration. Now to return to the 'advanced' circles, in which the dearest interest of them both lay, was quite impossible.

The position of Aveling was becoming difficult indeed. He was constantly traduced in the press. Bradlaugh and Mrs. Besant, who had provided him with both a platform and press in the secularist world, had cast him off. Hyndman, who had once regarded him as a promising recruit, had expelled him from the S.D.F., and William Morris, leader of the Socialist League, had quickly classified him as undesirable. The Fabian Society, knowing his reputation, had never admitted him to its respectable middle-class ranks. Keir Hardie and his I.L.P. had no place for him. But Eleanor's prestige with world-socialism kept him a foothold in international socialism, in spite of Engels' early denunciation of him.

Eleanor, although essentially a literary and theoretical socialist of the revolutionary and extreme wing, was by no means content with this type of work. On Bloody Sunday she was struck on the arm by a police truncheon. She fought in the Dockyard strikes, and even Annie Besant paid tribute to her eager service in the cause that day. She was an active practical organizer and administrator in trade unionism, most especially amongst the gas-workers, to which section she paid special attention. It was she who selected an illiterate gas-worker named Thorne (afterwards well known as Will Thorne, M.P.), taught him to read and write, and imbued him with socialistic theory until he was fit to stand for Parliament. Thorne never forgot the debt he owed this impassioned young woman during the rest of his career as an effective and greatly-respected Labour M.P.

Eleanor's throwing in her lot with Dr. Aveling effectually sundered Shaw from her. With his other women, his commencing journalism and his Fabian socialism, Shaw's hands were full. Hers, with her so-called husband, her trade-union work and her Marxist socialism, were equally full.

145

In a sense Eleanor's shame was a triumph. She had snatched her man from the lures of the greatest woman of the day, Annie Besant. Having regard to what that rival had published about her at an earlier date, it is plain that Eleanor can have been under no illusion as to Aveling's shady character, including his sexual and financial exploits. But she cherished other illusions about him and herself: that her love and her influence could redeem him, and that happiness for both would be the reward of her courageous self-sacrifice.

What manner of man was this frequently-condemned, unscrupulous scoundrel and seducer that he should ensnare women of such quality as Annie Besant and Eleanor Marx? Diametrically different physical descriptions of him are given. In one, he is said to have been horrible, an undersized man with the eyes of the basilisk; it was even said that he ought to have been a reptile in a museum. Many females were repelled by him, the most noteworthy of these being Eleanor's affectionate friend, the famous strong-charactered Olive Schreiner, whose novel *The Story of an African Farm* had gained a great success. She declared in letters to Havelock Ellis that meeting her on her honeymoon her beloved Eleanor 'looks miserable', and—

'I am beginning to have such a horror of Dr. Aveling. To say I dislike him doesn't express it at all. I have a fear and horror of him . . . this shrinking grows stronger. . . . I love her [Eleanor] but he makes me so unhappy. He is so selfish; but that doesn't account for this feeling of dread.'

Several of the women who began by hating Aveling at sight ended by being fascinated. But not Olive Schreiner, who was no fool or weakling. Aveling had publicly praised her book. But she was firm in distrust of him.

As against the repulsive portraits of Aveling, however, one must set others which declared him 'handsome' and 'magnetic'. His brilliance was undoubted, as was his adherence to his economic, political and religious principles, and his lack of all other principle whatsoever.

Intellectually, he had great talents of which he took every

advantage. He was that rare combination: an able economist with literary gifts in addition. He mastered Darwin as easily as he mastered Marx, and could expound both with equal facility; he was effective on the platform or in the press as he was in the class-room, lecture hall or in conference. Nothing but his own character could hinder the brilliant career confidently prophesied for him.

V

Time went on. Living in a cheap flat in Chancery Lane, Eleanor found it difficult to get work, for as she told Havelock Ellis: 'Respectable people won't employ me.' The tumult and the shouting over, the Marx-Aveling scandal died down. Thanks to Eleanor's tireless work for the cause, the comrades ceased from troubling and accepted the Marx-Aveling union as though it were an ordinary lawful marriage. He was to be Labour candidate for Northampton on Bradlaugh's death, but could not find the de-posit and the Socialist periodical *Justice* printed an exposure of him. Aveling turned over no new leaf: to Eleanor's distress his seductions and swindlings continued and were the theme of Socialist press and private denunciations. She would not leave him; convinced as she was that 'he needed her' she loyally held fast. Like her father, once she had given her allegiance, it was for life, however hard the journey and however long and bitter the travail.

The time came when Eleanor could no longer deceive herself as to her ability to reform her Edward. His real wife died sud-denly. She, and the whole Socialist world heard the news with relief, and it was confidently expected that he would regularize their union by marrying his partner. Nothing of the kind. He immediately went off and married a young unknown actress, sold the very house and furniture over the unfortunate Eleanor's head and temporarily disappeared.

This infamous conduct became known at once; indeed, the Marx-Avelings were too prominent as Socialist protagonists for it to remain hidden. Writing to Freddy, the son of the Marx family's lifelong devoted servant, Lenchen Demuth, upon the personal catastrophe, Eleanor showed clearly the quality of which she was made and how she looked upon Aveling's divagations:

'I know what friendship you feel for me and how sincerely anxious you are about me. But I don't think you quite understand —I myself am only just beginning to understand. I realize however, more and more, that wrong behaviour is simply a moral sickness and that the morally healthy (like yourself) are not qualified to judge the condition of the morally sick, just as the physically healthy can scarcely realize the condition of the physically sick.

'There are people who lack a certain moral sense, just as many are deaf or short-sighted or are in other ways afflicted. And I begin to realize that one is as little justified in blaming them for the one sort of disorder as the other. We must strive to cure them, and if no cure is possible, we must do our best. I have learned to perceive this amidst lonely suffering—suffering whose details I could not tell even to you—but I have learned it, and so I am endeavouring to bear all these trials as well as I can.'

Fate had not finished with this hapless woman, nor with Edward Aveling either. He did not long enjoy his second marriage. The doctors found that he was suffering from an internal cancer and that his very days were numbered. Eleanor wrote again to Delmuth:

'You haven't understood me at all. But I am too restless, too troubled to explain myself. Edward is going into a hospital tomorrow and the operation will take place in the middle of the week. There is a French proverb: "To understand is to forgive." Much suffering has taught me much understanding, and so I do not need to forgive. I can only love.'

Even more eloquent of the anguish and her loyalty is what she wrote in her last letter to the same friend:

'It is a bad time for me. I find there is little to hope for, and the pain and suffering are great. Why we all go on like this, I do not understand. I am ready to go and would do so with joy, but so long as he needs help, I am bound to remain.'

Edward Aveling's health after the operation appeared to

improve, and he must have made it clear that he no longer 'needed' Eleanor. Early on the morning of the 31st March, 1898 she received a letter from her paramour—a letter which, before anyone else could read it, he took care to destroy. Whatever it said, it was of such a nature that she instantly took a dose of prussic acid which Aveling had bought, one hopes for other purposes, and put an end to her tragic life.

She left a farewell letter of love for Aveling, who would have torn it up, the seal unbroken, had not the coroner's officer prevented him. He took the death calmly and made the necessary funeral arrangements with equal sang-froid.

But when a few friends gathered round poor Eleanor's coffin to accompany it to the crematorium, the burly form of Will Thorne, M.P., leader of the now firmly-established Gas Workers' Union, was seen to be shaking with uncontrollable sobbing. Tears coursed down his cheeks, and in uttering his valedictory address over the dead his voice was almost choked by his emotion.

His grief and pain were typical of what many others must have been feeling at the time. Eleanor was the second daughter of Karl Marx to destroy herself: one of her two sisters having faced death because she hated the prospect of old age.

VI

Edward Aveling now faced complete ostracism from every sect of the socialist movement. But that mattered nothing—for his mortal life was fast ebbing to its close.

The words that spring to mind over his death are hackneyed but appropriate; 'They say he made a good end' and 'Nothing in his life became him like the leaving it.' Sentences made respectively for the coarse Sir John Falstaff and the tragic King Charles I. However, strangely different stories are told of that end.

One story, given in his reminiscences, *My Years of Exile*, by Edward Bernstein, an international Socialist who knew both the Marx-Avelings at first hand very well, is that Dr. Aveling died 'a death which anyone might envy him: while reading a book in an

easy chair in the sunshine he fell asleep for ever'. But this is not
the generally received account, nor that which Bernard Shaw
knew, which is thus summarized succinctly by Hesketh Pearson:

'He died at last like an atheist saint, spouting Shelley in the
glory of the setting sun to the unspeakable edification of the
beholders.'

He was only forty-six when he died.

VII

Understandably, Shaw, like others, could never forgive Aveling.
Never did he speak of him directly without opprobrium as the
swindler and seducer that he was. But he essayed to be just, for
the contrast between Aveling's unswerving fidelity to Socialism
and atheism (in days when, and in circles where, such fidelity
could be disadvantageous and even disastrous) and his infidelity
towards women and creditors struck Shaw forcibly.

He knew Aveling well: once indeed in the middle eighties he
had played Krogstad to Eleanor's Nora and Aveling's Helmer,
Nora's husband, in Ibsen's play *A Doll's House*, though the performance of that then-idolized novelty in intellectual plays was
private and given to a select circle of the faithful in Bloomsbury.

There was a story put about in Fabian circles, which were a
hive of gossip buzzing about scandals in the private lives of each
other, that young Shaw, whose predilection for Eleanor Marx
was known, once said that he preferred Eleanor's ankles to her
speeches on the platform. As feminine ankles were then supposed
to be hidden by long skirts, this was considered a shocking thing
to say. The story came to Shaw's ears and he flatly denied its
truth.

Knowing Aveling as he did, and having suffered from his depre-
dations both in love and finance, when Shaw came to write one of
his plays, *The Doctor's Dilemma*, he could hardly help making use
of so unusual and picturesque a character as Edward Bebbins
Aveling presented; such a character was a gift to any author. He
drew him in that play as the painter Louis Dubedat, and could

have little difficulty in doing so since he knew the once-living model so well.

Dubedat, like Aveling, had a passion for having everything of the best and was wholly unscrupulous in getting that best for himself; like Aveling again, he shamefully borrowed even from his necessitous acquaintances where cash was scanty, for his selfish pleasures; again like Aveling, the painter by his aesthetics and affectations and flatteries fascinated and imposed upon women, making them mere conveniences for his own desires. Though Mrs. Dubedat is not Eleanor Marx-Aveling, each willingly sacrificed herself for the worthless philanderer and swindler to whose vices each deliberately shut her eyes and ears.

But the Dubedat situation, in spite of Louis's death-scene which closely parallels Aveling's, is only tragi-comic as painted by Shaw. He did not get—perhaps did not desire to get—the real tragedy of Eleanor Marx-Aveling; it may seem to those who know both the reality and the fiction he made out of it, as if he deliberately averted his eyes from the full horror of the destruction of the body and soul of the deeply-wronged daughter of Karl Marx.

No one will blame Shaw for that. Tragedy may have been foreign to his purpose in the particular play. Or he may have felt the woman's tragedy and his own failure to avert it too keenly to wish to make artistic use of it. One wonders whether Eleanor, a passionate lover and student of Shakespeare from childhood, realized what a Shakespearian tragedy her father's life and her own, a modern King Lear and Cordelia his youngest, were destined to become.

There is dramatic irony, too, in the fact that all these earnest men and women in the Socialist movement, striving for the betterment and amelioration of the lot of massed humanity as a whole or in herd-groups, remained onlookers, passively regarding the slowly-developing tragedy of this hapless woman. Not one of them held out a helping hand to her in her hour of need; nor did any one of them, when the deep waters of death rushed over Eleanor Marx-Aveling, utter a word of self-reproach at themselves for not having played the part of the Good Samaritan. They were all too busy caring in theory for the vast flocks and herds penned in sheepfolds to care to come to the practical rescue of merely one of their own sheep that had erred and strayed and finally fell—because none came to uphold her—into the valley of the Shadows for ever.

You cannot expect those vitally concerned in great matters, affecting the welfare of masses of humanity, to turn aside from their high talk to succour merely one more unfortunate weary of breath, murmuring as this one did, 'How sad has life been all these years!' before she becomes rashly importunate and goes to her death.

What is one compared with the many?

VIII

HIS FRIEND'S WIFE:
EDITH NESBIT

࿊࿊࿊࿊࿊࿊࿊࿊࿊࿊࿊࿊࿊࿊࿊࿊࿊࿊࿊࿊࿊࿊࿊࿊࿊࿊࿊࿊࿊࿊࿊࿊࿊࿊

'The frightful sensation of being always on guard when with another man's wife used to develop itself to such a devilish intensity . . .'

—G.B.S. on Himself

I

BERNARD SHAW believed himself to be especially attractive to women; and throughout his long life, and even at the age of seventy, there is a fair amount of evidence to show that the assumption was not entirely incorrect. Most young men are attractive as assets, even if only as prospective lifelong insurance in marital bonds. But in his first nine years in London young Shaw, as a non-earner, was a poor risk.

Perhaps that was why, in his twenties and early thirties, he attracted most those older women not in the raging quest for husbands. He himself thought that he was not safe in solitude with any ardent female; but few men are. He declared: 'Whenever I have been left alone in a room with a susceptible female, she has invariably thrown her arms round me and declared that she adored me.' In his fictional writings, as in Shakespeare's, woman is always the huntress; man the hunted, predestined victim.

It is difficult to see why young Bernard Shaw should have been physically attractive to females. His appearance, according to his contemporaries, was not prepossessing: in fact, the contrary. At this time his face is described as dead-white with sparse patches of orange whisker sprouting on cheek and chin; and H. H. Champion, a once famous fellow-Socialist, who had resigned his commission in the Guards to propagate his socialist faith, said that the effect of the white and orange in Shaw's face made him look like an unskilfully poached egg.

Wilfred Scawen Blunt, the poet, described him in his book, *My Diaries*, as:

'A grotesque figure. An ugly fellow. His face a pasty-white with a red nose and a rusty red beard and little slatey blue eyes.' But he added: 'Shaw's appearance matters little when he begins to talk—if he can ever be said to begin—for he talks always. . . .'

The grotesque figure was tall and painfully thin. He must have looked very like Don Quixote dismounted from Rosinante and divorced from Sancho Panza; and indeed at this stage in his mental development Shaw was quixotic—forever finding windmills to tilt at and wandering all over London and its environs to combat real or supposed evils in zeal for human betterment by collectivisation. Meliorists were common in Shaw's youth, but few were so zealous as he.

Later on in life, Shaw became much better-looking, as his innumerable later photographs show him to be. An actor always acting (as his wife later reproached him for being) and constantly studying how to make the best of himself before the camera, he never could resist the lure of being photographed or represented in painting or sculpture. But in young manhood when chill penury repressed the genial current of his soul, he was ill-looking and ill-dressed; one of the shabby-genteel.

In estimating the truth about Shaw's attraction to every susceptible female, allowance must be made for his ingrained habit of hyperbole. He exaggerated as heavily as Dickens. But undoubtedly there were times when a woman made a dead set at him. One of these huntresses was Edith Nesbit, the clever wife of his Fabian friend, Hubert Bland.

Half a century ago, the signature 'E. Nesbit', chiefly attached to children's poems and stories, was easily first in English magazine journalism. For ephemeral popular reading, her work excelled both in its quality and quantity. So good is it of its sort, that even today it is sometimes reprinted; but its commonplace content makes it poor food for the adult mind.

Her husband was also an able journalist, writing articles chiefly for the Sunday press from the Tory democratic viewpoint. Although one of the earliest of the Fabian Old Group and Treasurer of the Fabian Society, he was no Radical and only a Socialist in a manner of speaking; essentially he was a Tory Democrat or Imperialist. He was of the school of Randolph Churchill; the legislating not the litigating, the past, not the present, Randolph. In appearance this handsome man was monocled and moustached and aristocratic-looking; he had a taste for spiritualistic seances; a strong penchant for boxing and militarism; and an even stronger penchant for women.

Hubert had married his Edith when she was only seventeen and he twenty-five. They must have been a handsome couple then; and both of them were highly-talented. But Hubert at that time had no job, and the fact that he then already had a mistress and an illegitimate child was unknown to his girl-wife until three years after her marriage. Edith took the horrid revelation very well —so well, indeed, that Hubert was encouraged not to weary in ill-doing. He promptly fertilized one of Edith's friends who came to Edith for help, and Edith took the mother and baby into her home—not knowing her husband was the father.

But the presence of his mistress under his own roof was too much for Hubert and he 'carried on' with her there so that Edith learned the truth. She promptly decided to turn Mrs. Hagar and her Ishmael-babe out of the house, as Sarah did in the Bible, but Hubert threatened to go with them. Whereupon Edith surrendered, and was saddled eventually with husband and her own three legitimate children as well as the mistress and the bastards.

For a long time, the clever and industrious pen of Edith kept the household. But after a struggle, Hubert got a firm foothold in capitalistic journalism. But this, no doubt, encouraged him still further in his philoprogenitiveness, for—incredible as it may seem —he produced yet another child by yet another damsel, and again brought this mother and child to live with his long-suffering Griselda of a wife.

Shaw knew of Bland's promiscuous habits and tolerated, if he did not condone, them. He wrote to Bland: 'Imagine Mrs. Bland as the wife of a horrible city snob with a huge villa, a carriage and several thousands a year—which is exactly what, on moral principles, it was your duty to have made her. You and I have followed our original impulse, and our reward is that we have been conscious of its existence and can rejoice therein.'

But imagine Mrs. Bland as the wife of Mr. Bland and as her husband made her; the bread-winner of a bevy of her husband's bastards and mistresses! What was her reward and wherein could she rejoice?

However, Bland was useful to Shaw and Shaw was a useful recommendation to Bland in Fleet Street. Bland, as part-editor of a Socialist periodical *Today*, pushed Shaw's then failure of a novel *An Unsocial Socialist* for serial publication.

H. G. Wells describes Edith Nesbit and her extraordinary household: 'This tall, engaging, restless, moody, humorous woman . . . ran a great, easy-going Bohemian household at Well Hall, Eltham, a moated house with a walled garden. . . . The astounded visitor came to realize that most of the children were not Edith Nesbit's but the results of Bland's conquests; that the friend and companion who ran the household was the mother of one of these young people; that young Miss So-and-So who played Badminton with a preoccupied air was the last capture of Bland's accomplished sex-appeal. All this Edith Nesbit not only detested and mitigated and tolerated but presided over.'

Of Hubert Bland he says: 'He was under an inner compulsion to be a seducer.' (But all seducers are.) And he points out the incongruity of Bland's costume with his Bohemianism: the costume of a City swell: top-hat, tail-coat, greys and blacks, white slips, and that black-ribboned monocle.

II

One must diverge a little from the main Shaw–Bland–Nesbit topic here, to glance at the Fabian environment and understand how Shaw, Bland and Edith Nesbit were placed.

It might be thought, since the Fabian Society was nothing if not Socialistic, that Hubert Bland's position, prominent as it was, would be uncomfortable and highly anomalous. Nothing of the kind. To understand the strength of his position it is necessary to know something of the history of the Society and Bland's early connection with it.

The Fabian Society had been started by an idealistic moralist, named Thomas Davidson, as the Fellowship of the New Life. Its object at birth was to reconstruct society in accordance 'with the highest moral possibilities', so that its whole *raison d'être* was moral and ethical rather than economic and political. A community of the good was to be founded, possibly in Brazil. Havelock Ellis and a future British Prime Minister, the woolly-minded James Ramsay MacDonald, were original members. So, too, was Hubert Bland, who was always at odds with Sidney Webb.

Davidson went to America. But his society went nowhere, not even to Brazil, but led its precarious existence in Osnaburgh Street near Regent's Park. But Bland and others were not altogether convinced that the community could be reconstructed by ethical considerations: they wanted something more practical and down-to-earth. Between idealists and realists the Society split, and the realists carried on as the Fabian Society—an intriguing name that attracted the romantic intelligentsia who had heard the name of that ancient Roman, Fabius Cunctator, even if they knew next to nothing about him.

The Latin note was prolonged by what was thought to be a quotation from the classics, put on the title-page of the Society's first tract, as follows: 'For the right moment you must wait as Fabius did most patiently when warring against Hannibal, though many censured his delays, but when the time comes you must strike hard as Fabius did, or your waiting will be in vain and fruitless.' It is believed that this spurious quotation was invented by Frank Podmore, one of the earliest band, whose interests divagated to Psychical Research, in which he became well known. Whoever invented it, the invention was a stroke of genius.

'As Fabius did'—slow but sure—proved an irresistible appeal. It was one of those slogans like, 'What did Gladstone say in eighteen-eighty-blank?' or, ' "Sir," said Dr. Johnson,' that catch on irresistibly. Lots of earnest-minded folk were ready to do 'as Fabius did' without knowing what he did, or why he did it. But the 'Old Gang' of the early Fabians knew quite well what they were after. Being severely practical, they added the forthright and definite statement: 'The Fabian Society consists of Socialists,' thus nailing their true colours to the masthead. If they could not get Socialism by direct means—and they quickly realized they could not—they would get it by permeating Liberalism and Toryism with it.

On 16th May, 1884, George Bernard Shaw, who, like the Society itself, lived in Osnaburgh Street, came, out of curiosity, to his first meeting; the Fabian name proving an irresistible lure to him since it suggested something better-class and better-educated than the ragtag and bobtail of working men and foreigners generally associated at that time with the disrespectable propagation of Socialism. He realized that the Society was what he was seeking: a forum for ideas and self-expression on socialistic lines. In September he joined the Society as a member; the following January he was elected to the Executive Committee and wrote for the Society its Tract No. 2.

At that time its devoted Secretary, E. R. Pease, with Bland and his wife were the chief people running Fabianism. But Shaw brought in Sidney Webb, quickly followed by Sydney Olivier and his friend the academic Graham Wallas: a remarkable galaxy of budding talent.

These five men thrashed out together the creed that came to be famous as Fabian Socialism. Intellectually they were a formidable lot, aiming at what they believed was world-betterment through Socialism, and every one of them was a formidable character, notably in resolution and firmness of purpose. Theirs were the brains that, first, painlessly and secretly, inoculated the Tory and Liberal parties with socialistic and communistic doctrines; and next, formed the Labour Party based upon the rapidly-rising and power-getting trade unions which engulfed the old Liberals and survives in the political scene to this day. Once, the first five Fabians had believed in a swift, violent revolution by the oppressed proletariat on Marxist lines, but Bloody Sunday and much debate showed them the impracticability of that swift catastrophe for Britain. Quickly they adopted a permeation policy, much later defined by Webb, when he became Lord Passfield and a Cabinet Minister, as 'the inevitability of gradualness', and their method from the very early days was to permeate the great political parties with their ideas, and not at first to form any Labour Party at all. When the Labour Party was born they enthusiastically took it over.

The Fabians were the Jesuits of English politics. They burrowed like moles into the Liberals and Tories. They worked chiefly in secrecy in spite of their desires for the widest possible publicity and propaganda for their ideas. They knew Socialism was tremendously feared and hated in the Britain of that day. Socialism, Communism, atheism, anarchism, nihilism, revolutions, rebellion, sedition, not to speak of 'free love' and other deviations from righteousness and normality, were all lumped together in conventional British minds as diabolism and wickedness.

For many years the Press never reported anything the Fabians said or did: this press censorship, though merely imposed by convention, was as rigid and absolute as though imposed by law and enforced by imprisonment. On the other hand, behind the scenes, Cabinet Ministers of the first rank, like Balfour of the Tories and Haldane of the Liberals, constantly dined, and consulted, with Webb. Wives and intellectual spinsters soon reinforced the original Fabian Junta. Most of these, as is usual, were the mere reflection of their menfolk. Charlotte Payne-Townshend (Shaw) and Edith Nesbit (Bland) were of this kind, but Beatrice Potter (Webb) was very different. She was a political personality in her

own right, and when she and Sidney Webb married, as he told
her: 'one and one placed in a sufficiently integrated relationship
make not two but eleven'. In simpler words, 'You and I married
are not a pair but equal to eleven ordinary people.' Essentially
they were statisticians and researchers in political economy.

Sidney Webb soon became Bernard Shaw's political mentor and
closest friend. The Webbs were an extraordinary pair; caring only
for each other. Charles Sorley, the young poet killed in the
1914-18 war, talking of their conjugality, said the pair 'lived in
a perfect halo of mutual admiration and put their trust in figures'.
Indeed, they were the ideally married pair—the antithesis of the
Blands—inasmuch as they lived for each other and their shared
work; ideally married, except that they were childless. After
twenty years of marriage Beatrice could write of her Sidney: 'He
is the most perfect of lovers, by night and by day, in work and in
play, in health and in sickness.' And after thirty years' marriage
she could write of him: 'The days of his absence are weary to get
through. The sleepless hours of the night are haunted not by the
fear of death but the dread of life without him.'

Beatrice was good-looking, and wealthy. Amongst her rejected
suitors was the great 'Joe' Chamberlain himself. Physically, Sidney
resembled a small nanny-goat, and he was a poor speaker. But in
Committee and in compilation he was quite extraordinary: a
human computer that ate up Blue-Books and secreted vast information. Shaw reverenced him more than any living man, and
throughout their long lives never spoke of him except with the
utmost respect. It was probably the spectacle of the Webbs that
made Shaw believe that one day the pleasure of brain-work might
intensify to an ecstasy surpassing the sexual orgasm. No wonder
a poet of the day, contemplating the felicity of these soul-mates
and mind-mates, wrote:

> How wise it was of Mrs. Webb
> To mate with little Sidney,
> A man of slightly lower class
> But one of her own kidney.

'Dearest Ellen'—portrait
of Ellen Terry

. . . and on the stage

Annie Besant as a girl

> What fun that happy couple had
> As with a gentle laugh
> They added and subtracted
> And then drew another graph.

But even Shaw could not 'Blandulate Webb nor Webbulize Bland', hard as he tried to harmonize these opposites in the Fabian camp.

III

The history of the early Fabian Society belongs to fame and has been thoroughly revealed by Pease, its first secretary, and other writers, such as Lady Anne Freemantle. Here we are only concerned with it, so far as it was the setting for the personal relations of Shaw, Bland and Edith Nesbit.

It will now be clearer what Hubert Bland, that Don Juan and Conservative Democrat-Imperialist, was doing in that Fabian galley. He remained engrafted there firstly because of his original membership, and secondly as a Tory imperialist with private socialistic ideas, who could permeate the Tories as effectively as other comrades could permeate the Liberals and Radicals. Also, he was too formidable to be easily ousted from his entrenched position as Treasurer. Then again, as an accepted journalist writing popular politico-economic articles on the front page of large-circulation Sunday papers like the Hultons' *Sunday Chronicle*, he was a name, if not a figure, in the national consciousness. He and young Shaw as fellow-journalists were naturally friendly. Shaw's boxing-novel, *Cashel Byron's Profession*, was of interest to both.

If Webb and Bland got to loggerheads on dialectical grounds, Shaw would intervene to keep the peace. Webb and Bland remained antipathetic, however, beyond his skill.

IV

G.B.S. was at his extreme philandering stage in these early

Fabian days. His unpublished diaries with their bald, dull, brief comments—very unlike his usual writings in their bone-like factuality—make this Bland episode perfectly clear. He was in tow with six or seven women at once, and sometimes hard put to it to keep the affairs and the women from colliding with each other. They all frequented the same circles, that is to say, they were either his mother's music-pupils, like his Alice Lockett and Jenny Patterson, or they were in the Socialist circle, like his Annie Besant, Geraldine Spooner, May Morris, Eleanor Marx and Edith Nesbit. The time came when coterie actresses like Florence Farr and Janet Achurch had to be added to his life.

Edith Nesbit, though a Fabian by virtue of her husband's position in the Society, cared little or nothing for politics and economics. Both her tastes and her talents were literary. Except for Hubert's sake, she would have had nothing to do with the frumps and faddists of Fabianism and their interminable discussions. If she could not count intellectually with them, she was at any rate determined not to be ignored at their committee-meetings.

To draw attention to herself at Fabian Committees, she developed a technique of fainting-fits and creating scenes. The other women whispered that she had plenty to faint about, poor thing, in her domestic life, and out of commiseration they forgave her antics. When Shaw aroused her interest, she asked him to sit next to her at committee-meetings. He consented; but only conditionally. His conditions were: no faintings, no demands for sudden glasses of water and no scenes of any sort. For a time Shaw's proximity cured her behaviour. But fainting-fits in public were common in the women of that time, probably sometimes because they wore stays too tightly laced, or because their diet made them anaemic or tuberculous. Sometimes, as in Edith's case, it was pure exhibitionism.

If Edith cut capers amongst the Fabians, so did her handsome and formidable husband. Both of them, indeed, had a high nuisance-value and provided a pleasant theme for scandal and gossip. One amusing foible of Hubert's was the blackballing on moral grounds of candidates aspiring to join the Society, despite the fact of his being an irrepressible and unrepentant polygamist himself. Like Butler's Hudibras—slightly amended to fit him, he would:

> Compound with sins he was inclined to,
> By damning those he had no mind to.

When a drunken fellow-Fabian and fellow-journalist called J. F. Runciman once had the temerity to question the fitness of Bland for the Treasurership of the Society and the accuracy of his accounts, Bland proved his suitability by knocking down the critic with a well-aimed blow from his fist. Again, to parody Hudibras, he

> Proved his finances orthodox
> By apostolic blows and knocks.

There was no further criticism. The accounts were passed and Bland remained Treasurer.

V

Shaw, as his novel *Cashel Byron's Profession* proves, admired boxing. He was a bit of a boxer himself and would spar with Bland. In spite of Bland's High Toryism and Shaw's Extreme Socialism, which early became Marxism, they remained close friends. Necessarily Edith Bland saw a great deal of young Shaw. He visited their home. Sometimes he escorted her home, or to concerts and the like.

Naturally Edith Bland, herself a clever woman, was struck by Shaw's cleverness. His fund of dry Irish humour and wit she found 'irresistible'. But she was critical and discerned his faults—or some of them. He was, she declared, 'the grossest flatterer of men, women and children, chiefly women'. He did not always 'stick to the truth'. He was untrustworthy. Also (in emphatic italics) she wrote that he was 'very plain'—in that estimate agreeing with men like Champion and Blunt, already quoted.

Yet, in spite of all this, she found him 'one of the most fascinating men I ever met'. She noticed, too, that at this period—1885—people were constantly saying: 'Oh, it's only Shaw.' But, as to this fact, she told herself: 'Everyone rather affects to despise him—but everyone admires him all the same.'

From this it will be perceived that Edith Nesbit was a woman of rare perspicacity who had deeply studied Shaw. All the same, she fell head-over-ears in love with his 'maddening white face', as she called it.

Her growing passion for the young Irishman gave her a keen eye for any possible rival. There were plenty of these; some of them outside the Fabian circle and unknown to her. But she had no difficulty in picking one out. 'Miss H—— pretends to hate him,' she wrote, 'but my own impression is that she is head-over-ears in love with him.'

On such matters, the Fabian Society was a seething cauldron of scandal. Political collectivism was not the only collecting discussed by its females. Edith could not help giving away the secret of her feelings for the young Irishman. Besides, 'free love' manifestation was an oasis in the dull arid desert of Socialist politics and economics.

Edith's fellow-Fabians knowing all about it, as they thought, eagerly watched to see what would happen. The newly-married Mrs. Sidney Webb kept an eagle eye on Shaw: she had begun by disliking her husband's close friend but she now believed him irresistible to all women but herself. Sidney, to whom Shaw had confided some of his amours, had exclaimed: 'My! You do warm both hands before the fire of life'—a poetic allusion from Walter Savage Landor surprising in the walking library of blue-books that was Sidney Webb. The Webbs were therefore alert.

However, very soon Beatrice Webb came to the conclusion that Shaw was only flirting with women in order to get material out of them for his writings. He was not in earnest over Mrs. Bland or any other woman—Charlotte, his wife-to-be, not having yet appeared on the Fabian horizon. He was 'a sprite in such matters, not a real person', she thought. She began to accept Shaw as her husband's best, loyalest and most unswerving friend, admirer and supporter, though afterwards Shaw, at ninety-three, was still explaining that 'nothing amazed her so much as being suspected of any sexual attachment to me'.

Never was there the slightest ground for any such suspicion—especially not in Beatrice's conduct or words; but it shows how wide was the area of sexual suspicion that Shaw had created amongst his Fabian associates. Beatrice's affections were firmly fixed on her husband: from beginning to end of their marriage she literally worshipped him, and no man mattered to her except as he affected Sidney or his interests. This blissfully married pair—a pair in a million—have been happily described as so much united in heart and mind as to be 'two typewriters with a single click'. The description is worthy of Shaw, though it was by E. T. Raymond.

By now Shaw had determined that his connection with women was fundamentally Teutonic: they were the soldier's relaxation from warfare. 'I am fond of women (or one in a thousand, say); but I am in earnest about quite other things. To most women one man and one lifetime make a world. I require the whole populations and historical epochs to engage my interests seriously and make the writing-machine (for that is what G.B.S. is) work at full speed and pressure: love is only diversion and recreation to me.' This may have been true of him in general. But at least twice in his life-time he was very terribly in earnest and seriously infatuated: once in early manhood and again in late middle-life.

However, the increasing infatuation of Mrs. Bland, though it interested and flattered Shaw, did not rouse a corresponding passion of like character in him. He had other outlets. His attitude with Edith was that of playing with fire, but it was also the thus-far-and-no-further attitude. He was willing to meet her clandestinely for long solitary walks and conversations: to escort her to, and from, social occasions and entertainments; to miss last trains at night for the sake of her companionship; to talk endlessly upon literature, art, music, Fabian affairs, socialism, internationalism and anything objective; to lead her to believe and hope that he loved her. But when she called without permission at his home and interrupted his writing, and began to take him seriously, he grew restive. He had endured walking from her home at Black-heath to his own home in North London, arriving at 3.30 a.m., long enough.

Caution, too, came into the picture. Hubert Bland, immoral himself, was not the sort of man to tolerate unfaithfulness in his wife. This aggressive, pugnacious man was above all things likely to express resentment in physical combat; and physical violence was the thing above all others that Bernard Shaw hated and feared. Not once did he pretend to physical courage: indeed, more than once in his life he expressly disclaimed it for himself, notably, as we have seen, over the events of Bloody Sunday. He could not risk a collision with Bland for the sake of a woman for whom he had no real desire at all, and merely because he was (at first) flattered by her attentions, which, now becoming a nuisance, were beginning to pall.

Fortunately, she was of a mild temper and the 'scenes' that he had with her, destructive though they might be of his peace of mind and hers, were nothing like those he had endured from that scorned termagant Mrs. Jenny Patterson. Thus, on 11th July, 1888, after meeting Edith at the British Museum and having tea afterwards he says: 'She insisted on coming to Fitzroy Square. My mother was out and she went away after an unpleasant scene caused by my telling her I wished her to go as I was afraid that a visit to me alone would compromise her.'

VI

If Shaw was a writer, well, so was she—an almost equally industrious, and certainly at that time a much more successful, one. Shaw had not yet got into his later conquering stride. Her name now appeared regularly, attached to books as well as to pieces both in prose and verse in periodicals. Everyone in England was familiar with the name 'E. Nesbit' attached to a piece of writing, though no one considered that exceptionally important, for the rewards of a successful writer for juveniles were far less then than today, the payment-rate for juvenilia being excessively low. On the other hand, Shaw as a writer of books was utterly unknown, and his journalism confined to very few outlets was little known yet. Still, Shaw did not take the lady's mercenary writing seriously, skilled of its kind though he knew it to be.

She decided she too would write what he might respect; something fine and beautiful, different from the daily bread-and-butter grind. The subject lay to her hand: her beloved, himself.

Through the influence of her passion she now composed and published some passionate poems and sonnets, which though not ostensibly addressed to George Bernard Shaw were about him, as her fellow-Fabians guessed. One sonnet-sequence was aimed directly at him in the Socialist periodical *Today*, which was virtually the Fabian organ. It purported to be a description of one of Burne-Jones's pictures, then very fashionable. The poem was entitled *The Depths of the Sea*.

Irony was lent to this situation by the fact that at this time Hubert, her husband, was actually editing the paper. She did not sign the poem but merely appended her maiden initials: E.N. The opening sonnet ran:

> In deep vague spaces of the lonely sea
>> She deemed her soulless life was almost fair
>> Yet ever dreamed that in the sun-warmed air
> Lay happiness, supreme in mystery;
> Then saw him—out of reach as you I see—
>> Worshipped his strength, his brown breast, broad and bare
>> The arms that bent the oar and grew aware
> Of what life means and why it is good to be,
> And yearned for him with all her body sweet
> Her lithe cold arms and chill wet bosom's beat;
>> Vowed him her beauty's unillusioned shrine:
> So I—seeing you above me—turn and tire
> Sick with an empty ache of long desire
>> To drag you down—to hold you, make you mine.

(That is excellent poetry, and the second sonnet falls no way below the first in quality. One wonders what the editor-husband thought of it. Did he think himself the hero of the poem? Or that it was all mere imagination inspired only by the Burne-Jones picture? At any rate, his fellow-Fabians knew different.)

She showed some of her love-poems to Shaw, naturally enough, since his taste for poetry was a highly-cultivated one, apart from his being the inspiration behind them. Coolly Shaw sub-edited one that mentioned his 'maddening white face' by changing the second adjective to its opposite!

VII

But, by this time, a young man as acute as G.B.S. must have realized that, at any moment, there might be an explosion from the ferocious Bland. The situation was getting dangerous and beyond his control. He must make up his mind to control it. In its essentials, what he desired was simple enough: to retain the friendship and good-will of both husband and wife, especially the husband's, and to extricate himself and the woman from a perilous infatuation that could only harm them both.

He decided to play Joseph to her *rôle* of Potiphar's wife. Acting a part was fun and games to him, an easy and enjoyable activity. It was the easier in this case because in contrast to Bland's uncontrolled virility, Shaw was sexually sub-normal, as his own revelations show—H. G. Wells later in life publicly called him an intellectual eunuch—and he had no difficulty in sublimating his sexual urges into temperate friendships.

Controlling himself might be easy: controlling Edith Bland was more difficult. She had set her heart upon him. She was likely to prove recalcitrant, and determined not to relinquish him. He had encouraged her too much. That sort of behaviour would have to stop.

If the ferocious Hubert Bland found out, he might react violently at any real—or even supposed—trespass upon his marital preserves. He was of the type that made that kind of reaction a point of honour. The situation was one that called for quick action, for the longer things went on the more risky they might become.

In this very difficult situation Shaw showed a tact and skill worthy of a seasoned diplomat, or a very much older man. Realizing that to precipitate a sudden crisis or showdown with Edith might make matters worse, he resolved instead to change his tactics. He would cease philandering and flirting by degrees. Instead of making himself attractive to her, he would make himself as unattractive as he could.

When they met he set himself to bore the lady deliberately by long disquisitions upon the dullest and dreariest economic topics, steadfastly refusing to talk of anything likely to interest her. He cut down the time spent with her, excusing himself on the score of engagements. Of himself and herself he would not talk at all; and if he did, he would only joke and decline to take their conversations seriously. As far as he could, he arranged to have a third party present at their interviews.

Manifestations of her feelings for him he now treated with heartless and ruthless unconcern. He spoke of her to other Fabians in quarters where he knew he would be reported to her, so that she would think he thought her ridiculous while he himself was utterly insincere.

Shaw prided himself even at this early stage in his development, and not without good reason, upon his flair for managing awkward people and awkward situations. He had had a good deal of experience in this regard; as a Fabian committee-man he often had to compose differences of opinion and to conciliate opponents.

This carefully thought-out campaign took time: it was indeed a Fabian campaign both in concept and in execution. It would be too much to say it worked like a charm. But work it did. Such coldblooded tactics, steadfastly pursued over a period, fell like douches of icy water upon the febrile Edith's emotions. To be the target of ridicule and contempt in Fabian circles was intolerable. Under such slights, her rejected love remembered how she had formerly thought Shaw 'untrustworthy', and how this philandering, blarneying Irishman used to flatter everyone to get his way, both in public and private. Soon her rejected love wilted and withered like a tropical plant exposed to Arctic blasts. By these subtle means, the lady was weaned from her affection and her passion cooled rapidly.

Directly this happened, Shaw set himself to transform their relations back into the light, unclouded friendship of former times. Not surprisingly, he was not altogether successful. But that he reconciled her at all was a tribute to his skill as a peacemaker, often acknowledged later on in committee-work on many organizations. According to Edith Nesbit's biographer, Shaw transmuted the lady's feelings into 'a gay and untroubled friendship'. This is perhaps putting it too high.

Hubert Bland, a highly-intelligent and alert person, can hardly have been entirely blind to this episode. He must have appreciated Shaw's loyalty to their friendship, and his restraint in the face of temptation.

As time went on, when Shaw married and conditions changed, Bland and his Edith lost personal touch with Shaw. Whether this had anything to do with the affair is not known; friendships sometimes lapse automatically and Shaw's crowded working-life soon gave him no time for Blackheath. But on his death-bed, the former Fabian Treasurer had become a Catholic, and was no longer the old fighting Fabian. Troubled by financial doubt over sufficiency for the provision of a member of his family to finish his course at Cambridge University, the dying Hubert confidently said: 'If the money's not enough, ask Shaw.'

That was a tribute to the reality of their friendship, and to the generosity of Shaw's character. Bland knew that whatever Shaw's faults, an old friend could never appeal to his purse in vain, and that he could rely on his generosity.

Of all Shaw's pluralistic relations with women, perhaps this is the one from which he emerges with most credit. Cynics may ask, however, whether this happy ending would have resulted if Henry Sparling's champagne-bottle shoulders, instead of Hubert Bland's broad shoulders, had been in the case. If Bland had been May Morris's husband, perhaps that story would have been very different. . . . As it was, the upshot was entirely happy.

IX

HIS UNCONSUMMATED MARRIAGE:
CHARLOTTE PAYNE-TOWNSHEND

⁂⁂⁂⁂⁂⁂⁂⁂⁂⁂⁂⁂⁂⁂⁂⁂⁂⁂⁂⁂⁂⁂⁂⁂⁂⁂⁂

'What do you call married life? Real married life is the life of the youth and maiden who pluck a flower and bring down an avalanche upon their heads. Thirty years of the work of Atlas and then rest as pater and mater familias. What can childless people with independent incomes marrying at forty as I did tell you about marriage? I know nothing about it except as a looker-on.'

'The years make no earthly difference. I still fall for women but they regard it as one of my jokes and tolerate me. Charlotte took it very nicely and bravely: she wept and poured out her soul to one or two young men. I did not interfere. It will all come out when I am dead.'—G.B.S.

I

SIX MONTHS after 'Sonny' Shaw had been born in Dublin, a baby girl, Charlotte Frances Payne-Townshend, was born at Derry in the county of Cork in Southern Ireland. Not for almost forty years were these twain destined to meet, and then their convergence happened not in the land of their birth, but in England.

The little Townshend girl inherited wealth as the little Shaw boy inherited poverty. Her father, Horace Payne-Townshend, was

171

an Irish barrister and landowner, wealthy enough to be under no necessity of practising his profession; her mother, Mary Susannah Kirby, was an English lady from Worcestershire who disliked Ireland. Their two children were both girls; and the elder, Mary Stewart, the better-looking of the two, married an English Army captain, Hugh Cecil Cholmondely, who attained the rank of a general before his death.

Ironically enough, this was a related family of Townshends to that by which Sonny (at that period called by the name of George) was employed in Dublin as a youth.

In 1885, when Shaw was struggling to write novels in London Charlotte's father died and her sister married. From then until 1891, Charlotte and her mother lived together at their London house, 21 Queen's Gate, when her mother died—and Charlotte, aged thirty-four, was her own mistress. When the two sisters had lived together with their parents, their friends called Mary Miss Payne-Townshend and Charlotte Miss Plain-Townshend.

In 1891, a woman of thirty-four was regarded very much as on the road to becoming what was then opprobriously called 'an old maid', more especially if she was poor. But Charlotte was the reverse of poor, and now that her mother was dead, she fully intended to make a career for herself. As a small child she had declared that she would marry a 'genius', and though to her mother's vexation she had shown little inclination to marry, she was one of the 'New Women' of her day, with ideas of having a life of her own and developing herself.

But what sort of life had she led with her parents, and what manner of young woman had that life made her? She persistently detested publicity and in general self-expression of a subjective kind, just as Shaw loved both. Until she reached the age of seventy she shrank from telling her story; once, and once only, she broke her iron rule of silent restraint. She wrote an emotional letter to her then great friend T. E. Shaw (Lawrence of Arabia) author of *The Seven Pillars of Wisdom*, and painted a vivid and painful picture of her parents and home life.

II

That letter to date is not to be found in any of the standard biographies. But the original was found by Shaw after his wife's death; it greatly impressed him both by its eloquence and by the fact that, like him, she had a most hapless childhood, and cherished like him a grievance—deeper and more bitter than his—against her mother's upbringing.

The original letter is in the British Museum and it is dated 17 May, 1927. Just as Shaw told Ellen Terry he had 'a devil of a childhood', so she says to Lawrence: 'I had a perfectly hellish childhood and youth.'

Explaining that Ireland—unlike England — in her young days had only two classes: The Gentry and The People, and that her father of course belonged to the gentry, she went on:

'My mother was a terribly strong character—managing and domineering. She could not bear opposition: if it was offered she either became quite violent, or she cried. She constantly cried. She felt (genuinely felt) she had sacrificed her life for us and my father (We were two, my sister and myself) and she never ceased telling us so. She felt (quite genuinely) that we none of us loved her enough, or considered her enough, or helped her enough (she would not be helped—ever) or respected her wishes sufficiently, or cared to spend our time with her.'

Such, according to Charlotte, was her mother. The domineering female who, when opposed, is either violent or lachrymose, and who has egoistic grievances against those who co-habit with her, is a common enough type. Ridicule and contempt are an effective answer, but it is fatal to take her pretensions seriously when they should be laughed out of court. It would appear that the rest of the family took Mrs. Payne-Townshend too seriously; a great mistake.

Charlotte draw a very different picture of her father: 'My father was gentle and affectionate, well-educated and well-read; very, *very* good—honourable and straight. Trying to live with because he was slow and blundering about *little* things. He was a marvel of patience with my mother, which was terribly bad for her. I think, now, she ought to have been *beaten*: it would have been better for us all, especially for herself. As it was my father led a most unhappy life, and died comparatively young out of sheer tiredness.'

How much Charlotte must have suffered from her mother if fifty years or more later on she thought her mother should have been beaten! Ordinary folk might think she ought to have been laughed out of her self-regard, or that constant mental castigation by the others might have cured this ill-regulated matron.

How did her sister and Charlotte react? Charlotte goes on:

'It was a terrible home. My sister is as hard as nails, she takes after another branch of the family, and got through it best. I am in some ways like my father, but I have a lot of my mother's managing, domineering strain in me. I used to stand between my father and her, and stand up against her on my own account, but I have in me (what you have so much more strongly) a fearful streak of conscience, and sense of duty; complicated by a sensitiveness that is nothing less than a disease. The conscience has been my undoing! At that time I thought She is my mother: I owe her respect and devotion: I must bow to properly-constituted authority (fearful little prig that I was, I used to go about mouthing that phrase to myself—I got it in some accursed book—and crushing down all that was best in me with it—'Properly-constituted-authority'. Lord!) and so I was a kind of buffer she hurled herself against . . .'

(At this point in her story Charlotte actually asks her correspondent, who, remember, was Lawrence of Arabia, who had seen some dreadful aspects of life and war: 'I wonder are you dreadfully shocked!' That makes the reader smile; no doubt Lawrence smiled too at that idea.)

She explained that 'even in my earliest days I had determined I would never marry'; so, there being few career-women in those days, she had to stay at home. But she says:

'It warped my character, and spoiled my life and my health and my mind. The older I got the more I felt it and the more I longed for freedom.'

There you have it: the initial impulse that made this Irish gentle-woman of the 'New Women' order determined to lead a 'free' life on her own. They lived, she says, 'in one of the most lovely spots in the world, in a rather big rambling house all set round with yards and stables and gardens and woodlands and lawns and "our own people" (tenants!) for miles in every direction.' At that period her father in England would have been known as 'The Squire'.

She continues her story:

'Later we became rich by the death of relatives' (they had never been poor, and her father had the reputation of having doubled his personal fortune by wise investment) 'and she' (her mother) 'took us away to Dublin and London to "marry" us. One very vivid recollection of my London life is of her saying to me after my father had committed what she considered some little social *gaffe* (he had beautiful and considerate manners, but occasionally they were just a tiny trifle *too* good. You know.) She said: "Who could get into society dragging such an incubus as that——" I have never told a soul that before——.'

Evidently the husband and father was a weakling with no force of character, but he had Charlotte's love and sympathy and pity.

Her story, in its indictment of her mother, gets worse, for she says: 'It is my belief that she first killed my father and then killed herself. Oh! not murder in any legal sense—though it ought to be. But separated (mostly) from his home and his interests, and constantly snubbed and corrected he began to be often ill, and then he got internal trouble, and died, I think of pure unhappiness.

'Afterwards she died: of brooding, and self-pity, and—well—and selfishness. It is really awful to think how glad I was. I sometimes still wonder whether my constant longing for her death had anything to do with killing her.'

And she ends this part of her tale: 'Well, that's that' but adds the explanation; 'I said my mother killed herself. I am sure her little illnesses and "nervous depression" and final collapse were self-induced.'

Reading this, one can easily see that this mother was a pathological case, and that her behaviour was bad for those unfortunate enough to be constantly exposed to it.

Charlotte goes on to philosophize and to ruminate upon her parents' incompatibility and unlikeness to each other. 'Nature thrusts men and women into the arms of their opposites to stabilize the race. . . . But also marriage is not natural—but unnatural and disastrous.' She also sees clearly that the family was too weak and too afraid of this female dragon in their midst. Also she has the good sense to blame her own fears and says:

'If I had had the pluck, the courage, the determination, the decent straightness to say "Damn duty: I will take my life into my own hands and develop as I know I can develop and let other people face their own problems, no matter how 'wicked' it is according to my governors, teachers and spiritual pastors and masters"—I now believe that would have pulled her together, made her control herself, respect me and be a better and wiser woman.'

One may doubt whether the defection of one of the family would have redeemed the petty tyrant, who would have still had the weak father and elder sister Mary to wreak her feelings upon. But Charlotte goes on to say 'Then another thing' this time turning abruptly to a discussion about herself:

'I don't believe, as far as I can remember, that I was born with a dislike for children—perhaps I was. But, anyway, my own home life made me firmly resolve never to be the mother of a child who might suffer as I had suffered. As I grew older I saw many, and better, reasons for sticking to my resolution. The idea was physically repulsive to me in the highest degree, and my reason did not consent to any of the arguments brought to bear upon me.'

She points out that the country is already over-populated: and also, 'I did not desire to produce cannon-fodder. Then they said I was a remarkable person and should hand on my qualities. I said it did not appear that distinguished people had distinguished descendants: great men and women are "sports" usually. And so on.

'But there is another side to this question. No one must say "Because of my heredity, I will not have children". The finest people come from the most unexpected and, apparently, from the

most unlikely and unfortunate combinations. You [Lawrence] and
I and G.B.S. are all instances of this.' And 'Besides we do not
know what sort of men and women we want. We have no standard—Julius Caesar was an epileptic.'

It is evident from all this that Charlotte thought highly of herself
and romantically of Lawrence, though she changed her opinion
of Lawrence later on. He was a great *poseur* and more than a little
of a charlatan, though far from being entirely bogus. But it is of
course true that the wind of genius, like the other wind, bloweth
where it listeth and is not yet controlled by human engineers and
may never be. And it is clear from all this that, from whatever
cause, Charlotte Payne-Townsend was hardly likely to make an
ideal wife or mother. One may wonder, however, if her dislike of
the idea of marriage and child-bearing was not innate in her from
birth, and whether her unhappy home-life with her mother did
more than accentuate the natural—or unnatural—tendency in her.

She concluded this remarkable letter by saying:

'There! I feel so much better for saying all that. I've never put
any of it down in black and white before, and looked at it. The fatal
mistake, I find, is to keep these things locked up like guilty secrets
and brood upon them. Bring them out to the surface: let the
daylight shine on them and the Sun of Rightness [?Righteousness]
will shrivel up all the pettiness, and meanness, and make Wisdom
and Beauty.'

Then she signed herself with the imprudent signature of those
who do not realize how untrustworthy, in point of time, true
human feelings (including their own) may prove: she signed herself, 'Ever C.F.S.'

With the key of that letter Charlotte unlocked her inmost self,
not merely to Lawrence but to every reader of it. Of it and the
diary which he evidently destroyed, her husband said: 'She poured
out her soul to Lawrence.' And: 'There were parts of her character
that even I did not know.' And: 'Of all the women I have known
(and I have known many) I knew Charlotte least of all.' He only
realized this after her death.

III

When her parents were dead and her sister married, Charlotte Payne-Townshend was free to develop herself and her life on what lines she chose. Naturally she chose to make new friends amongst people of 'advanced' views like her own, especially as she was uncertain of herself and her destiny. Then she had a liking for travel, and untrammelled by relatives she joyously set out for continental travel alone—a much more original undertaking then for a gentlewoman than for any kind of woman today.

Adventures are to the adventurous, and Charlotte was therefore certain to encounter them. Two of her dissimilar adventures were important; one of them has not been told before, and it most certainly was calculated to confirm her prejudices against physical contact that might lead to child-bearing.

The story was told to me by a great friend and whole-hearted admirer of hers. It appears that while in Germany, she was so imprudent as to walk unaccompanied in the Black Forest. She was attacked by a man whose motive was sexual, and with great difficulty she escaped. One can well imagine the horrid effect of the highly-unpleasant experience upon a gently-bred lady.

Next, in Italy, she met a very remarkable man, the doctor, Axel Munthe, afterwards the author of that world best-seller, *The Story of San Michele*. It seems that like many others she fell in love with him, but he, so adept at self-expression and so ready to tell stories, has left no account of his feelings for her. But later, when she met and became friends with George Bernard Shaw, she told him of her former love for this Swedish lover of Capri and declared that she was broken-hearted over it. But for Shaw's retelling the world, nothing would be known of this association.

Returning to England, she met the Webbs and found them both, but Beatrice especially, congenial. The Webbs, of course, were only too ready to direct anyone from Cabinet Ministers downwards in the way they should go; and they directed Charlotte and substantial sums of her money in their direction. She became an ardent Fabian and subscribed £1,000 to their new scheme for the

London School of Economics, and even rented a flat at 10 Adelphi Terrace, in the Strand, to help the cause further.

For this heiress, Beatrice Webb had still further plans: namely, to make a Fabian bride of her. Beatrice thought of her Fabian male friends and from them selected one of the most academic and stable of them, a professor called Graham Wallas whom she thought well-suited for the Irish recruit and her money. The Webbs were in the habit of holidaying—if their never-ceasing industry ever took a holiday in the usual sense of that word—by renting a country rectory. In the autumn of 1896, Charlotte joined them in Stratford St. Andrew Rectory in Suffolk, and Shaw was invited, one of four guests, including Wallas.

Understandably, as an attraction, Wallas could not compete with Shaw, who very speedily fascinated Charlotte. His 'green-eyed Irish millionairess'—and her money—also fascinated Shaw. Those were the early days of bicycling and the two spent much time on the local roads together, enjoying the new and swifter mode of locomotion, then sacred to the better classes.

The picture which Beatrice Webb drew of Charlotte in her diary at this time is probably accurate, for Beatrice had a financial motive for correctly appraising the mentality of their new recruit:

'She is romantic but thinks herself cynical. She is a Socialist and a Radical not because she understands the collectivist standpoint but because she is by nature a rebel . . . She is fond of men and impatient of most women; bitterly resents her enforced celibacy, but thinks she could not tolerate the matter-of-fact side of marriage. Sweet-tempered, sympathetic and genuinely anxious to increase the world's enjoyment and diminish the world's pain . . . To me she seemed at that time a pleasant, well-dressed, well-intentioned woman . . . Now she turns out to be an "original" with considerable personal charm and certain volcanic tendencies . . . In a few days she and Bernard Shaw were constant companions. . . .'

Perhaps Beatrice was not, perhaps never was likely to be, in her entire confidence, for it was not the matter-of-fact but the sexual side of marriage that Charlotte could not tolerate. Also, as the

Lawrence letter shows, it was environment rather than nature that made Charlotte a rebel. However much of an 'original' Charlotte, in search of herself and her destiny may have appeared to Beatrice at that time, there was little of any real originality in her. Basically she was neither unconventional nor genuinely rebellious, as her acquiescent after-life shows clearly.

Beatrice also appraised her physically—as she was when she met Shaw. She called her 'a large graceful woman with masses of chocolate-brown hair, green eyes, *matte* complexion that sometimes looks muddy, at other times forms a picturesquely pale background to her brilliant hair and bright eyes'. No one called her a beauty.

Neither Shaw nor Charlotte was young at their first meeting. Both looked askance at marriage as an institution. And now—meantime—their friendship strengthened and deepened. It was not the sort of holiday-friendship that ends with the holiday; the very reverse in fact. Indeed, it was a working-holiday: as Shaw described the life it was 'an eternal political shop, mornings of dogged writing all in separate rooms, ravenous plain meals, bicycling, the Webbs incorrigibly spooning over industrial and political science; myself always tired and careworn and always supposed to be writing to Ellen (Ellen Terry, the famous actress).' Certainly it was not everybody's cup of tea. But 'Miss P.T.', as Shaw called her, found it all 'very interesting'.

Shaw made a confidante of Ellen Terry, whom he had not yet met personally. The Irish millionairess, he thought, had been successfully incorporated into the Fabian family—gang, perhaps, would have been a better word. She had cleverness and character enough to decline the station in life—'great catch for somebody'— to which it had pleased God to call her. Shaw was going to refresh his heart by falling in love with her; he loved falling in love, he said.

At this time Shaw thought himself 'no catch', as the cant phrase of the time went (even a plain girl with money, well-dressed, well-brought up and sensible might well expect something better). But he was not entirely ineligible. He was making a fair living in journalism: three plays, *Widowers' Houses*, *The*

Philanderer, and *The Man of Destiny* had been considered seriously, and he was busy upon a fourth, *You Never Can Tell*. In advanced circles he was a leading figure and an asset, even if his incorrigible levity caused the serious-minded to say: 'Oh, it's only Shaw.'

Like the timorous mortals in the Anglican hymn shrinking from the narrow sea of Death leading to heavenly bliss, Charlotte and Bernard lingered shivering on the brink of giving up freedom to attain matrimony. They had come to like each other very much, yet neither would admit to love, and certainly not such romantic love as leads to marriage. Besides, Charlotte was nursing her broken heart, though Shaw roundly told her that it was all nonsense and that her heart was not broken at all.

Ellen saw the matter romantically: 'You two walking in the damp and lovely mist, a trail of light from your footsteps.' But Shaw, a lover of beauty, had no illusions of that kind. Charlotte was not young, nor beautiful, nor a figure of romance. True, she was normally a lady-like person at whom nobody would ever look twice, so perfectly did she fit into her place. Perfectly placid and proper and pleasant! Bernard and Charlotte were certainly no Romeo and Juliet.

IV

This not-so-ardent pair hesitated. Holiday over, they continued seeing each other at Dorking, when Shaw was back in London. Next year, in the autumn of 1897, he and his 'Miss P-T' stayed with the Webbs in Monmouth. He was preparing his first dramatic book, *Plays Pleasant and Unpleasant*, with long prefaces, for publication by an enterprising, speculating young new-comer in publishing, Grant Richards.

Their speculation about each other did not wane. He called her 'a curious person' and she called him 'an utter brute'; but neither took offence. Shaw described her again to Ellen Terry: 'a restful person, plain, green-eyed, very ladylike, completely demoralized by my ideas, independent and unencumbered and not so plain either when you are in her confidence.'

'Plain', that good old English adjective, or what the Americans transmogrify into 'homely', seems to have been the *mot juste* to describe this woman, for everyone seems to have used it of her; Shaw certainly did, though one suspects, not to her face, for she was a sensitive woman. But when you can't flatter a woman upon her beauty you can always extol her brains, as Lord Chesterfield never failed to point out. If Charlotte was neither original nor creative, she was distinctly intelligent and cared for ideas, especially unconventional and advanced ideas promulgated by Shaw. Early in 1898, she had constituted herself his reasonably-efficient private secretary, and when he had a cycle accident, she did not disdain to give him personal nursing attention. (She had gone through a nurse's training.)

Then she started off for a tour of the world, and reached Rome with the Webbs to study municipal administration, when the rival Graham Wallas magnanimously telegraphed Beatrice Webb that Shaw was very seriously ill and much neglected by mother and sister in his Fitzroy Square house. Apprised by Beatrice, Charlotte immediately rushed back to London, and invaded her friend's home.

If she had not made up her mind on the journey—or even before—what she found in Fitzroy Square made it up for her at once. George, as his mother Mrs. Carr Shaw and his sister Lucy always called him, or Bernard as Charlotte called him, for he hated the name George and only now used it as an initial, was in a bad way. He had a fearful abscess on his foot which had attacked the bone, and it might entail amputation. Added to this was a mental breakdown through over-work. 'If I make another stroke with the pen I shall go mad,' he said.

His home horrified Charlotte. The study was sordid and squalid; dark, damp, dirty, with the remains of inadequate meals dumped about. Innumerable papers, pamphlets and books lay about in disorder. His mother absorbed in her music-teaching, his now-married sister ever absent on stage-engagements, entirely neglected him. Charlotte did not mourn or denounce the neglectful women. She showed the managing strain she was to complain of later in her dead mother. She acted; taking matters into her own hands, and brooking no denial.

She insisted on removing him into the country to a house she rented at beautiful Haslemere in Surrey, there to be nursed, doctored, and fed vegetatively as he insisted, by herself and her servants. His physical state was perilous. But he evinced scruples on the score of compromising her: she a Society spinster, he a bachelor. (They do not seem to have thought of a duenna or chaperone to keep up the Victorian proprieties.) Either they must be married or he could not elope with her.

She yielded. Or was it he that yielded? Or both? Anyhow, the marriage was agreed. Charlotte bought the ring and the licence at once.

V

Why did he give way when he believed, as she did, in freedom and not marriage? He told his friend Philip Wicksteed, 'For a reason I never thought possible,' he said, 'namely, that I think more of somebody else than I do of myself.' They had 'become indispensable to each other'.

But what kind of marriage was it that they agreed upon? Not, we may be sure, the ordinary conventional union: they twain becoming one flesh, as the Anglican prayer-book has it. Charlotte hated sex and the procreation of children, and she was too mature to change her strong feelings against conjugality and maternity. As for G.B.S., he had experienced sex in plenty with Jenny Patterson and Florence Farr, and he, as ever, was ready to explain his willingness to decline from bachelordom into the married state. And he did, in terms which, forthright as they remain today, were perfectly shocking to conventional Victorianism:

'When I married I was too experienced to make the frightful mistake of simply setting up a permanent mistress; nor was my wife making the complementary mistake. There was nothing whatever to prevent us from satisfying our sexual needs without paying that price for it, and it was for other considerations that we became man and wife . . . Do not forget that all marriages are different and that a marriage between two young people followed by parentage is not to be lumped in with a childless partnership between two middle-aged people who have passed the age at which it is safe to bear a first child.'

And had Charlotte any sexual needs for satisfaction? If she had, on her own later showing, there was something inherent in herself to prevent her obtaining such satisfaction according to her own confessions. She always displayed an antipathy to sex. No doubt there are, and most certainly ought to be, other considerations than sex in marriage, as the great poet John Milton has pointed out in his admirable and neglected pamphlets upon 'the godly doctrine and discipline' of divorce. Milton himself thought the mental and mutual comfort, society and helpfulness (the inward spiritual grace of marriage) far more important than the fleshy delights of the 'genial marriage-bed'. In one phrase: compatibility is more than concupiscence.

But Shaw—always too-fertile in explanations, never following the Disraelian formula 'Never explain'—explained still further in a letter to Frank Harris in 1930 many years later.

'Not until I was past forty did I earn enough to marry without seeming to marry for money nor my wife at the same age without suspicion of being driven by sex-starvation. As man and wife, we found a new relation in which sex had no part. It ended the old gallantries, flirtations and philanderings for both of us. Even of these, it was the ones that were never consummated that left the longest and kindest memories.'

Sexless marriage is nothing new though it is, of course, much the rarer kind. Old people's new marriages, in the very nature of things, can have little or no sex in them, and the statistics of the Registrar-General show that a small number of people even marry in their eighties and nineties. Charlotte was hardly a woman of 'gallantries, flirtations, and philanderings'; she was much too seriously-minded for that, and she fiercely despised and hated her husband's tendencies in those directions. Nor did marriage end Shaw's: there were new ones to replace the old. No doubt

Charlotte may have had a mild, girlish adventure or so, but there is a total absence of evidence, the only later one known being that with Axel Munthe. As to consummation, that idea, having regard to Charlotte's horror of it, must be applied and must have been meant to apply only to Shaw himself. Who can doubt, too, that money was a fundamental consideration for marrying on Shaw's side? For talking of his having hundreds a month by the marriage, he reminisced:

'I shared (deepened) my mother's poverty, that is, lived virtually at her expense for long enough. I began my literary career by writing five big novels and a host of articles which nobody would publish. My earnings for nine years were exactly fifteen shillings.'

And he got his wife-to-be to make a marriage-settlement upon him, on the plea that if he died he did not want his mother to have to beg from his widow.

Again, looking at his excuses for his sexless marriage: it is true that all marriages are different. Yet the more they differ the more they are the same thing in spite of that difference. As to the cry of 'Safety First!' there are times when that cry, so useful on occasions, is contemptible, and surely the risk of child-bearing ought to be bravely faced. Shaw might have put it more accurately: only the woman bears the child, and she alone is exposed to danger thereby.

But surely he did his Charlotte grave injustice here, and there is her letter to Lawrence to prove it. It was not personal fear for her own safety that actuated her refusal of a consummated marriage and of childbirth. Shaw was entitled to speak for himself, but he also spoke again for Charlotte when much later he declared: 'She married me because she thought I was a genius.' Of course, as a child Charlotte had wanted just that, but she had long ago recoiled violently from that early idea. It may well be that she had reverted to it. Or was she actuated by womanly compassion for the needs of a sick, neglected man with a mission in life that might be stultified by a lack of common care and sufficient filthy lucre?

VI

On 1st June, 1898, they were married at the Strand Registrar's Office in London. He was forty-two; she, forty-one. The bridegroom was ill and on crutches, dressed in an old jacket worn by the action of the supports. Graham Wallas and Henry Salt were witnesses, and Shaw joked that the groom looked so much like a tramp and Wallas so much the reverse that the Registrar nearly married Wallas and Charlotte but for his own intervention. A pretty Shavian joke, to which the antecedent circumstances lend special and subtle point!

Shaw wrote an amusing account of his marriage in *The Star* of 2nd June, 1898. He called it his second operation—the first having been on his foot. He declared that his friend Salt—as secretary of the Humanitarian League—would have protected him had there been time.

The bride's sister, Mrs. Cholmondeley, who was not at the ceremony, sent no felicitations. Quite the contrary; she wrote to the autumnal bride: 'Don't ask me to meet this man. And as a last kindness to me and for my sake, I ask you to secure your money.'

It was a well-founded suspicion. Arnold Bennett, the novelist, was told as a fact that G.B.S., some months earlier, had discussed with other male Fabians the question of whose duty next it was to marry an heiress and devote her and hers to the cause. Webb had captured Beatrice Potter; Costelloe, Miss Pearsall-Smith; Ramsay MacDonald, M. E. Gladstone. Too late, Mrs. Webb had intended the new-comer Charlotte for Graham Wallas, for Charlotte had been 'netted' (G.B.S.'s own word), by reading Shaw's *Quintessence of Ibsenism*, which chimed in with her own ideas of 'advanced' womanhood. Besides, Professor Wallas bored her. Later Shaw bragged to the two witnesses that, thanks to his career's success, he had not taken advantage of Charlotte's money.

Now, indeed, in this mental partnership Charlotte Payne-Townshend had found her purpose in life; domesticity and intellectuality in cohabitation with a nominal, but legal and respectable, husband.

From the first day of her honeymoon—if nursing of the sick man in her own home could be called a honeymoon—until the day of her death, she accepted the continuous task of a helpmeet, providing for her captive genius the conditions under which he could do his self-imposed work for world-betterment, as he conceived it, under conditions of comfort.

Shaw bragged to his witness-friends later on: 'Marriage has not made an iota of difference to my working. I write what I like and I do what I like.' This is as if Swinburne were to say that living in dull Putney under the care of the solicitor Watts-Dunton did not affect his poetry; or Kipling to say of his wife Carrie that she made no difference to his fiction; or G.B.S.'s friend Granville-Barker to say that his second wife Helen Huntingdon had not altered the direction of his writing. The truth was that Charlotte kept a careful check on him (as he later said): certain friends and certain books 'from Harris or Paris' she would not have in the house, and the dirty books she buried in the garden.

A Shavian and sexless marriage, however, is as likely, or unlikely, to be successful as any of the usual and normal kind. Marriages for money or convenience or both often turn out well, as in the case of Disraeli, of whom his Mary Anne said proudly: 'Dizzy married me for my money, but if he married me again he would do it for love.' Like nearly all unions, the Shaw marriage had its ups and downs. But the fair verdict upon the whole marriage is that, although there were troubles, and once the marriage itself was endangered when Shaw fell madly, if temporarily, in love with the highly temperamental actress, Mrs. Patrick Campbell, and was ready to risk all to possess her, the marital knot held firmly in spite of all the stresses and strains to which it was subjected.

In its first year physical ill-luck pursued Shaw. The sheltered Haslemere home was ideal in its peace and quiet for an author's work. In spite of his foot, Shaw worked hard on his pamphlet *The Perfect Wagnerite* and started a most ambitious new play, his *Caesar and Cleopatra*. But just as his foot was showing real improvement he fell downstairs and broke his left arm close to the wrist. Charlotte improvised two butter-patters as splints; and with arm and leg helpless he was incapacitated.

For change of air when he mended the newly-married pair went for a fortnight to the Isle of Wight, where Shaw never ceased working as usual. Coming back to Haslemere he felt so improved that he tried to ride his bicycle again using one foot only. He fell and badly sprained his ankle in consequence. This second accident gave him more pain than 'ten operations or two broken arms'.

They took a house at Hindhead, and again the bad foot caused a second sprain, and a little later a third, because he would go 'fooling with a bicycle'. In spite of all these disasters, he pursued his work unflinchingly. He was warned that the necrosed bone in his foot, which was constantly discharging, might turn can-cerous and finish him. He had to be operated upon, and was told he might die—a prospect he took calmly. But eventually the disease cleared up and his various breakages healed. Much of his restoration to health was due to the wifely devotion of Mrs. Shaw.

Though this companionate marriage went well enough between the parties to it, it did not go well with Mrs. Shaw's in-laws, the mother and sister of her husband. Charlotte disliked both of them. Lucy's health and musical and marital careers had alike failed, and she had become embittered. How bitter she was can be gauged from a horrible letter in which she calls her sister-in-law 'the drop of gall in our cup, all the more bitter that she is externally so charming and agreeable . . . *We* never dream of going near her!' The truth was that they were never invited. That his mother and sister never once crossed the threshold of the conjugal home Shaw himself attests, but he melioristically adds that though there was avoidance there was no bad blood.

Lucy's cynicism became so deep that when she published two booklets, *The Kildonnel Letters*, Shaw denounced them as 'terrible —like the grinding of teeth in Hell'.

Both mother and daughter harped on the theme that 'All love is Dead Sea fruit!'—to which Lucy added, 'whether parental, mari-tal or fraternal'. Both women, Shaw described, as unloving to himself, and in general to others, though Lucy had many admiring, affectionate friends. Everybody loved her but she loved nobody, her brother said. According to G.B.S., Charlotte objected to everyone who had a part in his life before her advent, including Mrs. Carr Shaw and Lucy, but this attitude is not uncommon in the very early stages of a marriage and soon wears off. Charlotte's dislike of her in-laws was much deeper and lasted longer than that. She was indignant that mother and sister should be friendly with such a woman as Jenny Patterson. Fortunately, Shaw, no enthusiastic partisan of his relatives, did not really mind their absence, to which he had always been accustomed.

Charlotte considered she had to 'civilize' this genius of hers; to weed out undesirable friends and guard his callers, his post and his writings. Of course, there were temperamental differences between the married pair. Shaw liked solitude, that necessity for literature, and cared nothing, or very little, for travel. Mrs. Shaw liked to have 'a lot of young men about her': she also adored travel 'for her happiness was always around the corner'. To Shaw publicity and the limelight were the very breath of his being, apart from their use in making himself and his work known and attracting a world-audience. He could never be photographed enough, but Charlotte Shaw loathed being photographed—as an excessively plain woman might well do—even when it was done by her camera-fiend of a husband. Still more did publicity, especially for herself, in all its forms disgust her; to her it was bad taste, bad manners and altogether execrable. Shaw said of her in this connection: 'I have never known a person who so hated the limelight.'

Today, when to attract publicity is widely regarded as a virtue and an attainment, that attitude of Charlotte Shaw's may seem eccentric. But the gentlepeople of her day held publicity for themselves in the utmost contempt; advertisement was for tradespeople and their goods. Mrs. Shaw was only expressing the ordinary views and feelings of her class.

Once this serious-minded gentlewoman showed a sense of humour over her husband's predilection for the limelight. St. John Ervine told me that she once turned to him and ironically exclaimed: 'Do you know, St. John, I almost believe that G.B.S. actually likes publicity?' It was a masterpiece of understatement.

As far as she could, she protected him from the grosser forms of it that would interrupt his work. Very capably did she manage the household and her servants; smoothly and efficiently she ran the domestic machine, giving him comfort, order, regular meals of the kind he wanted; the sheltered existence in which an author can concentrate in peace and tranquillity upon his work. Though the time quickly came when he had to have a professional secretary and she surrendered that part of her work, she managed the secretary and the rest of his physical life to perfection. She made an admirable hostess.

In the latter part of their lives, they had a London flat at Whitehall Court and a country house at Ayot St. Lawrence. These homes suited G.B.S. well enough. She did not care much for either of them: she, herself, would have preferred to live in Ireland, for which her affection was warm, and to travel. Very often she was restless and discontented, but later in life she found consolation and refreshment in the moral teachings of Dr. J. Paster Mills, and later on in the warm friendship she conceived for that strange character, Lawrence of Arabia.

But before Lawrence's death the warmth had cooled on both sides. Lawrence really thought her a 'plain, old stick' and a frump. And when her husband noticed the cooling-off and Lawrence's absence from the home, she explained it curtly: 'He is such an infernal liar,' she said.

The relations between this married pair were generally harmonious. Shaw always treated her with patience, courtesy and consideration. He was always first in her regard and her zeal for him was untiring. Their friends were always struck by the mutual devotion between them. Shaw's criticisms of her after death hurt and vexed them, though they were in keeping with Shaw's character and habit of blurting out unpleasant truth-as-it-appeared to him, oblivious of its effect on general opinion. He declared that she was always discontented, having everything to content her, and declared further that her death was a relief to himself, and his reversion to single-blessedness a pleasure. Below these surface expressions, in reality he cared deeply for her as she for him.

She herself did a little literary work but not of a creative kind. Diligently she compiled extracts of the wit and wisdom of Bernard Shaw. She also translated the social dramas of the French playwright, Eugene Brieux, which had considerable vogue in their day.

Just as the leopard cannot change its spots, neither could Shaw. He could not cease his philandering proclivities merely because he was married. A succession of women raised Mrs. Shaw's contempt; Shaw indeed boasted of how even after seventy he was pursued by women, and how, when they became too troublesome, he handed them over to his wife. If Charlotte Shaw was incapable of sexuality, she was not incapable of jealousy, and in this respect hers was the traditional dog-in-the-manger attitude. She was quite capable of defending her proprietorial rights in her husband against all comers—and she successfully did.

But the stories of those other women must be told later on.

VII

Years passed and the inevitable slowly came about. The physical machine of this devoted wife began to show signs of wear and tear; there were minor illnesses of bronchitis, asthma, and nervous troubles. Finally, she fell a victim to the incapacitating disease of *osteitis deformans*, with its slow, remorseless toll upon the appearance, health, strength and spirits.

Though the best medical and nursing attention was at her command, this of course was merely ameliorative. It could not arrest the progressive disease.

Shaw's behaviour throughout this long crisis was admirable. He did everything he could to show affection, consideration and attention. Once he had told his friend Ervine that if Charlotte were dying he knew an infallible way of restoring her to health. All he would need to do would be to go to bed and say *he* was dying. But alas! at this stage even that potent charm would not work the necessary miracle. It had become merely an effective way of paying tribute to her devotion.

Near the end of 1942 she was pronounced incurable, and of his 'poor' wife and himself Shaw wrote: 'Both of us deafish and rather dotty'. It was truer of her than of himself. And on 12th September, 1943, at Whitehall Court the end mercifully came when she was eighty-six years old.

VIII

Before the end came, a sad disintegration of the mental woman was slowly taking place. Her hearing and memory became bad. She suffered from hallucinations, at one time believing there were invaders in her bedroom. Her speech became incoherent at times but she became exceedingly exacting. On one occasion she complained that she had not seen her husband for two days, though he had been with her almost the whole time. On another she was found crawling on all fours on the floor to get to some books she wanted.

Towards the end Shaw noticed a change in her and told her she was looking better and younger. She smiled. Next morning she was found lying on the floor of her bedroom with a cut on her forehead. That day she was at last happy and uncomplaining and all her worries seemed gone. But on yet another morning the nurse woke her husband to tell him that his wife had died at 2.30 a.m.

Shaw went and stared at her, dead. She looked like her portrait at twenty-three—a portrait so flattering that beholders could not believe it was Charlotte. But within twenty-four hours that beauty had disappeared: she was her own old, worn-out self again.

She had desired cremation, and that her ashes should be scattered in Ireland on the Three Rock Mountain, but Shaw had told her he would keep her ashes to be mixed with his own at his death. At her cremation, his secretary, Miss Blanche Patch, and Lady Astor accompanied Shaw, and when the anthem was played Shaw stretched out his arms and sang the words quietly. He was cheerful and calm.

Edith Nesbit, 'his friend's wife'

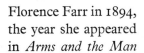

Florence Farr in 1894, the year she appeared in *Arms and the Man*

G.B.S. at ninety

A notice appeared in *The Times* saying that Mr. Bernard Shaw could not possibly acknowledge the prodigious mass of condolences on his wife's death. He assured their friends that what he called 'a very happy ending to a very long life' had left him awaiting his own turn in perfect serenity!

But he told Eleanor O'Connell, a friend, that 'Everyone tells me that I am looking well, and I can't very well say that it is relief at my wife's death, but it is, you know.' Similarly, when Lady Astor said how well he and his secretary looked since Charlotte's death, he commented, 'But you know if she had lived much longer we should have pre-deceased her. She completely wore us out.' Another week of her illness would have driven him mad. He spoke also to another friend of the abominable illness which took four years to kill her.

And on the point as to whether her marriage had made her happy, he replied, 'No. She was always discontented, with everything in the world to make her happy, but she had the idea that happiness was always in the place she wished to be or had just left.'

'Everything in the world to make her happy'? Except a physical husband and real children. Perhaps, like the Rachel of the Gospels weeping for her children, 'because they were not', she was sometimes conscious of what might have made her happy and fulfilled her womanhood. A barren woman who has no children to rise up and call her blessed, and yet also a husband who praiseth her, has little to make her happy in the wintry days of old age, looking back over the years and remembering that she might have been 'a mother in Israel'. Shaw, finding a Bible amongst his dead wife's effects, merely took occasion to write in it a scarifying criticism of its cover, its printing and its general appearance, and with that signed, to send it to Sotheby's to be sold to the highest bidder.

What, one wonders, would Charlotte have thought of that? There is no question that with all Shaw's gifts he had some strange insensitiveness, and atrocious bad taste both in action and in speech.

However, he claimed that after forty years of marriage something quite indestructible grows up between the pair; something which has nothing to do with emotions in any way. But what manner of something is that but something emotional in itself? Hesketh Pearson relates that he also told Eleanor O'Connell: 'If you had had forty years of love and devotion such as I have had you would know what freedom meant, and I am enjoying this, here, for the first time.'

Not surprisingly the woman-auditor retorted: 'You should never have been married.' To which he answered: 'No. That's perfectly true,' slapping his knee for emphasis. He had made the same point once before: 'I don't think I ought ever to have been married; I am not the marrying kind.' It was a belated recognition of the truth after a long forty—in banal fact forty-five—years of enduring a falsity in relationships. He added that Charlotte had helped him 'by her interest in intellectual things and I could not have been married to any other type of woman.'

It does not seem to have occurred to him that he might have grievously wronged Charlotte by marrying her, and that she might have been happier with a different kind of man, Axel Munthe, and that for her there had been endurances but no ardours.

IX

Charlotte's will did her infinite credit. She had always loved Ireland—unlike her husband—and she had dreamed of an Ireland peopled by refined, sensitive and educated Irish men and women with all that was best and finest in literature, art, music and grace-ful and gracious living. Her will tried to carry this ideal into reality.

She left £154,967. After bequests to her niece, Cecily Charlotte Colthurst, to various servants, and to Sidney Webb, Lord Pass-field, and an income for life to her husband, she left the rest for the aesthetic benefit of the Irish people. Unfortunately, certain expressions of hers in the will regarding 'awkward manners', 'vulgarities of speech' and the like caused some foolish people to mis-conceive the will as 'an insult to Ireland'—when it was, of course, nothing of the kind and nothing was further from the testator's intentions. She loved Ireland dearly and wanted to be there in death. She deserved praise and thanks, not blame, from her country.

And she left the Lawrence letters to the British Museum absolutely. Many women have found Charlotte Shaw a detestable and abnormal character, for they remember her remark to Shaw's secretary, Miss Blanche Patch: 'Babies. Who could like them? Disgusting little things.' This and her refusal to allow consummation of her marriage strikes them as treachery to the sacred fundamentals of womanhood, marriage and motherhood.

No doubt, to borrow an Ervine phrase, she was a vestal virgin who took her virginity very seriously, and was possessed by a deep and morbid aversion from the sexual act in marriage or out of it. But it is now clear from the Lawrence outpouring that her repulsion was real, not affected; innate in herself and not acquired by intellectualism, though she, of course, tried to rationalize it for justification's sake. It is but justice and good sense to recognize that in the populous hive of humanity not all can be queen-bees, but that there are born worker-bees who also serve the hive. Moreover, we are destitute of that diary found on her death and in no position to judge.

If we may trust the reports of his circle after her death, Shaw regretted that he had not been 'firmer' and 'more insistent' with Charlotte in the matter of having children. Would his insistency have prevailed? Perhaps the truth is that he was the wrong husband for her: it is, for example, difficult to imagine her former love, Dr. Axel Munthe, acquiescing in an unconsummated marriage. In this difficulty real 'love will find a way'. Nothing in Shaw's sexual history suggests that he was the right physical partner for a highly reluctant and physically over-sensitive wife. In this matter he was false to his own basic tenet of belief in production, and fulfilling the clearest purpose of the mysterious Life Force, in which it was his religion to believe and to serve.

It is only right to recognize that Shaw dealt with this theme of the woman refusing motherhood in his last complete play, *Buoyant*

Billions, and therefore he can be called as a witness for the prosecution against himself and his marriage on this question. In that play Miss Buoyant is afraid of the Life Force which is seeking to make her marry. Her solicitor points out that though marriage is often regretted, motherhood never is (this is questionable) and that 'celibacy for a woman is *il gran refuto,* the great refusal of her destiny and the purpose of her life, which comes before all personal considerations: the replacing of the dead by the living'.

Celibacy is not other than celibacy, even when disguised by the cloak of a marriage-ceremony and subsequent co-habitation.

It is only right to recognize that Charlotte Shaw's marriage was the kind of success that she wanted it to be, even if it was something quite other than marriage in its highest form, as most people conceive that institution. The world is heavily in her debt in so far as her ministrations and work in the fulfilment of her childhood's ambition made the work of her genius possible. That work in itself is part of her reward, perhaps even the best part of it, and it is known that she was the cause of his writing his greatest play, *St. Joan.*

Did she ever hear the ghost of her mother say after she had written what she did of her mother's marriage: 'And what of your own marriage, my daughter? At least I bore my children, but where are yours?'

Perhaps the triumph of Charlotte Shaw came when her husband's ashes, at last commingled with hers by his emotional desire, were scattered in their garden at Ayot St. Lawrence, between the statue of St. Joan and his writing-garden-shelter there. What had never happened or been desired in life had happened in death—the physical union of these twain into one, at long last. That was better than Westminster Abbey. . . .

. . . And yet one cannot help remembering Shaw's words, which he doubtless had forgotten when he directed the scattering of Charlotte's ashes in their garden: 'Charlotte hated Ayot.' She herself had wanted to be buried in Ireland, and that her ashes should be scattered on the Three Rock Mountain outside Dublin, as she directed in her will. It has been suggested that war-time conditions made Charlotte's wish impossible to fulfil. But the war did not last for ever and the kept ashes could have been taken over to Ireland when it ended.

Another strange fact is that G.B.S. did not like the house at Ayot either, and only bought it when he was told he must either buy it or leave it! There is indeed little beauty about the house that anyone should desire it. Long before his death, however, he was reconciled to life in it, hating as he did, especially in his latter years, to be uprooted.

And as Charlotte's will was dated 2nd September, 1937, and she did not die until 12th September, 1943, it is possible—perhaps highly probable in view of her wifely devotion—that she had acquiesced in the idea of their commingled ashes being scattered in their Ayot garden.

At all events, one hopes so, although what do the dead care about such things that they cared for so much when they were living?

X

Not seldom, relatives find amongst a dead person's effects things which surprise them. Amongst Charlotte's possessions Shaw found a little coloured poison-pill to be taken if her afflictions became more than she could endure. Shaw kept it, he said, for his own use in case he became a burden. The private correspondence she had kept was a great surprise; most of it he took the precaution of destroying, for she had 'poured out her soul' to some younger men such as Rilke and Lawrence in confidences she had never made to her husband. Some few letters he sent to the British Museum. Disconcerted by what he found, he was moved to say of the woman to whom he had been married for forty-three years: 'Of all the women I have ever known, and I have known many, I knew Charlotte least of all.'

That stresses the unreality of their marriage on the spiritual plane, and lends poignancy to his acute realization that, except as an onlooker, he knew nothing of marriage. Pathetic, too, is the letter to his estranged friend Granville Barker telling him of his wife's demise:

'Charlotte died last Sunday . . . She had not forgotten you.

'Since 1939 she had suffered much pain, and lately some distress from hallucinations of crowds of people in her room; and the disease, a horror called *osteitis deformans*, which bent and furrowed her into a Macbeth witch (an amiable one) was progressing steadily and inevitably. But last Friday a miracle occurred. She suddenly threw off her years, her visions, her furrows, her distresses and had thirty hours of youth and happiness before the little breath she could draw, failed. By morning she looked twenty years younger than you and I ever knew her.

'It was a blessedly happy ending; but you would not have believed that I should have been so deeply moved. You will not, I know, mind my writing this to you. She was eighty-six. I am eighty-seven.'

Granville Barker had been divorced from his actress-wife Lillah McCarthy, and had married Helen Huntingdon who loathed and detested Bernard Shaw, and set herself to break the friendship of the two men. She succeeded; and her influence was a great blow to Shaw who seems to have cared more for Barker than for anyone else. Shaw—in his writings a great foe to superstition—feared that Helen had bewitched him, and for a time physically disabled him; he regarded her with fear as an evil influence.

No reply from Barker is known. Probably the high-handed and hard-hating Helen did not allow a reply. A very few years later, Barker himself died, and Shaw lamented his death in a letter to *The Times Literary Supplement*, bitterly quoting a line from Swinburne:

'And marriage, and death and division make barren our lives.'

X

PHILANDERINGS AND FLIRTATIONS: GRACE GILCHRIST, GERALDINE SPOONER, JANET ACHURCH

⚜⚜⚜⚜⚜⚜⚜⚜⚜⚜⚜⚜⚜⚜⚜⚜⚜⚜⚜⚜⚜⚜⚜⚜⚜⚜

'I found myself suddenly magnetized, irradiated, transported, fired, rejuvenated, bewitched'
—Shaw on the actress, Janet Achurch
'You can have Janet'—Janet's husband to Shaw

I

FROM THE age of twenty-nine until he was over seventy, according to his own testimony, Bernard Shaw was liable to fall in love with women. But he did not put it that way as a rule. He preferred to say that it was the women who fell in love with him, and to play the part of the reluctant victim.

There can be no question, however, that if sometimes he was the pursued, he sometimes also was the pursuer. This was certainly the case with the Stella Campbell affair, when she was at the height of her beauty, her talents and her reputation as an actress. Shaw had the temperament of a male coquette, and it is significant that his second play bore the title *The Philanderer*. This play was, he admitted, based on his own experiences in that line.

This philandering was no mere trifling and time-wasting, though in his early and unpublished diaries he expresses disgust

199

of himself over two years' playing about with women on that very score. Like Charles Dickens, whom, emotionally, he resembled far more than he ever realized, he turned his womanizing to good literary account. The imaginative character-drawing type of author is never a one-woman man or one-man woman; and this is understandable, for such persons, from their mentality, must, like Shakespeare's Ferdinand in *The Tempest* for many things, like many women before—and perhaps after—meeting their Miranda.

Some of it was mere floundering, the sort of thing that makes for bewilderment and self-disgust in adolescence. G.B.S. developed late in sex, as in other directions, one of the less happy results of his curious upbringing.

But late as it was at twenty-nine, once he had taken the plunge with Jenny Patterson, his interest in women as a sex became vivid and intense. It startled his less ardent-natured friends like Sidney Webb, and naturally led to a lot of gossip in Fabian circles.

In the eighteen-eighties and nineties young women erupt into his private diaries suddenly; appear regularly and even insistently for a time; and then disappear as abruptly as they entered. From this it is fair to deduce that these birds of passage similarly entered and departed his life. There were some seven women on his hands at one time: Alice Lockett, Jenny Patterson, Annie Besant, Edith Bland, May Morris, Geraldine Spooner, Grace Gilchrist and Florence Farr. Following the belief of his friends, the Webbs, Shaw's apologists, such as St. John Ervine, baldly state that only two of these women were carnally known by Shaw. It is quite true that G.B.S. confessed to sexual intercourse with two of these, namely Jenny Patterson and Florence Farr. But in the nature of things, sexual intercourse is a secret matter usually and G.B.S. was not swearing an affidavit in making his voluntary confessions. There was a time when he talked of the women with whom he had sexual experience as to be counted on the fingers of one hand— which certainly suggests more than two sex-partners.

Also, there is no reason to suppose that his attentions were confined to these seven, merely because these are mentioned by name in his diaries of the time. His diary entries in general on whatever subject—even on the paramount subjects of his literary compositions and public speakings—are exceedingly laconic, factual and dull. The brief jottings were also irregular and clearly for himself alone. Only matters that specially engrossed his attention at the moment, for some reason or another, are entered. We are pretty safe in estimating that women of no, or little, importance to himself, whatever their emotional relationship to himself, are left out, and the affairs casually mentioned rather than recorded are merely typical examples of his flounderings and flirtations.

II

It was in 1888, when he was thirty-two, that the high comedy of Grace Gilchrist was played. This girl was a rank-and-file member of the Fabian Society and is said to have been physically attractive and by no means devoid of charm. Shaw's marked attentions to this young woman caused concern to some of the members, and they spoke to the girl's aunt, a Miss Emma Brooke, a well-to-do woman who wrote novels and who regarded herself as being *in loco parentis*. Miss Brooke spoke seriously to the young woman in private. Grace was at first reassuring to the older woman.

Satisfied for the moment, Miss Brooke let the matter rest. But her informants did not. They returned to the attack, and succeeded in impressing the now-alarmed guardian with a prospect of immediate danger to the young person's virtue and happiness. Again Miss Brooke interviewed her ward on the subject of young George Bernard Shaw: what occurred is not known, but whatever it was it caused Miss Brooke, a doughty and determined spinster, to carry the war into the enemy's camp.

At Easter she called on Shaw, reminded him of who she was and immediately tackled him on the subject of Grace. She bluntly told him that she regarded his intentions as strictly dishonourable and informed him that he was, anyhow, ineligible for her niece who was not altogether devoid of 'expectations', her aunt having some wealth. Taken by surprise and disconcerted by the spinster's plain speaking, Shaw reacted very much as might be expected: with equivocation.

This roused the lady's wrath. She told Shaw exactly what she thought of him: in Shaw's brief words 'she heaped abuse on me'. When she had gone, the young man wrote to this 'G.G.' (his habit of designating his women by their initials was incorrigible) and told her all about it. He was deeply upset over the unpleasant scene, especially as his 'J.P.' called the same day in one of her tantrums, no doubt, as usual. The effect was that a lecture he was to deliver that evening was incoherent owing to his emotional disquiet.

Anxious to justify himself, and now aware that repercussions were being caused in the Society where sex-scandals were always threatening to break, Shaw sat down and wrote a careful, serious letter to Miss Brooke protesting his innocence and his good faith. It took him all afternoon to write that letter, as he records. He saw clearly that Miss Brooke was fully determined to stick at nothing to protect her niece, and that his only course was to 'lay off' the girl. He had no livelihood and no means, so marriage was out of the question for him.

The letter did not placate Miss Brooke. Knowing Shaw's predilection for the British Museum Library, the determined enemy waylaid him there to demand an end to the acquaintance.

Shaw surrendered. Perhaps his heart was not deeply enough engaged, or perhaps, as he constantly professed in like cases, he did not wish to compromise a woman in days when respectable girls were easily compromised and their future marriage-chances endangered. But his motives can only be speculated upon. The fact is that he gave up the girl. Her name, so often mentioned briefly in the diary in a short space of time, disappears, without comment.

However, there is one later entry, probably nostalgic! He records the mere sight of her while going across Hampstead Heath. Did she see him? Did they speak? Did they even acknowledge each other's presence? The entry is silent except for the visual record, so it is a fair inference that all was over between them.

But there is a further entry regarding Miss Brooke's later behaviour to him. In Piccadilly Circus, he with other Fabians saw Miss Brooke waiting alone for an omnibus. Shaw, who was a great hand at helping women into omnibuses (he once said of this period that no man ever saw more women into omnibuses than himself) preferred to wait with her. (Only the most strong-minded women, such as Miss Brooke, would wait unescorted in Piccadilly Circus in those days.) She rejected Shaw's offer.

And in Shaw's own words, he 'retired, snubbed'. It was a complete victory for the redoubtable Miss Brooke, who had saved her innocent maiden from the maws of a male dragon, going about seeking whom he might devour.

By G.B.S. apologists, Miss Brooke is much castigated for officious interference and needlessly engaging in Rescue Work. She should have realized that Grace Gilchrist was in no real danger and that it was nothing but Shaw's easy manner and mildly flirtatious habits, manly affability and genial disposition. No doubt G.B.S. explained all that to her, even more convincingly (as usual) than his apologists, but somehow this recalcitrant lady refused to be convinced. Perhaps she knew too much. It is said that she should have minded her own business, but evidently and not altogether unjustifiably, she regarded it as her own business. It is also said that if she had done nothing the affair would have petered out. Thanks to her decisive action the affair swiftly ended; and that it would have petered out apart from her action is pure guess-work.

It would be interesting to know what Grace Gilchrist's attitude was to all this. Upon that, there is no clue either in Shaw's diaries or elsewhere, unfortunately. Shaw himself cuts neither a romantic nor a very Shavian hero in this comedy as the lover who surrenders to his love's duenna: a situation which would discredit an adolescent of spirit.

The main importance of it, perhaps, lies in further illustrating how late Shaw was in growing up.

III

About two years later—in 1890—Shaw was writing in his diary the brief revealing note: 'Rather in love with Geraldine.'

This was another Fabian, Geraldine Spooner. Shaw had known her during the Grace Gilchrist episode, and it is sometimes said that he was more enamoured of her than of the Gilchrist girl. The entry does not sound like it. However this may be, he seems to have been more easily detached from her, for there was no formidable aunt or guardian intervening in this case. It is also said that she was a high-spirited, as well as a good-looking girl, but practically nothing is known of her relations with Shaw, except that they were close and friendly.

By 1890 Shaw, from the earnings point of view, was in a position to marry, for journalists and schoolmasters and similar professionals at that date were marrying successfully on far less. That year he earned £250, and taxation then was negligible: moreover, both his mother and sister were earning their livings independently. But he had endured a long period of poverty from childhood to adult manhood, and he was reluctant to plunge into matrimony when he was just beginning to feel his feet amongst the uncertainties of London journalistic and literary effort.

So it is suggested that this is the reason why Shaw's interest in the fair Geraldine came to a full stop, and Ervine flatly commits himself to this view. It well may be so. But there seems to be no evidence one way or the other. What is sure is that the brief allusions to her, frequent as they once were, abruptly end.

IV

Very much more lasting as well as more important were Shaw's relations with Janet Achurch, the actress, who succeeded Florence Farr in engaging Shaw's interests. She was the wife of Charles Charrington, an actor, whose real name was Martin. Shaw first met her at a dinner to celebrate the production of Ibsen's *A Doll's House* at a London theatre. She had played the part of the heroine,

Nora; in itself enough to captivate Shaw's attention. His diary promptly mentions her as 'an interesting young woman'. Before this he had not even known her by name. Neither had the great British public, and the intellectual circles which Shaw frequented scarcely knew her either.

Rapidly, Shaw became infatuated.

She and her husband were a very Bohemian pair, genuinely keen on good literature and drama, but they were often in financial difficulties—as stage-folk often were in their terribly precarious calling in those days—and constantly having to be rescued by the charity of their friends.

Once Shaw's interest was aroused, their acquaintance rapidly ripened. The very next day, he sent her copies of two of his novels: *Cashel Byron's Profession* and *An Unsocial Socialist*. He sat up half the night writing her a long letter of admiration mingled with a pedagogic lecture upon her acting, of the characteristic kind he had formerly addressed to Florence Farr, and was later in life to address to Ellen Terry and Mrs. Patrick Campbell. It was easily the greatest recognition that her hitherto unknown talent had received from any dramatic critic.

He begged her to cultivate charm, the beautiful, reposeful, quietly expressive, infinitely inflexionable voice, the great charm of a fine speaker. G.B.S. had instantly resolved to share his discovery of this paragon amongst unheralded and unsung English actresses with his great friend and fellow-dramatic critic, that dour Scot and Ibsenite, William Archer. Friendly and Ibsenite though he was, Archer by no means shared Shaw's enthusiasm for the young woman, either as an actress or a person. But Shaw was now in full spate and was not to be discouraged: he persisted in preaching the genius of Janet to his friends and acquaintances. He only moderated his language when he found he had given some offence to Mrs. Archer by 'going-on about Miss Achurch'. (He had told Janet that nobody short of an archangel with purple and gold wings should be allowed to approach her.) Shaw was a good deal dashed at both the Archers' unresponsiveness to his great discovery. But he was beginning to plume himself on being as good as, if not better than, Archer as a judge of players and playing, if not yet of plays themselves. He was not to be put off Janet Achurch.

There was a hiatus, however. The needy Charrington pair had accepted an engagement to make a theatrical tour of Australia, having, at the moment, no prospects in England. Though Shaw had known them only a few weeks, he went to Charing Cross Station to see them off and to wish Janet—and her husband—good luck in this venture.

Meanwhile, Florence Farr was the destined star of Shaw's earlier plays, *Widowers' Houses*, *The Philanderer*, and *Arms and the Man*. But Shaw, 'despairing of his will-less girl' Florence, was already casting Janet in his mind for his principal female parts, and when writing *Mrs. Warren's Profession* wrote to her discussing what he was doing. But this play, unacceptable to the conventional morality of the day as expressed in the censorship, was banned from production until 1902, and even then, when produced in that year in America, the players of it were arrested in New York but let out on bail and eventually acquitted. It is perhaps not surprising that Janet Achurch did not appear in the 1902 production.

Certainly if she captured the up-and-coming Shaw, she, whom he called 'the greatest actress on this planet', not altogether seriously perhaps, was equally captured by him. She was the type of actress known as intellectual then, and when the Stage Society decided upon defeating censorship by giving plays before private audiences, Janet issued, with her husband and others, an invitation for Shaw's play *You Never Can Tell* in London on a Sunday evening. It was the first Sunday theatrical performance since the golden days of good King Charles II.

Janet and her husband were willing to take part in Shaw's private performances for a merely nominal fee of one guinea each, however onerous the part. Accordingly, the play had its first performance and was successful enough to make prominent actor-managers like Cyril Maude willing to consider its possibilities as a money-maker.

Shaw wrote many letters both to Janet and her husband of this.

In one of them he compared his struggle with Janet's struggle to gain public acceptance as follows:

'I got nothing for nothing; had to slave and plod for bare life to make myself at all current; and the result is the brilliant red-bearded creature you now see. Nature gave Janet a success half ready-made and enabled her to do things with impunity for which I should—so to speak—have been pelted from the stage and sacked next morning.'

What he said about his own struggle was literally true. But the probabilitics are that he put the inborn gifts of Janet Achurch too high; at any rate, in spite of his panegyrics, the world never esteemed her as more than an intelligent and competent actress; not of the first rank. One critic, by now, found her 'elephantine' on the boards. But when Shaw wrote his fifth play, *Candida*, he wrote it for her and gave it to her for performance in the provinces long before it reached the West End. He could write nothing beautiful enough for her, he told Janet.

In spite of Janet's liking for *Candida*, a liking not shared by either of such opposites as Ellen Terry and Beatrice Webb, G.B.S. had the greatest difficulty in getting the leading London actor-managers to take it.

Sir Charles Wyndham would not have it; Sir George Alexander demanded unacceptable alterations; Cyril Maude, on trying to rehearse it, found that his team, revolted by its talkativeness, walked out and abandoned it. In America, Richard Mansfield thought it 'delightful but not a play . . . but talk, talk, talk'. He declined to sacrifice himself to the (supposed) revenge of 'a bustling, striving, hustling, pushing, stirring American audience'. He wanted action, not words. Though he was willing to 'talk a little' to oblige Shaw, whom he liked and believed in, even in those early days, he was not willing to sit on the stage 'hugging my ankles for three mortal hours'.

Mansfield—who had already rejected *The Philanderer* and *The Man of Destiny* but later gave to G.B.S. his first real commercial success by producing *The Devil's Disciple*—by no means shared the G.B.S. enthusiasm for Janet Achurch. He was, in fact, brutally and horribly frank about her, and his own antipathy against her. He had previously declared, before criticizing the play itself:

'I couldn't have made love to your Candida (Janet Achurch) if I had taken ether!

'I never fall in love with fuzzy-haired persons who purr and are business-like and take a drop when they feel disposed and have weak feminine voices. My ideal is something quite different. I detest an aroma of stale tobacco and gin. I detest intrigue and slyness and sham ambitions. I don't like women who sit on the floor and kneel by your side and have designs on your shirt bosom. I don't like women who comb their tawny hair with their fingers and claw their necks and scratch the air with their chins.

'You'll have to write a play that a man can play and about a woman that heroes fought for . . .'

This is candour about one Candida with a vengeance. Shaw himself never hit harder at any woman. The year was 1895, so perhaps Janet had become what Shaw called 'a downstart', and had more than started to go downhill. Apparently, Janet's weakness was the weakness of Dickens's Sairey Gamp who 'took a drop when so disposed', and anyhow Shaw hated an aroma of stale tobacco and gin as whole-heartedly as Mansfield, so that the actor was hitting him in a vulnerable spot. Mansfield wanted an American actress, Minnie Seligmann, in Janet's place, but Shaw refused.

But six months later Mansfield atoned by producing *The Devil's Disciple* and making a great success of it. The detested Janet was not in the cast. The first run made £2,500 for the author, a sum considerably increased when Mansfield took the play from New York on tour. And in 1904 Arnold Daly made *Candida* the smash hit in the New York season.

That Mansfield's charge of addiction to drink against Janet was true is shown by one thing that Shaw himself related. He says:

'I remember addressing a meeting about Religion. My address was on a very high plane, but all I was thinking was that in an hour's time I'll be seeing Janet Achurch. When I did see her at last she was the worse for drink, and I had to talk religion to calm her, yes, gave her the speech all over again.'

The idea of the rabidly teetotal Shaw 'calming' a drunken actress with whom he was in love, by a repetition of an address upon religion, shows the hero of the episode in a ludicrous light.

It was not the only occasion when his calming influence on Janet was necessary. Once when he visited the Charringtons, he found Janet and her husband busily engaged in hurling the crockery at each other with objurgations of a lurid character. Shaw did not retreat—though retreat would have been in keeping with the character of physical coward that he gave himself, as it would appear, quite truthfully. Dangerous as intervention between a physically-quarrelling husband and wife is proverbially acknowledged to be, Shaw stood his ground and had the satisfaction (if such it was to him) of seeing the enraged couple melt into weeping repentance in each other's arms. Next day on a shopping-spree the reconciled couple replaced the crockery.

Speaking of these Charringtons many years after his acquaintance with them, Shaw wittily said: 'They married in a fit of love and quarrelled ever after.' On the china-breaking occasion Shaw says he pleaded: 'Leave some for tomorrow.' Whereupon Charles Charrington retorted: 'There's not going to be a tomorrow. You can have Janet,' blaming Shaw for 'destroying everything'. But by now Shaw preferred not to have Janet and to keep his own marriage intact.

In spite of his own knowledge of her weaknesses, and of Mansfield's strong opinion against Janet Achurch, Shaw would at first let no other actress play *Candida*. He refused the part to Florence Farr. He had behaved towards Janet and her husband with the greatest generosity, and in 1893, when he himself was badly off, even enlisted May Morris's sympathy to raise from that young woman £10 as a loan to Janet.

Again, two years later, noticing that Janet's wedding-ring had disappeared from her hand, he correctly assumed that it had been pawned to meet some pressing emergency of illness, he promptly sent money of his own to Charles saying he would 'observe the strictest duplicity with Janet if necessary'. He may have been grateful to the Charringtons for persistently playing his pieces in the provinces in days before Mansfield started general recognition of his powers as a dramatist.

Not that Shaw was capable of regarding 'the greatest actress on this planet', or any actress that ever lived, as immune from his unfavourable criticism. When Shaw wrote *Captain Brassbound's Conversion* for Ellen Terry and she could not, or would not, play Lady Cicely in a Stage Society copyrighting performance at the Strand Theatre in London, he fell back on Janet Achurch. There was general recognition that Janet was not a success in the part, and Shaw told her that, like the great French dramatist, Molière, he always tested plays by his cook's views.

His cook he declared an excellent critic. She esteemed actors and actresses 'as filthy rags in comparison to the great author they interpret'. She had said of Janet: 'No, she wasn't right: when she sat down she got her dress tucked in between her knees; no high lady would do that.'

And G.B.S. commented on this verdict, applying it to the whole of Janet's acting in the part:

'Now, that is an excellent criticism. You played the whole part as far as comedy went with your dress tucked between your knees.'

That was a devastating and mortifying criticism, but it was probably deserved. He lectured Janet severely on the difference between a lady and a middle-class woman.

The performance, though no triumph for Janet Achurch, was noteworthy because Granville Barker in it made his first appearance in any play by Shaw. Shaw had been at his wit's end for an actor who could play the part of Marchbanks, when he discovered Barker as the man for the job. Telling the two Charringtons of his 'wonderful discovery' of young Barker, they retorted they had previously recommended Barker to Shaw for that very part! Barker was one of the luckiest of Shaw's finds, for in the Vedrenne-Barker partnership at the Court Theatre in Chelsea he firmly put

Shaw as a playwright on the English map and was, up to the time of his second marriage, one of Shaw's closest friends; one for whom Shaw retained until his death a deep emotional feeling.

Janet Achurch claimed—and the claim may be true—that she was responsible for the genesis of Shaw's *Mrs. Warren's Profession*. She had read a French novel which she thought contained a good germ of a play and reported that to Shaw. However, Shaw never read French novels, so she related the highly-romantic story to him. Shaw promptly retorted: 'Oh, I will work out the real truth about that mother one day.'

The result, it is suggested, was the character of Mrs. Warren. But if anything is owing to the French novel, Shaw never acknowledged any debt to it or its author, whoever he may have been.

One of the more unpleasant traits of Shaw was in using other actresses as foils to each other. He told Florence Farr she was not good enough for Candida; her vulgarity, her vacuity and her lack of religion were against her, he alleged; but Janet was ideal for it. Florence was neither vulgar nor vacuous nor irreligious. Telling Ellen Terry he could not take the play—Janet's one ewe lamb— from her, he teased Janet by suggestions that Ellen could—and would—do it better than she. And he played on Janet's sympathies by telling her that he was suffering from overwork and overdoing it, while the doctor suggested under-nourishment, from his vegetarianism.

It is known that his infatuation with Janet reached a point where it nearly broke up the Charrington home—if these theatrical folk could be said to have a home. He admitted to her that 'as an Irishman, an irregular artistic person, an anarchist in conduct, he was a creator of an atmosphere subtly disintegrative of households'. Certainly that was the case with the Sparling household. But so far as the Charringtons were concerned, that dangerous phase passed.

Indeed, it may be said that he outgrew his infatuation for Janet as a woman and even to a great extent as an actress. As he went up in the world, he lost touch with her—perhaps because she had no more to give him. Suddenly out of the void, about the time of the Lillah McCarthy–Granville Barker divorce, news came to him that Janet Achurch was dead.

Thinking of her as she was, once young and beautiful and enthusiastic for the New Drama, he wrote: 'It is curious to see how, in the perspective of history which forgets the jerry-buildings and remembers only the cathedrals they had, Janet detaches herself from all the rest and stands memorable and prominent in the void.' And he prophesied that in fifty years' time she would be famous 'as the only woman who saw and took the really great chances of her time'.

This somewhat laboured and exaggerated tribute ignores the careers of much greater women like Florence Nightingale, Annie Besant, and even much more successful actresses who most certainly saw and took the chances of the time—even if those chances were not devoting themselves to the 'New Drama' of the day. The great world never regarded, and still does not regard, Shaw's Janet Achurch as one of the great actresses of all time, or even of her own time, fit to rank with Ellen Terry or Beatrice Stella Patrick-Campbell.

XI

MORE PHILANDERINGS AND FLIRTATIONS: KATE SALT, THE WAITRESS AT THE WHEATSHEAF, BERTHA NEWCOMBE, ENID STACEY, ERICA COTTERILL, MOLLY TOMPKINS

✽✽✽✽✽✽✽✽✽✽✽✽✽✽✽✽✽✽✽✽✽✽✽✽✽✽✽✽✽✽✽✽✽✽

'I, who have philandered with women of all sorts and sizes . . .'
—Bernard Shaw to William Archer
'Is it not delightful to be in love? . . . It has happened to me twice. It does not last . . . when you clasp the idol it turns out to be a rag doll, like yourself'
—Bernard Shaw to Molly Tompkins (June, 1924)

I

IN HIS very early London days, Shaw met a remarkable man who was a master at Eton College named James Leigh Joynes. Joynes introduced him to another Eton master, Henry Salt. Both these men ardently believed in 'a godly thorough reformation' of Society by individual human efforts, though not by 'fire and sword and desolation', but by preaching and agitating. To Joynes the chief enemy of the ideal society was poverty; to Salt it was cruelty. Each of them acted up to his belief, and was exceptional in being ready to sacrifice himself and his worldly interests in warfare against his declared enemy.

213

Joynes was a most unusual human being, inasmuch as he seemed entirely selfless and sincere. He gave up his Eton mastership to devote himself to the cause of human betterment, by discovering collective political and economic means of abolishing poverty and the need of the elementary necessities of life. Not unnaturally, perhaps, in his age and at the time of his young manhood, he became a Fabian; perhaps he was the noblest of them. But unfortunately for his cause, himself and his fame, he was destined to die prematurely before he had time to make his mark on the world. Salt who lived into old age was hardly less dedicated than his friend.

Salt had married Joynes's sister Kate. She was quite as remarkable as her brother, though in a very different direction. She prided herself on being different from ordinary women. She refused to allow her marriage to be consummated, proclaiming herself an Urning or a member of the intermediate sex; in fact, she was—according to Bernard Shaw—always falling in love with some other woman. In other words, she was what modern people call a Lesbian; a homosexual woman, though to what extent she gave rein to these proclivities is unknown. Yet she and her husband lived amicably together. Salt seems to have been a mild, amiable and kindly man who tolerated his wife's eccentricity and who founded the Humanitarian League to work devotedly against the cruelty he hated, as the League's honorary secretary. When, as an old man, he wrote his autobiography he called his book *Seventy Years Amongst Savages*—the savages being his fellow-countrymen in England.

When Salt gave up his mastership at Eton to live for his fellow-men and to follow the simple life in a country cottage on a small income of about £100 a year, Kate, entirely approving, flung in her lot with her husband. They went to live at Tilford in Surrey. Their house was a centre for remarkable visitors of advanced views, and perhaps their closest friends amongst these visitors were Edward Carpenter and George Bernard Shaw.

Edward Carpenter was a Socialist ex-clergyman who had resigned from the Church. Carpenter was an admirer and follower of the American poet, Walt Whitman, whose unrhymed verse he imitated in a book called *Towards Democracy*, which had a considerable vogue in Socialist circles. He wore sandals—a great eccentricity in those days—engaged himself in manual labour, and preached the simple life, speaking of civilization as a disease to be cured. He lived at Millthorpe, Derbyshire, quite openly a homosexual life with a low-class man called George Merrill, a drunken, brutal, worthless creature.

Carpenter had a slight but real literary talent and he composed the Socialist anthem, *England Arise!*, the music of which Shaw criticized as being 'the funeral march of a fried eel'. He had written pseudo-scientific books called *The Intermediate Sex* and *Love's Coming of Age*, in which he guardedly spoke of homosexuals as Urnings. It was from him that Kate Salt got the term; for Carpenter and she were close friends.

Shaw knew Carpenter very well indeed, but seems to have regarded him with a tepid distaste and dislike as something of a bogus individual with an inflated reputation. He described the ex-clergyman of Millthorpe as 'the ultra-civilized impostor'. But, for Henry Salt, Shaw had a genuine life-long respect that never faltered throughout both their lives.

Both the Salts liked and admired Shaw. Kate, indeed, not only admired him in the days of his poverty and obscurity but, in spite of her predilection for women, seems to have been genuinely attracted by him. Perhaps if Shaw had reciprocated her feeling, or set himself out to capture this wayward wife-who-was-no-wife, he might have redeemed her from her Lesbianism. It may be that he was too loyal to Henry, his friend, whose wife-in-name Kate remained to the day of her death.

As it was, both Carpenter and Shaw were in the habit of visiting, and being entertained by the Salts in their Surrey cottage, deep in the country. Kate, who was half-German and very musical, would play and sing duets with these two visitors whom she nicknamed her 'Sunday husbands'. She went to great pains to make Shaw's week-end visits pleasant in days when Shaw was struggling for a foothold in both livelihood and living.

As a very old man, Shaw said of her: 'Kate (Mrs. Salt) loved me as far as she could love any male creature.' Nor, later on, did his long years of neglect and absence from the Salts' home make any difference, for he relates of her: 'Once, towards her end, when I had been absent for years, and turned up unexpectedly . . . she actually flung her arms round me!'

Her affection for him took more practical forms. Not only did she cook for him; before his marriage, when he badly needed clerical help in his literary work, she acted as an unpaid typist and secretary to him. But her devotion seems to have been wasted upon Shaw, although she was, if not beautiful, at any rate a striking-looking woman who might have been described as handsome. She was very dark; indeed raven-haired, with large eloquent eyes and a Dante-like profile.

Shaw could write of her quite coldly: 'She was a queer hybrid —I never met anyone in the least like her.' Yet he admits that during their acquaintance Kate spoiled and pampered him 'most outrageously', and hazards a guess that it was their admiration for Shelley's poetry and principles that bound them 'in a congeniality so complete'. In considering this lack of warmth, it should be remembered that Shaw once wrote that his mother's death would vex him less than a misprint, and that, as already noted, Granville Barker, his friend, was scandalized by his gaiety at his mother's cremation.

It may well be that the friendship of Kate and Shaw was emphasized by their common feeling for Kate's brother James. In his too-brief life, this brother had a strong and deep after-influence on Shaw, both personally and professionally.

'You certainly have a talent for talking,' he told Shaw in his early days. 'Why don't you write plays?'

'I may descend as low as that,' retorted G.B.S. flippantly, though at that period he had possibly not even considered the idea.

It was Joynes, too, whose death—which Shaw bitterly attributed to medical incompetence—caused Shaw to become a fierce critic of the medical profession. It had led to the mordant satire of

Shaw's play *The Doctor's Dilemma*, and to Shaw's life-long distrust of doctors in print. Again, it is believed that *Pygmalion* owes its basic idea to Joynes suggesting to Shaw that the only difference between the State elementary school and the public school was the difference of accent, and that if a lower-class child could be taught correct speech he could mix with the best society, his origin undetected.

Perhaps one of the circumstances which made Shaw dislike Kate's friend, Carpenter, was the latter's reaction to the play *Candida*. Carpenter knew nothing of the stage at first-hand; had never written for it, and except in the study or in a theatre-audience knew nothing of the drama on the actual boards of a theatre. Yet when Shaw, greatly and justifiably cock-a-hoop over his writing of *Candida*, which he was struggling hard to get accepted, read the play to Kate Salt's little circle, Carpenter expressed himself rudely and forthrightly against it:

'It won't do, Shaw, it won't do,' he shouted loudly and emphatically, and went out of the room.

Now, Shaw had had to endure that 'won't do' proclamation for a very long time from very many quarters. There were the publishers and the publishers' readers who firmly rejected his novels, the work of many years. There was his hoped-for collaborator in play-writing, William Archer, a recognized authority on the drama who had roundly told him he had no gift for play-writing and urged him strongly to give it up. Finally, there was the general conviction of the theatrical world, the theatre-managers, the actresses and actors of the day, that Shaw's plays were not in the practical sense plays at all but disquisitions and discussions fit only for reading and not for acting.

So G.B.S. might well have been nettled by Carpenter's criticism and its form of expression. It is not clear what in *Candida* aroused Carpenter's hostility, but he perhaps fell foul of the Reverend James Mavor Morrell, the clergyman-hero of the play, based on the personality of the Socialist cleric, the Reverend Stewart Headlam, well known at the time. Thereafter, G.B.S. always alluded to Carpenter as the 'ex-clergyman of Millthorpe', and it seems clear had no further respect or use for one who was regarded as a 'prophet' by the general Socialist movement, if not by his fellow-Fabians.

II

However much, or little, Kate's feelings meant to Shaw, the time came when, immersed in his journalistic work and his lengthy struggles to get his early plays produced, his visits to the Salts inevitably became fewer. What put an absolute bar to them was Shaw's marriage to Charlotte Payne-Townshend. For Charlotte absolutely refused to have Kate Salt in her house on the ground of her character, and her husband had no option but to bow to the domestic decree.

The fact was that, in spite of her advanced ideas in many, perhaps most, walks of life and her strong feminism, Charlotte held firmly by conventional morality. She had no toleration for 'Urnings' or anything of that kind, and certainly did not accept the Carpenterian teaching that they were a superior race. She would not even have Frank Harris's books lying about, lest they corrupted the servants—but surely understandably in the case of one such book dealing with the alleged sex credo of her husband and his amorous divagations. She was rigidly determined to freeze out those of his friends whom she regarded as undesirables and to 'civilize her genius'. G.B.S. might cut such capers as he pleased in his own domain of print and paper, but his home was hers, and she threatened to leave home and husband, like Ibsen's *Doll's House* heroine, Nora, banging the door behind her.

Her ban did not extend to Henry Salt, and he, of course, with Graham Wallas, comprised the witnesses and friends of the bridegroom present at the Shaw–Townshend wedding. It would be, of course, difficult, if not impossible, for Henry to visit a house from which his wife was absolutely excluded; but the friendship between Salt and Shaw was not ruptured; and the fact that they remained loyal friends and firm allies to the end is a great tribute to the reality and strength of their friendship.

Shaw was reduced to apologizing to such friends of ill-repute as Kate for his wife's intransigence. His ingenuity was equal to the unpleasant difficulty, unlike that of Charles Dickens, when a similar situation arose between his Kate and the de la Rues. Shaw used to explain that it was because his wife, though she had no personal animus against, or objection to, the proscribed visitor, just could not tolerate those of his pre-marital world 'who formed part of a world in which she had no part'.

But he could not truthfully use this excuse in the case of Kate Salt. What Kate was told and how she took it is not known. Perhaps she was not unused to this situation arising. At all events, the association between her and Shaw ended.

III

Like many, perhaps most, *bourgeois* democrats, professing human equality, Shaw had little taste for women of the lower class and infinitely preferred those of his own, or a higher, class. Whatever he might profess in print, Shaw was always personally class-conscious, a tendency accentuated by conjugal influence after his marriage.

But when he was young and poor, he habitually used a vegetarian restaurant off Oxford Street called the Wheatsheaf. It was cheap and, of its kind, good; and vegetarian restaurants, then as now, were infrequent even in London. As an *habitué*, he always sat at the same table, which soon came to be reserved for him. The same girl-waitress always served him; and, as almost always happens in such cases, soon began to take an increasing interest in 'her' customer.

She was by no means an ill-looking young woman, and it may be that young George Bernard Shaw took, or seemed to her to take, a reciprocal interest. His poverty was no doubt apparent from his well-worn clothing and the cheapness of the menu he selected. However, he never failed to leave her a penny as a tip for her service—and if to a modern reader that seems incredibly little and socialistically speaking a 'sweated wage', it must be remembered that a penny was then an acceptable sum; that G.B.S. had few pennies of his own at this time and none to spare; and that most customers left nothing, the gratuity system not then being firmly established in England as it was on the Continent.

Since G.B.S. made no appreciable advance in personal relations, the young girl decided to take the initiative. She boldly suggested to the young man that he should 'walk out' with her— what a modern waitress would call 'making a date'—and announced that she (like Barkis) was 'willing'.

But young Shaw (unlike Barkis) was not 'willing'. He firmly declined. And there—for that day—the matter rested.

She did not ask him again. The next time he entered the restaurant—it is believed to have been the very next day—she announced, no doubt with satisfaction and sniff, that she had accepted another offer and, indeed, to the fullest extent, since she was now engaged to be married.

Shaw showed a very proper recognition of the situation. That day, instead of leaving the usual penny under his plate, he substituted a gold sovereign for it. (Evidently he, too, was in exceptionally acquisitive luck.) He also left a message for her: 'Come back when you are tired of him.'

It is a pretty and a pleasant story, though cynics, with perhaps more knowledge of the psychology of girl-waitresses than young Shaw possessed, may wonder if the story of the swift engagement were truth or fiction. But Shaw, after all, knew the waitress and the cynics do not.

IV

About the same time as Shaw was occupied with Janet Achurch he was paying open attentions to a Chelsea artist, Bertha Newcombe. She, too, was a rank-and-file Fabian and the Webbs would have paid no attention to her, had it not been for Shaw's interest, keen and openly-displayed as it was. Constantly he visited her studio in Chelsea and was prodigal of advice to her, not merely upon her painting but also upon its merchandising. No more didactic creature than Shaw ever breathed. Without the slightest invitation he would advise his friends on any aspect of their lives and work, as though he were their solicitor, doctor, and chaplain combined.

Beatrice Webb was especially agog at this development. Indeed, since Shaw was to be seen with the Newcombe young woman 'everywhere', it was strongly rumoured that the pair were likely to marry—'sprite' in matters of love though Beatrice Webb held Shaw to be. Promptly Beatrice laid plans to help forward the good work.

She, being happily married, was anxious for the more un-attached important Fabian men and women to marry and settle down. It would keep them from sexual pre-occupation and enable them to concentrate single-mindedly upon Fabian work. In her mind's eye, she thought Professor Graham Wallas an ideal mate for the heiress, Charlotte Payne-Townshend, now firmly en-webbed in the Fabian meshes. Bertha would do very well for G.B.S.

With this idea in her scheming brain, Beatrice invited all four down to the Rectory at Saxmundham, in Norfolk, for a feast of Fabianism—and whatever might come of that. Such a feast of reason might well give rise to a flow of soul afterwards. It was a typically calculated piece of Webbery; in this case harmless enough.

It succeeded brilliantly—though, as we know, not at all on the lines Beatrice Webb expected. It was Shaw and Charlotte who paired off together, leaving the professor in the cold. As to Bertha: that particular fly did not even walk into the spider's parlour. She discussed her invitation with Shaw. He advised her not to go but to get on with her pictures. He himself might not go, he averred. What he wanted was 'silent communion'. However, when Bertha had decided against going, he changed his mind and went.

Perhaps it was a Shavian manœuvre to get away from Bertha. Perhaps not. But that was its effect. And probably as an accidental and unforeseen consequence it provided G.B.S. with an heiress-wife.

Bertha had met Janet Achurch, for Shaw had introduced them.

They professed liking for each other, and certainly both were interested in each other as rivals in Shaw's regard. Bertha thought Janet charming, 'so accessible, generous and responsive—but, and here with unerring feminine cattiness she put her finger on Janet's weakness, she said Janet gave her 'an uncomfortable (did she mean comforting?) feeling of elephantine grace'. It was a true bill of indictment. Janet needed a large stage for her acting; on a small stage there was too much of her and she seemed gigantic.

One feels sorry for Bertha. There is no doubt that, to put it vulgarly, this incorrigible male flirt, G.B.S. 'led her up the garden'. He was always discussing marriage with her, its advantages and disadvantages; even condescending to talking of her available cash in such an eventuality. He went so far as to tell her of his 'dislike of the sexual relation and so on'. His everlasting talks, she declared, created between them 'an atmosphere of love-making without any need for caresses or endearments'. A sort of mustard-without-beef kind of love-feast, apparently.

It did not altogether suit nor satisfy this particular young woman, though possibly she may have put up with it as mere talk, for she accused him of 'talking, talking, talking'. She concluded that this strange suitor had not the 'gift of sympathetic penetration into a woman's nature'. Soon Shaw was explaining to their Fabian friends that he was only continuing with her 'to prevent her worrying herself into a state of broken-heartedness'.

She wormed certain information out of Janet Achurch—but what did Janet confess or complain of, to her? (Possibly she learned of his association with Charlotte.) Disillusioned by what she now learned, whatever that was, she wrote a pungent letter to him:

'I feel dazed and must rearrange my ideas and take you away from the position you have occupied in my life. . . . You say this and you preach that, and then I hear all I have heard from Janet. What can I think? How is it possible to think of you as anything but a hypocrite and to feel anything but contempt for your writing?'

'To feel anything but contempt for your writing'; that surely was the awkwardest cut of all! It was bad enough to be stigmatized as a hypocrite. She had said in the same letter that she could not understand how he, who professed admiration for whatever was just and honourable, could choose 'the lowest way of life'. Then came the stinging *finale*:

'Nevertheless I acknowledge now that the hand of Providence —with Shaw's consent and guidance—intervened with good results on his behalf in warding off any possibility of a marriage with me.'

A hit—a very palpable hit—as Osric said in a play by one of Mr. Shaw's predecessors, Master Shakespeare. It was, in fact, the *coup de grâce*. Thereafter no more is heard, and Bertha Newcombe vanishes from the Shavian story. This is a pity; one would like to hear more of this spirited young woman who so attracted G.B.S. that it was generally thought they would marry.

It is something that her real—or professed—opinion of Shaw as a lover is on record. She found him unsatisfying because 'he refused to give more than amusement'. She said: 'Shaw was, I should imagine, by preference, a passionless man. He had passed through experiences and he seemed to have no wish for, or even to fear, passion, though he admitted its power and pleasure.' Of herself in connection with G.B.S.'s intimacy she says: 'Love making would have been very delightful, doubtless, but I wanted besides a wider companionship.'

To understand exactly what she meant by that last remark is difficult, for it was not in 'companionship' that Shaw was wont to fail women in general, or seemed to Fabian onlookers to fail her. Shaw was blowing hot and cold with her, and his lack of passion in his relations with her was not by preference—or deliberate choice—but his natural reaction to this one particular woman, who did not rouse his sensuality as Jenny Patterson, Florence Farr and later Mrs. Patrick Campbell did. As men go, Shaw was decidedly less sensual than the average: he seems to have been under- rather than over-sexed. One can only conclude that his commerce with Bertha was no more than indefensible philandering. Certainly, the philandering went altogether too far in rousing hopes that he did not fulfil, and possibly never intended to fulfil. Bertha Newcombe's words make it clear that she expected a marriage, and was thoroughly disillusioned by what she considered his contemptible hypocrisy in not acting up to his professions.

The affair over, Bertha retreated into the obscurity of her career as an artist, from which Shaw's attention had caused her to emerge for the attention of a posterity curious about Shaw's women. It is difficult to assess the importance, if any, of the Newcombe affair in Shaw's development; but it may well be that it proved slight and he might well be anxious to forget it, as his meeting Charlotte Payne-Townshend followed hard upon it, and that was so much more important. In his garrulous eighties and nineties he often dropped remembrances of his women into the eagerly-cocked ears of his men-cronies who had not known them personally. Many years later he mentioned her work in a 1950 letter to another artist:

'You can't paint half as well as Bertha Newcombe whose portrait of me on the platform is still the best vision of me at that period; and yet Bertha did not go on painting.'

The chief biographers of Shaw, such as Archibald Henderson, St. John Ervine and Hesketh Pearson, do not mention the name of Bertha Newcombe. It looks as if they had never so much as heard of her. Stephen Winsten gives her name and an adequate account of her place in the Shavian saga.

IV

Few young women, indeed, can boast that the matrimonial disposal of themselves attracted the interested and detailed attention and advice of one man destined to be England's Prime Minister, and another destined to be her foremost man of letters. But Enid Stacey, a young woman-teacher at the London School of Economics, could make that particular claim.

A fellow-lecturer of hers was James Ramsay MacDonald, later the first socialist Premier of England. He fell in love with her, and carried on a long correspondence with her. When she was touring the country to give socialist lectures, he invited her to Lossie-mouth as his guest. The greatest asset of MacDonald was his personal appearance, which was handsome and striking; but his mind was decidedly second-rate; his integrity dubious, his charac-ter wobbly, and his socialism only skin-deep. He had literary as well as political pretensions, but his letters, aiming often at arch-ness, are flatulently feeble and facetious.

It is ironic, in view of his later reputation as the Iscariot who sold his party, that one of his letters to his Enid was signed: 'Jim with the Lip, or the traitor in the Labour Government . . .' His innate snobbery, which grew obvious later to the political world in his fascination over Lady Londonderry, artlessly reveals itself to Miss Stacey. He speaks odiously of 'his mater, a kind of rough diamond', a former 'day-labourer on a farm', and unforgiveably calls her an 'animal' in the passage: 'When a raw animal on a farm she trusted my scoundrel of a father too much but, poor soul, she has done her best for me and I am now trying to repay her'. To interest Enid still further, he heavily emphasizes his poverty and ill-health, and prophesies his early death from Bright's disease. In another letter, this democrat speaks of 'being alone in the house with servants—and they are nothing!'

Enid Stacey did go to Lossiemouth, but although the visit in-creased MacDonald's ardour, it may have diminished hers, for she suddenly soon after got engaged to an Anglican clergyman, the Reverend Percy Widdington, who had also visited there. It may be that she gauged the character of her political suitor too accu-rately to choose him. Ramsay MacDonald made the best of his rejection by giving her matrimonial advice.

The news of her engagement also roused George Bernard Shaw, who was yet unmarried and staying in Monmouth. He, too, wrote matrimonial advice to her in a lengthy screed which was marked by sound common-sense.

They first met at Bristol. She had charmed and touched him at that first meeting, and, as usual with women who appealed to him, he had a sense of being refreshed and rejuvenated by contact with her. Thereafter, as Fabians, they frequently met in London, and as Shaw was not yet married, Enid was a distinct possibility since she had roused his imagination. However, like the lady in *Twelfth Night*, he never told his love until he heard of her engagement, when he confessed to her that he always had a greater regard for her than he had ever told her of.

He did not hesitate to urge Enid to the hymeneal altar. He imagined that she might have misgivings, and he set himself to dissipate them. If she did not marry she would most certainly regret that. Her clergyman must want her badly to want her for keeps, and his wanting her permanently was the best of reasons for marrying him. Any marriage was risky, and no other marriage was likely to be happier. Long engagements were the devil and she should not delay.

He spoke to her of himself, as he saw himself at the time. Probably he would never marry. The reason for that was that he didn't need a woman in his work. No woman could make any real difference to his work, he bragged. He often fell in love with them—'with all the customary infatuation'—but he didn't want them except for playtime occasionally, and certainly not for always. He had felt all sorts of things for various women, from the commonest kind of feeling to an entirely noble tenderness—but never indispensability.

Then he made his main point about himself. If ever he had to say to any woman, 'I can't do without you', then—he did not add, 'I will marry her' but—'She will marry me'. Evidently he realized that in any sincere encounter with a woman she, and not he, would be the top dog. It is worth remembering that his chief explanation of his marriage with his Charlotte later on was the very point he makes here about himself to Enid Stacey.

Shaw's letter to this prospective bride is that of a parent or brother, and it does him every credit. There is no attempt at paradox or cleverness; his letter is perfectly plain, pedestrian and prosaic. It does no more than hint at the warmth of his friendship, and does not pretend that he suffers by the marriage, or that she fulfilled the 'indispensable' condition for his helpmate.

Enid married her clergyman and in due course bore him a son.

She died soon after the birth. Her husband attained to the dignity of a canonry in the Church and, as is not uncommon in clerics, especially those of the Anglican persuasion, lived to a ripe old age.

V

In extreme old age, his friends tell us, Shaw was seriously worried about his posthumous fame being smirched by his own indiscretions. It is certain that he deliberately destroyed large quantities of documents, and burned many hundreds of letters, as perhaps he had every right to do: it will be remembered that Charles Dickens took the same precaution of burning private correspondence.

But Shaw went further than Dickens. His close friend, neighbour and biographer, Stephen Winsten, tells us in one of his books, *Jesting Apostle*, that Shaw even created fictitious matter to put people off the scent. His formula, we are told, was: 'I may tell a lie about a person and the whole world will believe me, but I will arrange that if the truth is told about me, nobody will believe it.' We are told, further, that when such correspondents of his as Lord Alfred Douglas and Erica Cotterill died, he made every effort to get hold of letters they might have left behind them.

We can believe and understand this. Shaw, when he plied even a public pen, could be supremely indiscreet, self-contradictory and altogether incalculable. Still more so when he plied his private pen! It so happens that I knew Lord Alfred Douglas personally, and he showed me some of G.B.S.'s supremely friendly and appreciative letters to himself, usually calling him 'Childe Alfred'. Shaw greatly liked Lord Alfred's sonnets and lyrics, but Douglas did not care either for Shaw or his writings—quite the contrary—but was flattered by his homage and attention. He made no scruple about selling Shaw's letters, and was amused and pleased at getting £20 for one of them, I remember.

VI

The story of Erica Cotterill and Shaw is a strange one. Erica Cotterill was a young woman who conceived first an admiration for Shaw as a writer, which fact was normal enough, but later the literary admiration passed into an intense personal infatuation for the much older man, and a quite frenzied desire to capture 'him whom I love', as she called Charlotte Shaw's husband.

Her campaign began when Shaw was at the height of his fame as the star-playwright of the Vendrenne–Barker seasons at the Court Theatre at Chelsea. She was only one of a cohort of strangers who pestered Shaw with letters of appreciation, and Shaw, like other authors, generally neglected his 'fan-mail', and returned no answers to stranger-correspondents of the merely enthusiastic variety. Authors, like other celebrated and public people, are obliged to adopt this attitude in self-defence of their time and postage. Unfortunately, in Erica Cotterill's case, for some inexplicable reason Shaw weakened and replied.

That was, in this case, a fatal error. Erica, delighted that she had got in touch with her target at her first attempt, lost no time in replying to the reply, as persons of her kind can be counted upon to do. Even then, Shaw did not see the red light of danger. Soon he was having to deal with requests for a personal meeting, with protestations of devotion and discretion. The ever-didactic Shaw, instead of dropping her, could not refrain from giving her good advice.

She did not take the advice, which, amongst other counsel, warned her that her efforts towards friendship could come to nothing. Instead she asked for more advice—and Shaw could not resist the temptation of giving it to her. For one of his weaknesses was his passion for advising other people for their supposed good. Either Erica guessed this weak point of his, or by luck hit upon it.

The merry game went on. She had plenty of personal and intimate problems to put up, and Shaw had an unending stock of good advice to proffer in return. The correspondence became interminable, and both the parties to it were thoroughly enjoying themselves. But Erica kept her steady purpose in view: to meet Shaw and try the effect of her charms upon him. She was not a bad-looking girl, and she was young and hopeful. She begged hard for a meeting—just one, only one.

Weakly, Shaw gave way. They met. Shaw afterwards said he did it to disillusion her. Of course it did nothing of the kind. She was a highly determined young woman who knew what she wanted and was resolved to get it. Probably, if there had only been Shaw to consider, she would have prevailed. She forgot that there was Charlotte Shaw, a watchful wife, in the background.

At first Charlotte knew nothing of Erica and her passionate correspondence. Suddenly Erica, presuming upon Shaw's attitude towards her, which cannot have been discouraging, to say the least, invaded the peaceful hamlet of Ayot St. Lawrence where the Shaws lived. To add to the sensation, she arrived by motor-bike. Shaw was horrified. He strongly advised her to remain invisible, so Erica went to stay at a cottage in the village, announcing that if she could not obtain a lodging there nor stay at Shaw's house, she would sleep in the woods or fields, for, be near her beloved, she must.

Thoroughly alarmed by this recalcitrant pursuer who so exactly carried into practical effect the Shavian theories about woman being the pursuer—and rightly so—Shaw, fearing that Charlotte would certainly find out, confessed to his wife about his entanglement with this girl. Charlotte Shaw was very angry, and her anger was increased when Erica, thinking perhaps that Mrs. Shaw knew nothing about her, and that she could conquer the wife as she had conquered the husband, actually went so far as to call at Shaw's Corner, as the Shaws' home was called. It was a major blunder.

Mrs. Shaw, outraged and enraged by the uninvited caller's impudence, harshly forbade the girl the house. She wrote forbidding her to call again, and made it crystal-clear that her presence would not be tolerated. Erica at once wrote back to Shaw. Whether Mrs. Shaw intercepted this letter or whether Shaw felt compelled to show it to her, the letter contained expressions which raised Mrs. Shaw to fury, not only against the girl but also against her husband.

Some of those expressions, to say the least of them, were highly ambiguous: one is said to have been, 'At night when I have you to myself. . . .' Mrs. Shaw accused her husband of encouraging the girl—a charge which was not perhaps entirely ill-founded. She regarded the affair with icy distaste.

Erica, however, went on writing to Shaw, but Charlotte soon put a stop to that. She wrote to the girl in the plainest possible terms that, G.B.S. being married, and the girl having acquainted him with her feelings, they could only break off acquaintance. 'I could not trust him,' Charlotte confessed, 'to keep you at a distance. He has already allowed you to become far more attached to him than he should, and I do not intend to let you drift into an impossible position.' But this did not prevent her from pretending to the girl that her husband's attentions were no more than the 'universal friendliness such as he showed to all, from dogs and cats to dukes and duchesses'. Moreover, she suggested that they were 'not a special regard' for the recipient.

Finally Charlotte indicated that she would tolerate no argument or reply, and that there was to be no further correspondence or interviews. An irrevocable decision had been taken: there was to be an end—at once!

And an end there was. Shaw bowed to the storm, for Charlotte —not for the first time—threatened to leave the home for good.

However, there was a sequel. Erica Cotterill wrote a series of six books, which were privately printed and published. Vols. 1–4 *In Woolwich*, Vol. 5 *In Chelsea*, but Vol. 6 is untraced to date, if indeed it was published at all. The first four volumes are harmlessly entitled: *An Account*, Vol. 5 is called *An Account through letters*. Vol. 1 is dedicated 'To Bernard Shaw', Vol. 2 'To Bernard Shaw whom I love'; the remaining volumes bear no dedication.

Copies of these books are of extreme rarity. Even in the British Museum Library only the first two volumes are to be found; the London Library possesses none of them; but the Woolwich Borough Library possesses the five.

These outpourings are semi-mystical, autobiographic musings— an unkind critic might say ravings—of a pronouncedly egotistical character, meandering both in form and content. They are difficult and wearisome to read since a single sentence may be so lengthy as to occupy anything between thirty-nine and forty-five lines of print. In the whole text there seems to be only one reference to Bernard Shaw by name, and then only as an illustration. Vague references to a so-called 'this person', and expressions such as 'it came to me that' and 'it grew on me that' are typical. The following brief extract will serve to illustrate the verbose style of the contents:

> 'Let me come to you, let me give you what it's in me to give you through my hands and my lips and my face and through all that I can do or feel or know or be.'

The authoress expresses a fear that her work may be dismissed by its readers 'with perplexity or contempt or ridicule as a thing which was strange or mad, or without meaning, or worse'. Perhaps in general this fear is well-founded. But Vol. 5 is sharply different from the other volumes, not only in introducing a set of characters with such fanciful names as Lott, Loom, Layos and Surch, but also in a sharp change of style in quoting letters, which in their style and content are characteristically those of Shaw.

No one reading them who has any knowledge of Bernard Shaw's mind and the way it works, as well as his literary art, can doubt the identity of Shaw in pages 137–143 of the fifth volume. The short, sharp sentences ring like current coin after base counterfeit; unmistakably true.

In giving her account of these letters, Erica tells how she submitted a piece of her writing to her beloved. He replied: 'It's a literary masterpiece . . . showing a talent as Shelley's and Tolstoy's rolled into one. You will either die a lunatic before you are thirty-three or be the greatest English woman writer—indeed one of the greatest of English writers.' Later he wrote: 'You are certainly a clever young devil and I suppose I shall have to treat you as a friend.'

This might not be convincing, but she continues: 'Then I wrote a play and I sent it to you and you sent it back with the way I was to alter it and make a different ending and then you wrote: You had better definitely make up your mind to adopt literature as a serious profession. You will, if you work hard enough, succeed in literature.'

'Then you wrote: You must come to London, then you gave me directions about it, not suggestions or advice, orders; they began with, You must . . . then you wrote to me to go and see you! I went and you scolded and goaded me from the minute I went up to the minute I went . . . I didn't want to be scolded, I wanted to be loved and perhaps I nearly cried.'

These indeed—these directions couched as peremptory musts and the scolding and goading—are nearer the Master's Voice.

She goes on to tell how Shaw explained about Life and the Life Force, love, seducers, curates, socialist orators, divine sparks and ultimate goals, things to do with *prima donnas* and athletes and things about saints and pacts. This might well be Shaw, but yet it might be the imitation of one who knew his style. At last comes the original undoubted voice—very different from her Cotterill-isms—in telling her she must marry and how to choose a husband:

Marriage, he told her, was mostly an acquired taste like olives or eating winkles with a pin, not a ready-made one. She should choose a husband in the same way as choosing a horse, to demand no more than that there should be no vice (in the horse-dealer's sense); that he be healthy and wealthy (in reason) and 'of the colour you like. You will acquire a taste for him and make a pet of him with surprising celerity. Even if you don't, you will be all the less anxious about him and will have all your energy for your own business'.

Who but Shaw would look upon marriage in this light?

Soon he is again his typical self as she describes his reactions about her intention to publish a book. She reports his words on this subject thus:

'What's all this about publishing a book? How are you doing it? Where are you doing it? Who is doing it? Why don't you consult me about it? Sign nothing until I have time to explain it to you. Don't write them any letters . . . Don't do anything, don't say anything more on the matter until I tell you what to do.'

He offers to readapt any literary agreement she may receive, and suggests either a subscription to the Authors' Society (Shaw was a member of its Council and its tireless advocate) or negotiating through a solicitor.

He calls her 'a luxurious young devil with the ethics, and something of the figure, of an ant-eater . . . the very worst brought-up young woman I have ever met in my half-century of taking notice'. He also calls her 'a grown-up baby' with whom he couldn't be bothered. At another time: 'You are a woman of exceptional strength, well-bred, refined and of altogether superior quality. Even your appearance is extraordinary: you are like the edge of a knife.'

Still summarizing his letters to her she goes on as if directly addressing him:

'In the next letter you explain that when adult women and adult men caress one another the result is not the same as it would be if I kissed my mother. Then you explain that the very first time that I behave in that perfectly natural or beautiful and happy and innocent way the person I behave to, in that way, will lose all power of doing anything but the thing which will result in my having a baby, that's to say, you explain that I mustn't caress you in the perfectly natural and beautiful and happy way that I wanted to caress you in, because the very first time I did, you'd have a baby—I mean I should.'

She continues:

'In the next letter you explain that just as you have to take care of me in literary matters, you have to take care of me in "more personal matters; and some of these matters are so delicate that delicacy in dealing with them is intolerable". Then you say it's very difficult for you to educate me in this matter. Then you say—I beg you to spare me as much as you can.'

One need not accept as factual evidence everything this young woman writes in relation to Bernard Shaw: it would be indeed the height of imprudence to do so without corroboration. But that Shaw was indiscreet in encouraging her by letters and personal interviews, as his wife Charlotte thought and said, can be accepted.

Also that he may well have feared what she would say of him, for nobody reading her lucubrations can doubt that this supposed combination of Shelley and Tolstoy, destined to rank high in English letters, was a highly-dangerous young person for any male to be acquainted with. One can easily believe that Shaw came to fear her.

However, Erica's pursuit of her beloved eventually ceased, of her own volition, much to Bernard Shaw's relief. But as there was no formal break between them, he lived in a state of uncertainty for many years, until quite suddenly and unexpectedly an anonymous communication announced her death. He wrote to a friend a letter which may serve as the young woman's epitaph:

'E.C. lived on a farm in North Devon with some children she had adopted.

'Forty or fifty years ago, she imagined herself violently in love with me, and being about one-third quite mad was a terror and a nuisance as she would arrive at ten or eleven on a motor-bicycle and assume that my house was her own and I her husband. When we were driven to tell her that if she did not go away, we should have to call the police she either slept in the woods or planted herself in the nearest farmhouse. Yet she was an exquisite sort of person, and had literary talent, nullified by an aphasia which made it impossible for her to mention the nominative in a sentence; so that in her private books I got so mixed up with Rupert Brooke that no one could tell which of us she was writing about in any sentence.

'At last she dropped out of my life; but I never quite got over my dread that she would turn up again, and her death is a relief, though it is at least forty years since I saw her last.'

'An exquisite sort of person'—it is something to have dragged that tribute out of so fastidious and contemptuous a critic as Bernard Shaw, the inveterate philanderer and poseur. The Erica Cotterill episode does neither of the parties any credit. What is it but an undignified demonstration of the fact that befooled by young womanhood, herself besotted, the elderly sage may become a noodle. Erica never became even a competent writer. But it is a remarkable fact, pointed out by Dr. Farmer in his biography of Lucy Shaw, that only one of Shaw's biographers 'breathes the name' of Erica.

VII

Shaw fully expected that, immediately after his death, there would be fresh revelations of his philanderings with the opposite sex. But he had not reckoned with the slump in public interest which generally comes hard upon the demise of an author, however popular and celebrated he may have been in his lifetime. Or perhaps he imagined that his memory would be immune from it.

The customary decline in interest came. There were no fresh disclosures immediately.

But in 1961—eleven years after his death—some of the letters of G.B.S. to the American actress-author Molly Tompkins (Mary Arthur) from 1921 to 1949 were published. The title given to this lavishly-illustrated compilation was: *To an American Actress*, and the letters were reproduced in facsimile by photolithography. The correspondence is far from complete, amounting in all to some 125 letters and postcards, for a great quantity of Shaw's communications had been either lost or destroyed. Of the lady's replies, none are included for all are lost, but it is suggested that there were about 1,000 of these.

It appears that in 1921, a young American married pair, Lawrence and Molly Tompkins, who were Shaw-devotees, invaded England with their baby son to meet their hero, the High Priest of Creative Evolution. They came; they saw; they conquered. They succeeded in making enduring friends and patrons of both Shaw and Mrs. Shaw—a friendship that was personal as well as epistolatory. Their initial enterprise—never fulfilled—was that Lawrence should build a Shavian Theatre in which Molly would be a Shavian actress.

The 125 letters and postcards are typical of Shaw, flirtatious and didactic by turns, often genuinely amusing, sometimes artificially and laboriously so. The correspondence is much on the same lines as that exchanged with Ellen Terry and Stella Patrick Campbell. Molly both acted and painted; Shaw of course considered himself an authority on both those arts, and he plentifully advised her on these and almost every other personal subject under the sun. Shaw considered that Molly had a not inconsiderable literary faculty, but in the absence of her replies no one can judge that.

It was he who got Mary Arthur to adopt the name of Molly Tompkins. He thought her birth-name characterless, schoolgirlish, with no bite in it. Molly Tompkins he considered memorable, a challenge, a gesture, one that no one else would take. He warned his *protégée* that she must choose a professional name most carefully and 'build it up from the beginning'.

In this correspondence Molly is addressed as Bellisima Molly, Cara Molly, Mollikins, Mollemolli, Mollimolli, Dearest Molly, Molly Bawn, and by similar appellations. Very frequently she is not addressed at all. He tells her—what indeed the correspondence itself bears out—that 'coquettes and philanderers are incorrigible'. She was, according to him, really pretty, with grace and a fine shape, and in temperament a seductive siren and he warns her, 'When you go husband-stealing, don't forget your grin.'

In one mood, he tells her not to show his letters to Lawrence, for then they won't be torn up and will probably be much franker. 'Domestic censorship is always crushing.' And he confesses that when he reads aloud her letters to his own wife, he occasionally skips bits of them. He exclaims:

'Why a poor old domesticated drudge striving to keep pace with his work (and worse his business) should be suspected of being Don Juan, heaven only knows!'

After Charlotte's death he tells her, 'We can write more freely now that Charlotte can never read our letters. I could never bring myself to write a line that could hurt her (a statement not strictly true). But now I can write *anything*.'

In another mood, he is exclaiming: 'Is it not delightful to be in love . . . It has happened to me twice.' (Query, Florence Farr and Stella Campbell?) He continues: 'It does not last because it does not belong to this earth; and when you clasp the idol it turns out to be a rag doll like yourself; for the immortal part must elude you if you grasp at it. But it is impossible to write about it; nothing that can be said about it is true.'

Easily 'the best love-poem ever written, he says, is The Song of Songs'. But not everyone will agree that the Biblical 'Song of Songs which is Solomon's' deserves that rank.

In this correspondence rarely does Shaw touch on either politics or economics. When he does it is merely to register a slapdash judgment in passing, as where he says that 'for coarse, savage, bloody-mindedness it would be hard to beat the orations of Birkenhead, Lloyd-George or Churchill', and contrasts these characteristics with the 'good sense, unaffected frankness and educated mental capacity of Trotsky'.

On personal and professional matters his advice to Molly is generally sound, shrewd and sensible, being based on personal knowledge of the theatrical and cognate worlds. Obviously her welfare, and that of her husband and son, was a matter for concern to him; even if that concern was spasmodic and fitful. Unquestionably, Molly, like most men and many women, found him a good friend.

The note struck most often and most sombrely in this correspondence is his detestation of his own old age, upon which he painfully insisted. It is clear that Shaw grew old neither gracefully nor willingly, and that he was in bitter revolt against the burden of the years and the physical and mental disabilities that these entail. This realist hated having to face reality, but he sought no refuge in romancing about his deafness and his increasingly defective memory, and his descriptions of himself, such as 'a ghastly old spectre who has outstayed his welcome', and 'old and gagga', are brutally frank and pathetic.

Later in their friendship, in late 1945, Molly gave her old friend a shock. For some years she had been divorced. Shaw's wife was dead. Now she proposed to come to England to live with her G.B.S.

Shaw was horrified, and fully determined that nothing of the kind should happen. Other women had suggested that, and they had to give up the idea as she must.

'No woman shall ever live with me again in that sense,' he declared. He was 'a Great Man living in dignified retirement'. If she came, his stern, indispensable Scottish housekeeper—a treasure—would leave instantly. So would his devoted Irish Catholic housemaid. He told her plainly that the village scandal, the degradation to Literature, the insult to Charlotte's memory, would justify himself in shooting her. If she came, she would be told 'Not at home', and she would never see or hear from him again. He ended this repudiation of her idea with the words:

'No more atomic bombs, please.'

That ended Molly's unwelcome proposal. But Shaw continued to write to her up to the year before his death. He was shocked at her proposing to become a shop-assistant in Brentano's (the bookshop) and strongly advised her to re-marry her divorced husband, for both their sakes and that of their son. At ninety-three he sent her a photograph of 'The Old Man at his gate of Shaw's Corner awaiting news of thee'. It was not his last word; he wrote two more letters to his Molly; but they are lost.

It was the last and longest of Shaw's philanderings on paper, of which he was so fond, and certainly it is one of the most pleasant, being creditable to both of the parties. Its epitaph was written in verse when he, obsessed with the passage of years, urged her to:

'Turn from the setting to the rising sun,
Love bettering men and let the worsening die
For I, dear Mary, am no longer I.'

It was only too painfully and pathetically true that the nonagenarian Shaw was no longer the former G.B.S., as he himself clearly and bitterly recognized; though sparks of the old fire leapt up in him every now and again. But even genius cannot defeat the slow invasion of senility.

XII

PENNY-POSTAL LOVE: ELLEN TERRY

✤✤✤✤✤✤✤✤✤✤✤✤✤✤✤✤✤✤✤✤✤✤✤✤✤✤✤✤✤✤✤✤✤✤✤✤

*'It was a wholly satisfactory love affair . . . She got tired of
five husbands, but she never got tired of me'*
—G.B.S. on his association with the great actress, Ellen Terry

I

THIS ACCUSATION of five husbands is one of the many indefensible inaccuracies of Shaw, who, a former journalist himself,
scathingly sneered in later authorship at journalists as a class for
inaccuracy. The fact is, as Dame Ellen Terry's solicitor reminded
me, Ellen never did have five husbands to get 'tired of'. Perhaps
one should compare the facts of Ellen's married life with Shaw's
fiction about it.

She was first married to the famous painter, G. F. Watts. He
was forty-seven; she not then sixteen. The separation that was
arranged after a few years was much against Ellen's wishes, and
she grieved over it. Undivorced, she fell madly in love with E. Wm.
Godwin, the architect, and he was the father of her two adored
children, Edward Gordon Craig and Edith Craig. It was not she,
but her paramour, who broke the liaison.

When Watts divorced her, as he ultimately did, she married an
ex-army officer, Charles Clavering Wardell, who went on the
stage as Charles Kelly. She said of him, 'one cannot live with a
steam-roller', and as he was addicted to the bottle and bad for the

239

children, she was judicially separated from him in 1881. After Wardell's death in 1907 she married the American actor, James Usselmann, whose *nom-de-théâtre* was James Carew.

It will be observed, therefore, that she had only three and not five husbands, and there is no truth in the statement that she tired of them all.

Shaw further declared of his association with Ellen: 'The ideal love-affair is one conducted by post.' That is the point of view of a highly literary person with an opposite number able to express herself in words; and so far as Shaw was concerned, it might well be so. But it will not be the view of any Romeo and Juliet, or of anyone passionately in love, or of those with normal sexual inclinations. Doubtless postal affection had its advantages in avoiding the dangers, disillusions and duties that may arise out of physical contacts; but most lovers of both sexes look upon the post as a mere adjunct to intimate acquaintance, and as not to be compared with the delights of personal physical presence.

Ellen Terry (1847–1928), admittedly the greatest actress of her generation, the darling of English theatre-goers, was the child of Benjamin Terry, an actor, and his wife, Sarah, an actress. These parents were the progenitors of one of the renowned theatrical families in Britain, and Ellen herself is imperishably linked with the greatest actor of her day, Sir Henry Irving, for she played the leading lady in all his Lyceum theatre productions between 1878 and 1902. (That theatre, once the very cathedral of theatrical art in Britain, where Shakespeare was the chief god worshipped, is now degraded into a popular dance-hall at cheap prices.)

Trained from earliest infancy to the stage, Ellen soon won all hearts, and attained the unique topmost place in her profession. Her face, figure and movements were beautiful; her trained voice perfect in its articulation, enunciation and carrying pitch—you could hear her lightest word at the back of the gallery; her enchantment, charm and vitality, quite extraordinary. Nor was that all. She had qualities of intelligence and emotion that instantly put her upon the same wave-length as her audiences, and created a sympathy between actress and audience that was unextinguishable from the first rise to the last fall of the curtain. To these natural attractions, the gift of the gods at birth, she fortunately added a passionate love of her art, which meant that she spared no pains in perfecting any part given her to play. Yet her great art expressed itself with apparent spontaneity, and not as something artificial and studied in preparation beforehand.

She was indeed a paragon of an actress; quite incomparable upon the stage. In addition, she was a thoroughly womanly woman, notably sweet-natured, kind and good, with a natural goodness of both mind and heart. Yet there was nothing insipid about her; rather was she dowered with a native intensity, both as an actress and a woman.

There was no section of the British public that did not adore Ellen Terry; she appealed as strongly to the intellectual as to the uneducated, and to the gallery quite as much as to the boxes and stalls. Of course, these were days when all classes took the most passionate and vivid interest in the personal theatre; there were no cinemas, no radio and no television then to compare or compete with it. But the universal concensus of opinion regarding this actress is testimony to the genuineness of her genius.

Even Bernard Shaw, that Ishmael amongst the critics, did not dissent from the majority view—for once. He, a most skilled and discerning judge of stage-playing, flattered himself that her genius meant more to him than to his fellows. Bitterly he criticized her Irving-slavery, her being walled in by popular old-fashioned melodrama, and even in Shakespeare, when her divine gifts marked her out as born for the 'New Drama' of such playwrights as Ibsen and, of course—himself!

Naturally, any ambitious dramatist might well desire to capture the matchless talent of so superb an actress and so acknowledged a premier performer as the peerless Ellen Terry. A laudable and high aim to set oneself. Shaw braced himself to capture her if he could and, since it might be impossible to get her away from Irving, to capture them both, should that be possible.

II

As a very young man, new to London, he first saw Ellen acting in a small theatre in the Tottenham Court Road. The play was T. W. Robertson's *Ours*, and Shaw was not greatly impressed either by the piece or the actress. That very same year, 1887, he saw her in another Robertson play: *New Men and Old Acres*, in which she had more scope for her talents. At once Shaw recognized her as a great, a very great actress.

Thereafter he watched out for her. He had little difficulty. For Ellen was on her way up and he could see her whenever he had the price of or a free theatre-ticket—which was not often in his early London years. But after his novel-writing and music-criticism phases were ended, and he became a dramatic critic and Ellen had become Irving's lady at the Lyceum, there was more chance for his taste and his talents. He freely exercised both, as was his excellent way in life.

These were the days when Shaw's sister Lucy, Dickens's young love Ellen Ternan and other young women of the stage were priding themselves upon their real (or fancied) likeness to Ellen Terry. Nor was it only young actresses who did this. And Shaw himself frequented the Lyceum on every 'first night' there to laud Ellen and—at first—to flatter Irving, though in his view Irving had only one part in him and that was Irving.

Now actors and actresses regard the lucubrations of dramatic critics with the greatest possible interest, as is only natural, since they are the watchdogs of the public. Naturally the players hope for the critic's good-will and favourable opinion. When a critic like Shaw is difficult to please and rarely favourable, his good opinion seems more valuable than that of his fellows, and possibly more effective. Players are sensitive folk as authors are, and in their estimation one unfavourable notice may outweigh a whole bushel of others.

The great Sir Henry regarded Shaw in his obscurity and early criticisms as a squalid nuisance. He thought at first that he could disregard the fact that even in early flattery Shaw was not uniformly laudatory of him. Incense from the press was plentiful enough. It was through an accident, not by design (although it was Sir Henry's policy to keep on friendly terms with the critics 'with thanks for favours received and with hopes of favours to come', like Calcraft the hangman with the hanging judges of his time), that the Irving-Terry partnership first got acquainted personally with G.B.S.

Ellen was interested in a young singer and composer with the queer-sounding name of Elvira Gambogi. She wanted to help her, so she wrote to Yates, the editor of the *World*, to ask him how to do it. Yates passed the letter on to Shaw as his musical critic and Shaw answered Ellen's letter.

'I didn't like you when you first wrote to me,' Ellen afterwards confessed to him; 'I thought you unkind and exceedingly stiff and prim.'

But to do him justice, Shaw went to great trouble over the matter. He even listened to Miss Gambogi's singing. His view was that she was no better than many others, and he wouldn't go a hundred yards to hear her again. Ten years' work, if she took care, might make something of her.

The young woman became in fact a music-teacher, a living demonstration of Shaw's acute aphorism: 'Those who can, do: those who can't, teach.'

At that same time, and in the same place, the Lyric Club in 1892 where Shaw heard the Gambogi sing, he also heard Ellen Terry recite Monk Lewis's poem *The Monk*. He waxed lyrical upon the reciter and the recitation, telling Ellen she had made herself one of the best actresses in the fourteen hundred million of people in the world, and by his praise brought tears to her eyes.

No actress of forty-five could resist that! The correspondence between Shaw and Ellen was now fairly launched. It continued, with broken periods, for twenty-six years. It deserved Shaw's satisfaction in it as ideal, for none of Shaw's love-affairs, except the one that ended in marriage, did him half as much good as his long-continued paper love-making with Ellen. That correspondence satisfied both the parties to it. It hurt and harmed no one—except at long last Ellen's son, Gordon Craig, and Shaw's elderly wife Charlotte when it was published. Even then it was only the publication that hurt.

But its publication is far from regrettable by the world at large. Ellen, though no professional writer, and 'not clever' as she called herself in the sense of not being what is commonly called an intellectual or high-brow, certainly could express herself well. Shaw, too, in general, was at his best and sincerest; and each had no motive for hiding their genuine selves in the privacy and fancied security of these letters, originally meant for no eyes but their own. The result was an epistolary masterpiece, ranking amongst the classics of its kind in the English language.

Of course, there is dross amongst the gold. Shaw was not only writing for the *beaux yeux* of Ellen: he had one eye firmly glued to the main chance of getting her, or both her and Irving, into his plays. She, too, was not impervious to flattery, and perhaps sometimes a shade disingenuous in repelling Shaw's efforts to make use of her; efforts that he had the audacity to avow quite plainly. It is always good tactics to admit what the other side is clever enough to detect and will know even if you disavow. Shaw was always a master-tactician in such diplomacy as this.

The great Sir Henry, at this beginning of the correspondence, was showing himself impervious to Shaw's flatteries. He disliked and distrusted Shaw, and besides, flatteries were his daily diet. Also he was quite as ferocious an egoist as Shaw himself.

But having made friends with Ellen, Shaw wrote a short play expressly for the famous pair, *The Man of Destiny*, in which Irving would be the great Napoleon and Ellen, of course, the Lady in the piece. (He told the American, Richard Mansfield, that he had written the play for him!) Through Ellen, Shaw offered the play to the actor-manager. Ellen loyally urged Irving to take the play, but he told her he detested 'Your Mr. Pshaw' and thought the stuff no good. In particular, he did not see himself declaiming criticisms of England before a popular Lyceum audience. However, the heroine, Shaw said, was 'a delineation of Ellen—imperfect it is true, for who can describe the indescribable?'

Irving felt that Shaw, by his solicitation, had delivered himself into his hands. Anxious to silence Shaw's criticisms, and to bribe him, he offered to take an option on the play for £50, but with no guarantee of production. Irving had rather a habit of buying up playwright-critics in that fashion, and from one point of view it was legitimate business enough. He might need plays at short notice. Also, an author's reputation might rise and make production suddenly well worth while. Anyway the press had its remedy: in not employing aspiring dramatists seeking the good-will of actor-managers, to criticize the productions and acting of those to whom they were suppliants and suppliers.

At this stage of his career, production—especially production in which Sir Henry and Ellen might figure—was everything to Shaw and money a quite secondary consideration. Sensibly enough, he wanted to stipulate for production not at once but within some stated period. To this Sir Henry would not accede. It is only fair to Shaw to say that he was not to be bribed: in money-matters, even when in pecuniary distress, he was most strictly honourable; indeed, beyond the ordinary standards of the profession.

Over this particular piece, one can quite see Irving's difficulty. He was an actor specializing in highly-romantic myths about eminent people; this irreverent and short *Man of Destiny* was no more really in his line than Shaw himself. But an opportunity came for fitting in a short piece and Irving asked Shaw to come to the Lyceum office to negotiate.

Unfortunately, Shaw, irked by the delay and his failure, had gone over to the attack. He was now decrying in print what he called Irving's 'fretful little handful of hackneyed stage-tricks'. The very day he went to the Lyceum, his critique of Irving's production of Shakespeare's *Cymbeline* appeared in the *Saturday Review*. The critique was butchery. Not only was the play 'vulgar, foolish, offensive, indecent and exasperating beyond all tolerance; but Irving was held up to execration as a disemboweller of plays who should expiate his artistic crimes on the scaffold. 'A man who would do that (i.e. play as Irving played) would do anything,' Shaw asserted.

It was little compensation for the frightful attack that he had praised Irving's rendering of Iachimo.

The interview after this onslaught must have been highly embarrassing to both parties: Ellen intended to be present, but her courage failed. Upon the doormat, she heard their voices and fled.

In spite of—or perhaps because of—Shaw's fierce criticisms, in the negotiations Irving raised his price to £50 each Christmas for a sole option upon the play with an understanding upon production upon an unspecified date. Whether Irving was buying an abstinence from criticism or a production of the play he was refusing Shaw's conditions for production, and Shaw withdrew the play. Inevitably the negotiations proved abortive.

Richard Mansfield the American actor-manager also requested the play. Within a few days of this defeat Shaw was writing to Ellen about 'going to refresh his heart by falling in love' with his 'Irish millionairess', and receiving Ellen's warm, womanly encouragement.

III

The time came when Ellen Terry had the opportunity of beholding her lover-on-paper. She took eager advantage of it by looking through the peep-hole of the Lyceum curtain at G.B.S. sitting in the stalls.

She told him: 'I've seen you at last. You are a boy, and a duck.' The year was 1896. She was nearing fifty and he about forty-two years of age.

Still in spite of this inspection they wisely abstained from meeting each other, and their paper-affection deepened. Ellen did all she could to reconcile Irving and Shaw, but it proved to be all in vain. Things between them got worse. Criticizing a revival of *Richard III* when Irving, a temperate man as regards drink, made many slips of speech and gesture, Shaw said that Irving was not 'answering his helm very satisfactorily'. He went on to talk of how the great Edmund Kean, in playing Richard, had been 'too tired or too drunk to keep his feet'. Readers instantly read into the passage that Irving was drunk—and Irving was furious!

His anger was reported to Shaw, who wrote to him of his criticism that he never meant that; if he had, he would have said so plainly. Irving at once mounted his high horse:

' . . . Your criticism—as you call it! I never read a criticism of yours in my life. I have read lots of your droll, amusing, irrelevant and sometimes impertinent pages, but criticism containing judgment and sympathy I have never seen by your pen.'

All good will between these two men was dead for ever. Ellen Terry, greatly distressed, wrote to Shaw: 'Oh dear, my dear, this vexes me very much. My friends to fight! And I love both of them and want each to win.' But the temperamental differences between the two were more than Ellen could bridge. Moreover, her influence with Irving was on the wane as she grew older. She had been playing away from him in Germany when he played Richard III.

Shaw might bravely tell Ellen that he would fight both Irving and Mansfield and 'toss them about the stage as Cinquevalli (the juggler) tosses oranges and dinner-plates'; but his stage-ambitions were doing badly at this period. His newest play *You Never Can Tell*, of which he had conceived high hopes, had, it is true, been put into rehearsal by the well-known actor-manager Cyril Maude at the Haymarket Theatre. But the rehearsals went badly; my friend Judge Maude told me how his mother Winifred Emery flung up her part, and others openly expressed doubt and dislike of the piece. Ultimately, Maude decided against any public performances and dropped the play.

Promptly G.B.S. sent it to George (later Sir George) Alexander, the fashionable actor-manager of the St. James's Theatre who had backed Pinero and Oscar Wilde. As promptly, Alexander returned the play with a note saying: 'When I got to the end, I had no more idea what you meant by it than a tom-cat.'

But with dogged persistence and unshakeable confidence, Shaw went on. He wrote *Caesar and Cleopatra*, and Ellen again tried to get Irving to consider that play. All Irving would say was, 'It's like a comic opera,' and he rejected it out of hand. He said that he would willingly pay Shaw's personal expenses, and Shaw noted grimly that Irving, while refusing his *Man of Destiny*, had accepted a French play on the Napoleon subject. Ellen was forced to confess: 'Henry will never do a play by you.' To which Shaw retorted: 'Except through you he won't get the chance.'

In these days of struggle and failure as a dramatist, Ellen and her letters were a tower of consolation and strength. His wife Charlotte knew nothing of the theatrical world, and could do nothing more than secretarial work to help him. As Ellen said, he had by now written 'a crowd of plays' and it was imperative to get them acted. But the commercial theatre boggled at Shaw's work, in much doubt as to its value. Eight more years were to elapse before the Vedrenne–Barker management at the Court Theatre in Chelsea made Shaw an accepted playwright in his own country. Those were years of a long and hard struggle against the existent theatrical fashions.

Not for a moment did he slacken his efforts. Directly one play was finished he began another. When managers refused his plays he decided to publish them as books, and when William Heinemann produced accounts to show that there was no money even in publishing the successful Pinero plays, he looked elsewhere. The young enterprising publisher, afterwards well known as Grant Richards, rose to Shaw's bait, and *Plays Pleasant and Unpleasant*, against the rules, succeeded in book-form after an interval.

Meantime Shaw's ill-luck with the stage continued. William Terriss the actor asked Shaw if he could write a melodrama for him, to be produced at the Adelphi Theatre. Shaw produced *The Devil's Disciple*, which was a melodrama with a Shavian difference. Before Terriss could do anything with the piece he was stabbed to death by a madman at his theatre-door. Shaw sent the play to America again for Richard Mansfield's consideration. Mansfield had already abandoned Shaw's play *Candida*, which Sir Charles Wyndham had also declined.

At this point Fortune relented and smiled upon his effort. Mansfield liked the play, and produced it, himself playing the title-*rôle*. It was an immediate success. Its first run made £25,000, on which Shaw says he got ten per cent. With that and his lucrative marriage, Shaw resigned his journalistic job as dramatic critic to the *Saturday Review*. He was now economically independent. Jubilantly he told Ellen: 'I roll in gold . . . I will take a theatre presently and engage Henry for eccentric comedy.'

The book-market and the American production definitely put Shaw on the map; Archer and others were publicly asking why *The Devil's Disciple* and *Candida* could not get produced on their merits in London. Intellectual enthusiasts came in and founded the Stage Society for the production of 'New Drama' plays. Shaw's *You Never Can Tell* was shown, and soon the commercial theatre found such curiosity about Shaw's plays growing that they were obliged to consider him again.

IV

Meantime, Ellen Terry had reached a time of life when even a great actress has difficulty in finding leading parts in new plays to suit her. When her beloved son, Gordon Craig the theatrical designer and producer, became a father she wrote to Shaw saying no one would write plays for a grandmother. Thus challenged, Shaw wrote *Captain Brassbound's Conversion*, and its heroine Lady Cicely Wayneflete was exactly modelled on Ellen. But Ellen could not see herself in the part. She said she 'hated' it, and she told G.B.S. that he must have intended the part for 'Mrs. Pat Cat', as she called her rival Mrs. Patrick Campbell. Shaw told her he had not, and amongst other things declared:

'In every other play I have ever written I have prostituted the actress more or less by making the interest in her partly a sexual interest, in Lady Cicely I have done without this and gained a greater fascination by it.'

When the Stage Society first produced this play, Janet Achurch, not Ellen Terry, played the heroine. But Ellen saw Shaw at the theatre and estimated him—to her surprise—'a good kind gentle creature'.

Meanwhile the 'incomparable' Max Beerbohm—Shaw's successor as critic on the *Saturday Review*—was urging the commercial speculators who control the theatres to run Shaw for all he was worth, assuring them of profits if they did. Success was on its way, but Shaw told Ellen Terry: 'I dread success. To have succeeded is to have finished one's business on earth, like the male spider who is killed by the female the moment he has succeeded in his courtship.' But events show that that sentiment was only momentary. He survived initial success and went on succeeding.

Before the long Irving–Terry partnership ended, Ellen was no longer the actress she had been. Her memory was starting to fail; she could not remember all her words and her powers of concentration were affected. One day her maid, told to read her 'a dull book', read *Captain Brassbound* to her and exclaimed: 'Lady Cicely is just like you! She gets her way in everything—just like you.' It made her reconsider the play. Shaw had declared it to be a perfect delineation of her—as far as herself, the indescribable could be described.

She now wanted to do the play. But Vedrenne and Barker paid poor salaries and they would not pay Ellen, who had in the past often got £200 a week, more than £5 a week. She was her characteristic sweet self about it. But the play she had once 'hated' she now 'adored'—and was only too willing to play in it. Later she took it on tour.

The whirligig of time had indeed brought its revenge. For Ellen was in the decline of her powers, and anyway was no longer as vital as an actress to the now-successful Shaw's career as she had been in her prime so many years ago. She was now too old to give her best powers to 'her' play. Still, it was a success and she a success in it.

V

In earlier days, when Shaw first met his wife-to-be, Charlotte Payne-Townshend, he was regarded by her 'as always writing to Ellen'—but she was not jealous of this other woman in his life. She knew that Ellen's 'Bernie' was after the actress not the woman, and Charlotte was too sensible a woman to mind that. The fact that the women did not meet, and the other fact that she remained in ignorance of the endearments in the letters and much of their contents, reconciled her to G.B.S.'s spate of correspondence with one of the most famous women of the day.

In later years when Shaw, after resisting proposals for publication, finally consented, neither Charlotte nor Gordon Craig, Ellen Terry's son—who disliked Shaw—were so tranquil about it!

Shaw tried to behave well over Ellen, and on the whole succeeded very well in this. He was genuine in his admiration and affection for her, just as she was for him. Perhaps he was at his best and most sincere in early days when he told her:

'I will try not to spoil my high regard (for Ellen), my worthy respect, my deep tenderness, by any of those philandering follies which make me so ridiculous, so troublesome, so vulgar with women. I swear it. Only . . . keep out of my reach.'

That was written in a moment surely of deep insight into his weakness. It is saying in effect: 'If you were within my reach I could not trust myself.' The day was to come, not so many years later, when Mrs. Shaw would be writing to yet another woman, a very young woman, Erica Cotterill, warning her off the ageing G.B.S. and adding bluntly: 'I could not trust him to keep you at a distance.'

In their later years, Shaw and his Ellen did not encounter each other often, and when they did, their meetings were usually in public and of the briefest possible character. Upon such occasions both displayed nervousness. Shaw writing to his 'blessedest darling Ellen' said it was because people were watching them, and 'the way I want to, and ought to, behave would be ridiculous and indecorous'.

Soon she was asking him for a mere 'charwoman's part' in a new play—and Shaw said they both felt inclined to cry.

A little later she was reproaching him over his passion for Mrs. Patrick Campbell: 'So now you love Mrs. Pat Cat.' But she had another hour of triumph when the book of their correspondence was a financial and literary success.

The Ellen Terry idyll, while not flawless, was Shaw's most prolonged and most literary romance. The Shaw-Terry letters are as likely to give pleasure to generations yet unborn as to ourselves. And surely posterity, reading it, will take to heart Shaw's striking epitaph on the correspondence given in his Preface to it:

'Let those who may complain that it was all on paper, remember that only on paper has humanity yet achieved beauty, truth, knowledge, virtue and abiding love.'

That, if accepted, is a sobering reflection, for these virtues are surely to be lived, not merely to be put into words upon paper.

XIII

CUPID'S LAST SHAFT:
MRS. PATRICK CAMPBELL

❖-❖

*'I want my plaything that I am to throw away. I want my
Virgin Mother enthroned in Heaven. I want my Italian peasant
woman. I want my rapscallionly fellow-vagabond. I want my
dark lady. I want my angel—I want my tempter. I want my
Freia with her apples. I want the lighter of my seven lamps of
beauty, honour, laughter, music, love, life and immortality. I
want my inspiration, my folly, my happiness, my divinity, my
madness, my selfishness, my final sanity and sanctification, my
transfiguration, my purification, my light across the sea, my
palm across the desert, my garden of lovely flowers, my million
nameless joys, my day's wage, my night's dream, my darling and
my star.'*

—G.B.S. yearning for Mrs. Patrick Campbell

I

TAKEN INTO captivity by his Charlotte, rather than into Holy
Matrimony, Bernard Shaw sometimes strained at his conjugal
fetters. Only once, however, was his domesticity in deadly peril.
Then, indeed, his ladylike Charlotte became frightened and
furious; thinking (according to Shaw) of murder and suicide, and
actually likening his conduct and character to that of Bluebeard!

253

This affair—sharply different from all others during his matrimonial career—only came to Mrs. Shaw's notice when it was approaching its climax. Accidentally, she overheard her husband talking on the telephone to the second most celebrated actress of the day. Now Charlotte, despising and disliking the indignity of her husband's frequent philanderings though she did, knew perfectly well that none of them had been serious or any menace to her conjugal position. But she sensed at once that this one was different in kind. Alarmed for her marriage, as indeed she had need to be, in this particular instance, and aware of the weakness of her unconsummated union, she flared into ferocious and jealous fury.

That was over Stella Beatrice Campbell, the actress who took London by storm, in one night, as Pinero's *The Second Mrs. Tanqueray*. She alone—of all Shaw's women—could have broken up his marriage, and almost did!

But she preferred as her second husband the Society figure, George Cornwallis-West, once married to Lady Randolph Churchill, the American Jenny Jerome, the mother of Winston Churchill.

Incalculable and temperamental as lightning, Stella had brains as well as beauty. She was the song of all the sirens incarnate; the most alluring woman of her age. 'Nobody could resist her when she was out for capture,' was truly said of her.

But, to say the least of it, her temperament was shrewish both on and off the stage. Though she could be so alluring in private life, and so effective upon the boards of a theatre, she was a great contrast to Ellen Terry whose native sweetness made her adored by all who came into contact with her, as well as by her audiences. Stella had a most cutting tongue which she used freely, and she was no respecter of her fellow-players, even when they were actor-managers. She, it is safe to say, was the best-hated and most-feared woman in her profession when at the height of her fame.

Once at rehearsal in Shaw's play *Pygmalion*, she flung a pair of slippers into the face of Sir Herbert Beerbohm Tree with such force as to cause him to collapse in tears. Shaw knew what he was about in creating the part of the virago flower-girl, Eliza Higgins, for her; no living actress could have uttered the then-shocking words in public, 'Not bloody likely' with the same native force of reality as Stella. On another occasion, she told a hapless actor to move a chair 'as much like a gentleman as you can'. She insulted George Alexander *sotto voce* while he was making love to her during a performance; and her asides to her fellow-players were often cruelly disconcerting.

In brief, she was a holy terror. Nothing but her fame and talents caused her to be tolerated. Fortunately for her, and her fellows, she was not always at her worst. At her best she was admittedly magnificent, carrying all before her, both her audience and her fellow-players.

Her mother, an Italian, was Count Romanini's daughter; her father, John Tanner, a once-rich Anglo-Indian. At seventeen, Stella eloped with young Patrick Campbell, son of a Hongkong bank-manager. In three years she had two children, and her husband had left for South Africa in search of wealth and health.

Perhaps it was not only in search of health and wealth that Patrick left country, wife, and children and stayed away so long. There is no doubt of his love for Stella, nor of Stella's love for her young husband. An aura of mystery that never seems to have been cleared up hangs over his exile; perhaps, like Shakespeare, Patrick Campbell had got into some youthful scrape of which his friends and family had no desire to speak. If so, Stella would stand by him; she was no quitter, being intensely loyal to those she really loved. Indeed, from the day of her marriage to the day of her death, she clung to his name, using both his Christian and surname, thus identifying herself with him completely in the eyes of the world.

II

Sending his family more endearments than money, Patrick was away for more than six years. In this difficult time, young Mrs. Campbell, faced by her children's needs and her own debts, unsophisticated and untrained, bravely attacked the stage.

She had been successful in amateur theatricals, then a most popular form of amusement for the upper and middle classes who were always 'getting them up'. This had given her a taste for acting. Besides, what else could she do? Most careers in those Victorian days were closed to women. She might become a governess or a nurse, but that would mean grinding hardship and semi-starvation. The stage clearly called.

Now, in those days the stage was not regarded as respectable by large numbers of English people, amongst whom were Stella's family; especially not for women, and most especially not for their women. It was one thing to go to a theatre for enjoyment; quite another to degrade oneself into a public performer, and it was then well known that actresses led Bohemian and amoral lives; indeed how should they do otherwise, unchaperoned and in constant contact with males as they were, often needy in a precarious livelihood and living unprotected in theatrical lodgings away from home? Consequently, Stella's affectionate Aunt Kate, regarding this prospect of a niece going on the stage with revulsion, told her with grief that she was a lost soul going straight to hell, and repudiated her!

But a still more affectionate Uncle Henry, who adored and believed in her, and for whom she could do no wrong whatever she did, supported her decision because it was hers. . . .

She came to London and sought an engagement. Her plight was frightening, but nerved by the thought of those two infants she flung herself at the stage. Leaving her lodgings she went to call on a theatrical agent. Walking along the Strand, she saw a mother-cat licking its two dead kittens drowned in the gutter. Thinking of her two children, she burst into tears.

At her agent's she could not control her distress; and touched by it, the man doubtfully recommended her for a small part. She was launched, at least. Another engagement followed; then another; but nothing of importance until she was taken on at the Adelphi, then the home of melodrama, in a melodramatic part.

At a fortnight's notice the Adelphi Theatre sacked her. They said: 'Her voice was weak, her gestures ineffective, and she did not get over the footlights.'

But the fashionable dramatist, Arthur Pinero, saw beauty, elegance and distinction in her. He wanted to try this innocent beginner for the difficult *rôle* of the heroine in his newest play, an ultra-fashionable society worldling. The piece was destined to fame as *The Second Mrs. Tanqueray*.

For Stella, it was a daring part in a *risqué* play. Quite inexperienced in such a demanding part, she rehearsed badly; and there was great anxiety over her competence. Only the author believed in her.

But on the opening night at the St. James's, this tyro, ill, bewildered and overwrought as she was, more than triumphed. By a performance of tremendous power and passion, she mesmerized both the audience and her fellow-players and swept the play to victory.

And when the curtain-calls had been taken to impassioned applause for the cast and for the author, she crept home, shaken and in a crisis of nerves after her tremendous effort. She had not so much acted Mrs. Tanqueray as been the woman herself, giving the breath of life to Pinero's creation.

III

Next morning the critics lauded her to the skies—including that grudging critical ogre, 'G.B.S.' At this period Bernard Shaw was one of the best-known dramatic critics, ranking with Walkley of *The Times* and William Archer of the *Daily News*. For the commercial and fashionable drama of Pinero, Sutro and Henry Arthur Jones, the successful English dramatists of that day, he had little respect, being the confirmed Ibsenite and 'New Drama' adherent he was. Of most actors and actresses he was highly critical. Not even the great Irving in Shakespearian parts at the Lyceum escaped his castigation, as we have seen, and even actresses who were his personal friends were criticized, often severely. Indeed, his own sister Lucy, appearing in a light-opera, *Dorothy*, did not escape somewhat severe handling, for Shaw's standards of competence in acting were strict. But he could not praise the new young actress's achievements as Mrs. Tanqueray highly enough; for once, he was in agreement with all the other critics about this newcomer to the fashionable St. James's Theatre.

Fame and her babies' future were secured. Thereafter, with Ellen Terry, she was at the top of her profession.

Unlike Ellen, Stella was no piece of sugar. Her acid wit, her self-assertiveness, her strong and difficult personality, quickly came into operation, once her success was assured and her position in the London theatrical world secured. From the 'first night' of Mrs. Tanqueray, she never looked back.

Up to this date, as a mere nobody, she was of course unacquainted with the leading London dramatic critics, except by name. Now they were in thrall to her, and the one on whom she had made the greatest impression was the most intransigent Ishmael of them all: George Bernard Shaw, who was not only a critic but also a budding dramatist of the Ibsen school.

She was certain, of course, of taking the leading part in the next play by Pinero. Meanwhile Tanqueray played to capacity; everyone wanted to see the newcomer in the part. When Pinero's next play, *The Notorious Mrs. Ebbsmith*, was produced, Shaw denounced the play as shoddy; 'Nothing would induce me to say anything good of it,' he declared. But Mrs. Patrick Campbell's performance of the part was warmly praised, although the play was thought unworthy of her genius.

IV

Naturally enough, Shaw wondered if he could not secure Mrs. Campbell for his plays and harness her to the New Drama chariot. She had far more intelligence than the average actress; that was clear. Besides, Shaw, although a middle-aged and married man, had been attracted by the woman as well as the actress. He, to whom love had been unimportant, a mere diversion at best, a distracting nuisance in general, was destined to become its helpless prisoner.

Other plays of his, such as *Caesar and Cleopatra*, were driven out of his head because he wanted to write a play in which she should be 'an east-end donah in an apron and three orange and red ostrich feathers'. That was the genesis of *Pygmalion*. Before that, he had tried to get the famous Forbes-Robertson and her in the first piece, but the play was expensive to produce and G.B.S. not yet sufficiently important, and so it was not accepted. But at least it enabled him to have an excuse to write to her. So he wrote his first letter, talking of his health and trying to interest her, if not in the play, in himself.

It took nearly nine years before Shaw got this play produced, and then instead of Stella he had to be satisfied with Gertrude Elliott, afterwards Lady Forbes-Robertson, at the Savoy Theatre. But Shaw had the consolation that his inamorata had given a copyrighting one-performance of it at Newcastle, earlier. So successful had been his correspondence with Ellen Terry that he naturally tried the same manœuvres with Stella Campbell.

Epistolatory blarney proving not enough, he sought her company. Much to his chagrined surprise and against his will, this contemner of romance, at the age of fifty-six, fell head-over-heels in love with her. He started the famous passion-ridden extravagant correspondence with her. She was interested and intrigued, and willing to play at extravagant letter-writing with 'Joey-the-Clown', as she called him. But she was not in the least in love.

His best friend, Sidney Webb, regarded Shaw's besotted infatuation for Stella as 'a clear case of sexual senility'. Hardly, at fifty-six, when Shaw was at the zenith of his powers! But Webb was firmly anchored to his wife Beatrice, and only understood women in statistical masses, when properly classified. Charlotte Shaw had the perspicuity to understand the real seriousness of the situation. She let her husband see not only her fury but her suffering and her jealousy.

G.B.S., who at one time told Stella everything, told her how his wife had overheard his telephone-talking to her. 'The effect was dreadful. It hurts me miserably to see anyone suffer like that. I must, it seems, murder myself or else murder her . . . Well, I daresay it is good for us all to suffer; but it is hard that the weak should suffer the most . . . I throw my desperate hands to Heaven and ask why one cannot make one beloved woman happy without sacrificing another.'

Caught in the trap of monogamous marriage, many a polygamous male has asked himself that question. If Mrs. Shaw saw her husband's tropical love-letters to Stella, she must have inevitably contrasted them with the temperate and tepid letters (notable for the absence of endearments) that Shaw wrote to his wife up to their marriage, and she must have suffered still more.

Shaw had introduced 'Mrs. Pat' (as nearly everyone called her) to his sister Lucy, divorced and in ill-health, and then living at Denmark Hill. Perhaps because she detested Charlotte, perhaps because Stella was famous and Lucy was flattered by the siren's enchantments, certainly because Stella was sorry for Lucy, the two women became good friends. (It had been one of Charlotte's grievances that Lucy and her mother had remained friends with that immoral woman Jenny Patterson, of whose connection with her husband before marriage she now knew.)

Realizing keenly the anguish he was causing his wife, and deploring it as he did, Shaw did not alter his course. While there was hope of attaining Stella he was quite incapable of giving her up. Yet he knew very well that domestic cohabitation with her would be fantastic for an author used to an efficient and unobtrusive, orderly-run household like Charlotte's. He was simply reckless of consequences, in spite of his 'inflexible domesticity'.

He was behaving like a love-sick youth: 'as if my next birthday were my twentieth', but he could think of nothing but 'a thousand scenes in which she was the heroine and I the hero' and his years had fallen from him 'like a garment'.

The situation was doubly dangerous, since Stella's husband, Patrick Campbell, was no longer any obstacle to her re-marriage. After six years' absence he had returned to his wife and children, to be welcomed warmly by them but to be little noticed by the rest of the world. Then, when the South African war broke, out he went to the front as an officer and was killed fighting bravely. His commanding officer's tribute to him was such as any family might be proud of, and it was to prove a source of inspiration to his only son, Alan, later fated to be killed in the First World War.

Stella was in no hurry to re-marry, indeed rather the contrary at first; and she was a warmly-affectionate mother deeply interested in her boy and girl for whom she had struggled so long and so hard. But from Shaw's point of view, the important point was that she was free. He had not yet reached the point of contemplating a divorce from Charlotte, but had he sued for a decree of nullity on the ground of wilful non-consummation of their marriage, if he had decided upon divorce, Charlotte would have been ready to leave him, as she frequently had threatened to do.

But, characteristically, Shaw vacillated as he usually did in emotional matters. Clearly, however, the situation was unstable. It could not possibly go on. If Stella took the initiative, there was a moment when Shaw could have been captured easily; she had only to raise her little finger. When the moment of destiny arrived, however, Stella's heart, unknown to Shaw, had been engaged elsewhere.

v

She had fallen in love with a prominent Society figure, the Duchess of Westminster's brother, George Cornwallis-West, a handsome, picturesque, romantic, extravagant, fashionable, spendthrift playboy. What sort of competitor was George Bernard Shaw to this paragon in her eyes?

Imagining, foolishly, that he was the only Richmond in the field, Shaw had nerved himself to decisive action. She had left London for Sandwich to escape him, she who was his 'Stella Stellarum', his 'Beatricissima', his 'beautifullest of all the stars'. He, 'the greatest critic in the world', had proclaimed her 'the most wonderful woman'.

Once more he is writing to her in the same strain as he had written to Florence Farr—when he was in his twenties. He told her, in the words heading this chapter, words eloquent enough to bear repetition:

261

'I want my plaything that I am to throw away. I want my Virgin Mother enthroned in Heaven. I want my Italian peasant woman. I want my rapscallionly fellow-vagabond. I want my angel—I want my tempter. I want my Freia with her apples. I want the lighter of my seven lamps of beauty, honour, laughter, music, love, life and immorality. I want my inspiration, my folly, my happiness, my divinity, my madness, my selfishness, my final sanity and sanctification, my transfiguration, my purification, my light across the sea, my palm across the desert, my garden of lovely flowers, my million nameless joys, my day's wage, my night's dream, my darling and my star.' . . .

All this—and Heaven, too!—as Browning might say. But G.B.S. wanted his Charlotte and his home-comforts, as well. Moreover, he was word-drunk.

His pursuit of her to Sandwich put Stella in a real difficulty. That he hoped and intended to seduce her there is undoubted; that she had led him on, must be admitted. But she was not going to risk endangering her longed-for second marriage. She would not be compromised. She fled, leaving him this brief note:

'Please will you go back to London today—or go wherever you like but don't stay here—if you won't go I must—I am very, very tired and I ought not to go another journey. Please don't make me despise you.

Stella'

It was the brutal brush-off. No consummation—yet again! He was unspeakably humiliated by his frustration. There was nothing for it but to go back to London, nursing his humiliation and to resign all hope of possessing her.

Not awaiting his answer, she had fled. In his disappointment and despair, Shaw—on paper—raged at her:

'Infamous, vile, heartless, frivolous, wicked woman! Liar—lying lips, lying eyes, lying hands—promise-breaker, cheat, confidence-trickster . . .'

He exhausted the vocabulary of vituperation. She retorted in kind, but less vigorously, for she was no born writer like her antagonist. Soon she married her George, with whom she remained deeply in love; but the marriage had no lasting quality and there was a divorce.

By then Shaw had recovered from his infatuation, and he never forgave her for his being so deeply humiliated by her. For her he had risked his domesticity, his wife's peace of mind and his own in transparent deceptions and lies. He had indulged in false pretences by reading the innocuous bits of her letters to mislead his wife's suspicions. There had been secret visits, telephonings, and love-letters. There had been lovers' raptures, quaint comforts and happinesses and close-togethernesses and babes-in-the wood-nesses. She had betrayed him, this Circe, this *femme fatale*, this Delilah. He said:

'I, the greatest living Master of Letters, made a Perfect Spectacle of myself with her (a monster of illiteracy) before all Europe.'

Pygmalion, on which was founded the comic-opera, *My Fair Lady*, which, long after the deaths of both author and actress, was such a stupendous success, was his greatest public tribute to the acting powers of Stella. When Tree, at its rehearsal, mischievously suggested giving the vegetarian Shaw a juicy beefsteak for lunch, 'to put some red blood into him', Stella retorted: 'For God's sake, no. He's bad enough as it is. If you give him meat, no woman in London will be safe.'

And when Stella, on the opening night of the play, uttered the then-sensational line: 'Walk! Not bloody likely!' those words, carefully-articulated and perfectly-enunciated on Shaw's theories of phonetics, brought the house down. They did more for Shaw's fame among the illiterate multitude than all his life-work to date. While *Pygmalion* was being rehearsed, dire predictions of utter failure were made, for Stella seemed utterly indifferent to, and contemptuous of, the piece, being now absorbed in Cornwallis-West.

For Mrs. Patrick Campbell, too, he created Orinthia in *The Apple Cart*. The physical struggle between the King and his mistress in that play actually took place in life, between the dramatist and the actress at her London home.

Shaw wanted to get back to his wife for tea. She refused to let him go. When he insisted, she held him fast and prevented him. Locked in a fierce struggle, they were on the floor when a maid-servant entered the room. Understandably Stella hated the vulgarity and bad taste of this 'Apple Cart' exposure of their quarrels and begged for mercy. She observed that in his play Shaw had painted the woman as the rejected one, when in truth it was Shaw who was rejected by her. Years after she explained with equal untruth: 'I ran away from you at Sandwich because I wanted to remain Queen of my Heart.' It was, of course, another man who reigned there, and she fled to protect her physical self from Shaw's importunities.

In this falsification-contest Shaw reached the limit in lying when he told a woman-friend: 'The moment I discovered that Stella merely wished to humiliate Charlotte by weaning me away from her I was through with Stella.' But this was, after all, only his Roland for her Oliver. For in one of her letters she told him: 'Next time you try to fascinate an actress don't use her as a means of teasing Charlotte. That was the ugliest thing you did.'

The impartial and amused observer of these indictments will acquit each of the accused upon the other's charges. It is quite certain that Stella no more wished to humiliate Charlotte than Shaw desired to tease her.

VI

Authors not infrequently improve with age; and, if they do not, their harvests are reaped late in life. The reverse is true of actresses. Sirens and enchantresses of seventy are unknown. A play by Stella's other great admirer, Sir James Barrie, specially written for her, failed—her one great failure! As the years passed, Bernard Shaw's star rose while that of Mrs. Pat-Cat began to fade. He rolled in wealth and fame; for her, evil days dawned. Eighteen years after his father's death, her brilliant, dearly-loved son, Lieut.-Commander Alan Campbell, M.C., was killed in the war. It was a terrible blow for Stella, this loss of a promising son whose soldier's death was directly inspired by his father's example. Even Shaw expressed his sense of tragedy to her, though his love had long been quenched.

After that, what was there in life for Stella as the years rolled on? Struggling on the stage at home and abroad; frightening managements with 'temperamentalism'; oppressed by financial stringency and debts, the ageing actress applied to Shaw for help.

Would he not give her permission to publish his love-letters, since he had allowed Ellen Terry to publish their correspondence to her enrichment?

Shaw was afraid of, and considerate for, his wife's susceptibilities and he refused, though he knew that Stella badly needed the money.

Later on, their correspondence was published; after Charlotte's death and, under the terms of Shaw's will, the proceeds were to be expended for the benefit of Stella's grandchildren. Earlier under Stella's will she had laid it down that the book should be called *The Love Letters of Bernard Shaw to Mrs. Patrick Campbell*, so that all who read them would realize that the friendship was *l'amitié amoureuse*. Upon publication in full, the word love was omitted from the title, and rich reading the collection makes. Much earlier she had written a bulky tome of her life, but it was mere hash for cash. She could talk, act, inspire, live magnificently, but anything more than an epistle was beyond her writing-powers.

Dying as an old woman of seventy-five in France, her last letter to Shaw began, 'Dear, dear Joey.' After her death, she was called a monster and a devil by her quondam lover, and no doubt there were times when this proud, brave woman made others feel that she was.

But her love-affair with Bernard Shaw, as told in their letters which are very far from being merely sentimental on either side, will always hold their fascination for readers of them. The impression made by the book as a whole is tragic, as it moves slowly but surely from fantastic adoration to undeserved abuse. There is no monotony in these cat-and-dog exchanges, however, but what hurts the reader is to see the two partners to the sexual combat

changing *rôles*; the once-triumphant queen becoming the beggar
asking a crust from the former beggar who asked alms from her.
It may well be that this correspondence may rival the much
pleasanter letters to and from Ellen Terry, for it is the more
realistic, and though full of artifice is not fundamentally artificial.

Perhaps the best verdict upon these letters is Shaw's own.
When Stella had complained that G.B.S. had, as a critic, 'maligned
her for years and years,' he replied: 'Dearest Liar—Never did a
man paint his infatuation across the heavens more rapturously and
shamelessly.' And for consolation in his folly of 'writing idiotic
love-letters' he reminded himself that the great musician
Beethoven had done the same, adding: 'Whatever they may contain they cannot be more fatuous than Beethoven's.'

But Beethoven did not set up as a super-man to guide mankind
in wisdom, righteous conduct and human betterment.

XIV

THE SUMMING-UP

✢✢✢✢✢✢✢✢✢✢✢✢✢✢✢✢✢✢✢✢✢✢✢✢✢✢✢✢✢✢✢✢✢✢✢✢

'If we had to write down what we have made of our lives, what a hotch-potch of ineptitudes and muddle-headedness we would reveal . . .'

'It will all come out when I am dead'

—G.B.S. on his own life

I

To WHAT conclusions should we come regarding the psychology of Bernard Shaw, using the word in its widest meaning? Shaw himself was at pains to show that he himself had arrived at clear and emphatic conclusions upon it, as indeed he did upon most topics upon which he exercised his strong and agile intellect.

What he said and did is always worth examination. But in connection with that, it is necessary to consider the circumstances in which he thought and said it. And before one considers these, there are conclusions so obvious that they may be stated at once.

For example: if most men found it necessary or desirable to tell of such intimate relations as Shaw enjoyed with Jenny Patterson, they would refrain from giving the particular name to the world. Why did Shaw give her name? It was the conduct of a cad. It added nothing to the story. It must have hurt those relatives (if any) and friends who thought well of her. Why did he do it? Admit, if you wish, that (as his youthful diary shows) she made herself an unmitigated nuisance and caused him the maximum annoyance and inconvenience. So be it. It should not have been his hands that put her in the pillory for the scorn and amusement of posterity.

Shaw seems to have had not the slightest scruple in doing so. It does not seem to have occurred to him to sit in judgment upon himself, or that others might sit in judgment upon him and justly condemn him, firstly, for giving this poor wounded name to a censorious world, and, secondly, for being so obtuse as not to realize that his lack of sensitivity and delicacy might shake even his staunchest admirers. Not that it appears to have done so, to date. His biographers are content to relate Shaw's story.

There must, of course, be another side to it. And there would have been no loss if he had given Mrs. Patterson a *nom d'amour* and so protected the dead woman.

No doubt he wanted to shock the *bourgeoisie*. That seems to be the only rational explanation for his conduct.

And if Jenny Patterson had exhibited an angelic instead of a diabolic temper, would she have escaped calumny? Judging by the case of Florence Farr, who was chaste as ice and pure as snow in that particular regard, if not in her morality, Jenny as an angel of light would have fared no better at Shaw's hands. The easy virtue of poor Florence was similarly betrayed to the world 'to tickle the ears of the groundlings'. And May Morris, similarly, had to have her unhappy married life butchered to make a Shavian holiday, Shaw boasting himself as the cause of the breakdown of the marriage—May taking no steps to deny it.

The conduct of Shaw towards women shows him at his worst and weakest. He had not even the excuse that he was a rake and a libertine at heart, sex-driven like his friend and benefactor, Frank Harris.

II

It was to Frank Harris, under something approaching duress, that Shaw made most candid revelations regarding his 'sex-credo', as Harris called it. And to understand the circumstances fully it is necessary to look closely at this fellow-journalist and fellow-author, and to consider his relations with Shaw.

Now, Harris was by general testimony a bad and unscrupulous man, but he was also a most remarkable one. Famous in his day: Arnold Bennett rated his short-story, *Montes the Matador* as one of the best *contes* in English. He was a controversial critic: his creative and highly-imaginative study called *The Man Shakespeare and His Tragic Life-Story* challenged received opinion and made a sensation on both sides of the Atlantic. Successively he had been editor of the London *Evening News*, the *Fortnightly Review* and the *Saturday Review*, and from these journalistic eminencies had fallen to less respected periodicals.

Reputedly, he was a blackmailer and a swindler. High as was his standing as a writer, he became shunned except in Bohemian circles. Eventually he landed in an English prison, but only in connection with some journalistic indiscretions. Released, he left England for America and carried on a vindictive pro-German campaign during the First World War. Finally he made his home on the Riviera, where, after making some money by a fictionalized and pornographic autobiography, *My Life and Loves*, he died.

It was a piece of characteristic generosity, gratitude and kindness on the part of Bernard Shaw to supply material for Harris's biography of Shaw, for which he deserves nothing but praise. Shaw's task cannot have been easy or pleasant, for Harris, besides being difficult by temperament and anxious to exploit his subject, believed that nothing sold in literature more readily than pornography. He suspected that Shaw's patent puritanism and advertised asceticism were rooted in physical sexual impotence, and he was anxious to proclaim this to the world, as he had formerly proclaimed Shakespeare's supposed or real unbridled sensuality for the 'dark lady', the Maid of Honour, Mary Fitton.

It was in these peculiar circumstances, partly to help Harris and partly to stop his allegations of Shaw's impotence (for Harris had made a similar allegation about Thomas Carlyle) that Shaw made the frank and forthright confessions and explanations in an extant letter to Harris in June, 1930, which Harris printed in a chapter of his Shaw-biography entitled *Shaw's Sex-Credo.*

III

Let us first see what Shaw said, and whether it is or is not substantially true. Let us then see what he did *not* say, but what is apparent from the facts about his known affairs. By considering the whole of this available evidence we are likely to arrive at a just and true verdict upon Shaw in his relations with women.

In an earlier letter to Harris in 1930, Shaw had stated roundly: 'I had no love-affairs. . . . Women got interested in me . . . but there was nothing in it on my side.' Taken literally, that statement of having no love-affairs is neither true nor accurate. But if by no love-affairs is meant no romance of the Romeo and Juliet or the Antony and Cleopatra variety, the world-well-lost for love kind, it is probably true enough.

Four days later Shaw was writing to Harris of 'gallantry'—his euphemism for fornication—'every such adventure that I have enjoyed'. Such ecstasies were, he said, 'irresistibly desired and rapturously executed'. He stoutly claimed normal virility. He denied impotence, homosexuality, and sterility. He asserted that he was 'extremely, though not promiscuously, susceptible'.

He associated sexual intercourse 'not with guilt or delinquency but with delight'. He preferred the initiated female to the virginal. He had scruples, however, about getting women into trouble.

Perfectly continent until the age of twenty-nine when 'an enterprising widow, one of my mother's pupils, appealed successfully to my curiosity'. (This enterprising widow, of course, as he had revealed elsewhere, was Jenny Patterson.) Up to that date, except for 'the involuntary incontinencies of dreamland which were very infrequent' he was perfectly continent.

Except for his very late start at twenty-nine, this story of early amours might be the story of the majority of males in Shaw's day in the temperate Anglo-Saxon climate.

After twenty-nine, until his marriage, 'there was always some kind lady available'. Then comes an assertion which could have many meanings. He continues: 'I tried all the experiments and learned all there was to be learned from them.' The curious reader may ask, 'Does he mean literally what he says? *All* the experiments?' Does this mean all the physical, as well as all the mental, experiments in love?

Knowing Shaw as the Puritan he was, it is probably safer and truer to read this as referring to his flirtations and philanderings, rather than to physical perversities. He says, too, that he 'put everything else before sex', never dreaming of marriage in connection with it (a strange confession this last, indeed). But he liked sexual intercourse for its own sake, 'because of its amazing power of producing a celestial flood of emotion or exaltation of existence'. He was pursued by women and never needed to pursue them, he declared.

He thought sex 'hopeless as a basis for permanent relations'! Without accessory or ancillary relations, sex may well be. Some of his women, he tells us, were 'sexual geniuses unbearable in any other capacity', others did not want sexual intercourse. No two cases, he averred, were alike.

It was for other considerations that both he and his wife married. (This, as we know, was undoubtedly true.) Finally he asserted: 'In permanence and seriousness my consummated love-affairs count for nothing beside the ones that were either unconsummated or ended by discarding that relation.'

Here is the man who wrote only four days earlier, 'I had no love-affairs', talking now of 'my consummated love-affairs and the unconsummated'. Here is, of course, a direct contradiction in terms.

But perhaps the contradiction may be resolved by attending to the last words of his letter to Harris. 'And now no romance; and above all, no pornography.' His *affairs* were not affairs of romantic love: they were affairs of sex. Not that Shaw was absolutely incapable of love in the romantic sense. There can be no doubt that in the cases of Alice Lockett and Stella Beatrice Campbell he was genuinely and sincerely in love, in the real sense of that phrase.

271

But neither love-affair reached consummation and, in each case, for that non-consummation the woman's failure to respond was responsible.

The candour of Shaw may be accepted. Clearly he was less libidinous by nature than the ordinary sensual male. Further, his mode of life, his spartan and spare diet, his intense, cerebral habits of work would militate against sexual excess. By long habit, chastity becomes as much ingrained as any other mode of life. It was a case of

> Nuns fret not in their narrow convent room,
> And hermits are contented in their cells,

as we are told by Wordsworth; and as a generalization the Words-worthian doctrine on the whole may be endorsed, though there are exceptions to the rule, as Heloise and Abelard show. Upon this evidence it may be accepted safely that the heterosexual Shaw was rather under- than over-sexed.

v

But if he was no rake and despised libertinism, Shaw was, as he bragged, 'a born philanderer'. He cast himself for the part of Charteris in his 'unpleasant' play, *The Philanderer*. Again, there is no reason at all to doubt this diagnosis of himself and his recon-struction of the scene between himself and his first mistress.

St. Bernard was also Joey the Clown. He philandered not only because 'it was his nature to', like the dogs that bark and bite in Dr. Isaac Watts's didactic verses for children. He also philandered because that behaviour brought him rich literary material, as it has done many another fiction-writer and man of letters. We have seen the stinging comments of the defeated Bertha Newcombe upon this side of his conduct.

Charlotte Shaw knew this facet of her husband's character well enough. She regarded it with the contempt that King David's wife had for that monarch's dancing before the Ark of the Lord. 'She despised him in her heart.' But Charlotte also knew its essential unimportance, though that knowledge did not prevent her jealousy. Nor was Charlotte the only or the first woman to perceive this trait in Shaw. Edith Nesbit knew and recorded it. Indeed, it was common gossip amongst the Fabian women of his premarital days, and the Webbs even in criticizing excused it, realizing that it was literary exploration akin to their own more austere economic researches into real life rather than books.

Much of this philandering was merely time-consuming, and quite fruitless. Indeed, in his diary, as we know, the young Shaw records his own shame and disgust over his trifling with women to no purpose. But that momentary recognition did not cure him of his self-indulgence—for mere self-indulgence much of it was.

It came easily and naturally to him, as to many Irishmen, and it readily and irresistibly appealed to English women unaccustomed to Irish blarney. He tells us how surprised he was when English women took his flatteries and courtesies and endearments for serious intentions instead of lighthearted attentions. Often he had hastily to reverse his engines.

But as life went on he soon learned to put his philandering to severely practical uses, and to employ it as a means of obtaining first the interest, then the goodwill, and finally the co-operation and services of famous actresses. Through them he hoped, not altogether unreasonably, to obtain production of his plays. Women have always been a power in theatreland, and Shaw's early days in play-writing were the days of actor-managers whose leading-ladies could greatly influence their production of plays.

Shaw's first endeavour in this line began with Florence Far True, when he first met her she was not then a famous actress, r was she associated either with any ruling actor-manager. But Sh thought he saw a real future for this coterie player as an Ibsen actress who might rise to conquer the West End for him. He n e her both his mistress and his pupil. We have seen how and wh ne failed him, though she did not fail to gain a *succès d'estime* tha as some slight fulfilment of his purpose.

A much more ambitious attempt was Shaw's effort to gai llen Terry, and—at first—through her, the head of his professi , Sir

273

Henry Irving. Again Shaw failed; and yet in the very long run he gained a Pyrrhic victory. He secured the famous actress's warm postal friendship; he failed to get her and Irving to play *The Man of Destiny*; and it was not until Ellen Terry had become a grandmother that, after her first instinctive rejection of it, she played in *Captain Brassbound's Conversion*.

At this point, indeed, the tables turned. Ellen was now past her best, and needing parts was reduced to beseeching Shaw to write for her. It was too late in the day, however. From playing Juliet she had been reduced by age to playing the Nurse—a real but inevitable declension—if she was to stay on the stage at all.

Morover, Shaw was now besottedly interested in her younger rival, Mrs. Patrick Campbell, not merely as an actress and not merely postally but personally. The sage, it must be said, does not come out of this pursuit well. But even in this instance, which alone amongst his divagations seriously threatened the viability of the Shaws' marriage, Shaw did not lose sight of the main chance. If he wanted the lady for himself, he equally wanted the actress for his plays.

But Stella at first was far shyer of the playwright than of the man. At first, like Ellen Terry, she saw nothing in his plays for her talents. Even Eliza Higgins, the cockney flower-girl of *Pygmalion*, destined to be one of her greatest successes, did not attract her at first, and it took a great deal of cajolery to induce her to take the part.

Shaw, in love in his fifties with his Stella, cuts a ridiculous figure, acutely realized that fact, and left to himself would never have published their correspondence. He never did publish his doggerel verses to her, for the excellent reason that they are, as he must have recognized in his saner moments, too poor and too revealing. Shaw was no poet and his verses were as feeble as those of Charles Dickens. Two of these effusions called *Taste* and *Cock Robin* have come into my hands, the first I think never having been published before. The reader may judge their quality for himself.

There are some twenty lines of verse in *Taste* and most people would think the verses both vulgar and in execrable taste. However, there is this to be said: that they were probably intended for the eye of the lady referred to in them alone and not for publication at all. They are mildly erotic to a degree that would scarcely shock the present generation.

To show their quality one need do no more than instance a single line of this composition:

'Oh God' (he cried) 'take off that gown: resume your silk chemise.'

The lady obeyed this injunction if the versifier's account is to be believed. They were on kissing terms at least. The gown in question was a dressing gown; and it will be realized that the verses show the degree of intimacy between the two persons concerned.

Cock Robin is even poorer in quality than *Taste*. For example: 'Who kissed her toes? Who d'you suppose? And also her nose?' Extraordinary to the ears of his worshippers, it was this great master of letters who, besotted by a temporary infatuation in his middle-fifties, composed these utterly trivial, vulgar and seemingly juvenile verses. Again the excuse must be that they were intended for nothing more than the private eye of their heroine Mrs. Campbell and her tolerant amusement, provided by that small side of G.B.S. that was Joey the Clown.

What will surprise many of Shaw's readers, accustomed as they are to the generally Puritanical nature of his writings, is the declension from his ancient wisdom and strict control in these compositions. Like the poet Roscommon in Charles the Second's day, generally speaking Shaw can 'boast unspotted bays'. He was fundamentally too serious—even as a jester—to indulge in erotic literary antics generally.

One description of himself in their piece of rhyming as 'Stella's true friend, world without end', cries loudly for comment. When Stella, towards the end of her life, fell on evil days, and was financially embarrassed and miserable, she turned for aid to this true friend and found herself unwelcome. Yet Shaw was in general (and a hundred instances might be given to prove it) a staunch and generous friend.

Generally speaking, Shaw has been fortunate in the so-different biographical works by Henderson, Ervine, Pearson, Winsten, Harris and others. They are accorded the tribute of well-deserved notice, quotation, and appreciative identification in this book. Classics in their field, they are indispensable to those interested in Shaw's work or personality.

It is not their fault if they omit, or insufficiently stress, the importance in Shaw's development of the Lockett episode. When such letters as survive or any substantial part of them, on both sides, are published this importance will be manifest, though many readers may find the petty disputing rather dull.

But how hardly, slowly, reluctantly, even grudgingly does knowledge unroll her ample page, as Gray knew. Sometimes it seems as if those who hold the keys are as unwilling as the Anglican episcopate to unlock the prophetess Joanna Southcott's once-celebrated box of religious secrets.

It is staggering to reflect that the Alice Lockett episode happened some eighty years ago, and that so little of the existent knowledge of it has yet been made available to the generality.

VI

Shaw realized and regretted that he was no poet. He said he could think of no rhyme for Stella but 'umbrella', 'and only too damn well I love Mrs. Campbell', and horrors of that sort.

More excruciating even than his verses was Shaw's change of attitude when this beggar attained horseback in later years, and his erstwhile princess had become beggar-maid to sue him as once he had sued her for favours. The letters during the last years of their correspondence make painful reading, and may be contrasted with his later letters to Ellen Terry. Ellen in her decline was in exactly the same plight as Stella Beatrice Campbell in later life, but Shaw still retained some chivalry and consideration for Ellen. It may be argued that the sweet-natured Ellen was the more deserving of the two and had never humiliated or rebuffed him, but the governing principle in human relations is surely that put by Shakespeare in the mouth of Hamlet: 'The less they deserve the more merit is in your bounty.'

The pattern of Shaw's behaviour towards beautiful and talented actresses is remarkably consistent. At the back of what he genuinely felt by way of appreciation, admiration and affection was the settled determination to make capital for himself out of them and his relations with them. We need not be too censorious over this fact. What he was trying to do was both human and natural. It does show clearly that if he was both saint and sage in some respects, in others he was no more elevated in his aims than the vulgar, practical person with an eye to the main chance.

VII

All this posing, posturing and philandering forces one to point out the gulf between Shaw's preachings and his practice. This early Ibsenist was, in respect of his personal relations with women, a fine example of the adjuration: 'Do as I say, not as I do.' Like the tired warrior—Shaw was often the tired mental warrior—he regarded love as mere recreation and refreshment, utterly unserious and not to be mistaken for the serious purposes of life. He regarded women as a mere plaything to be flattered, caressed and as unceremoniously left as his hero Conolly in *The Irrational Knot* left his Eleanor. In theory and in his writings Shaw repudiated such ideas with contempt and was an ardent feminist, proclaiming the equality, if not the actual superiority, of women. Intellectually, he did not see the destiny of women as being houris in Paradise for the delectation of males. But in practical life and in private conversation when he dropped his pose Shaw was no feminist.

This inconsistency and contradictoriness in Shaw need not detain us. It was a feature of his intellectual and emotional make-up which he himself recognized as inherent. If he had been the simple, consistent, all-in-one-piece character that he, in order to create a public image, often reported himself as being, instead of the extraordinarily complex, kaleidoscopic and baffling character that he in fact was, he would be much less interesting than we find him. In a word, he would not have been George Bernard Shaw at all.

He said quite often that he saw no reason why a man might not love two women at the same time. But, as usual, with women brought up in a monogamous society, neither Charlotte nor Stella encouraged that idea. Though he proclaimed himself, over Stella, 'a mere predatory creature seeking my prey', his appetite for her would not allow him to be late for dinner with Charlotte. And when she foiled, by flight, his attempt to seduce her, and unforgivably humiliated him, he returned to married sexlessness with Charlotte, to that lady's great relief—and no doubt to his own—giving up intimacies he had childishly described as, 'Such quaint comforts and happinesses, and close-togethernesses, and babes in the woodinesses.' Like Pegeen Mike in Synge's play, Stella had lost for ever her Playboy of the Western World. And not only for ever but also completely, for though their correspondence continued it is plain that he was no longer her lover, and scarcely to be described even as a friend; rather, indeed, an old acquaintance turned cold as charity and censorious as hypocrisy.

Professor Archibald Henderson, Shaw's 'official' biographer, who knew him personally over long years, and whose loyal admiration and continuous labours for his fame were unbounded, is forced to admit that 'the emotional upheaval is a far from edifying spectacle as it reveals Shaw on his weakest side'. The Webbs, whose sincere friendship for him was lifelong, like the St. John Ervines' affection, detested the Circe and sympathized with the wife. But in his fifties Shaw was certainly not senile in this aberration, or anything else. It is more probable that his foiled attempts to kick over the marital traces were a manifestation of his rebellion against the dull, dreary and unnatural union with Charlotte.

Perhaps he would have been wiser to have kept Charlotte as a woman-friend rather than as a nominal wife. For Shaw was capable of true friendship with women, as his relationships with such diverse women as Lady Astor and the Abbess of Stanbrook clearly showed.

VIII

As is natural and inevitable, Shaw's interest in women waned with the years. At sixty-six, writing to Beatrice Webb, he says: 'I grow old apace. . . . I have lost all differentiated interest in women and am bored by their redoubled interest in me. Probably I ought to die.' But even in his seventies, he strongly cherished the old idea that women eagerly pursued him, and still later, after his Charlotte's death, he thought of himself as still a great catch in the marriage-market at ninety. Indeed at over eighty-eight—a year after Charlotte's death, he told the American actress, Molly Tompkins, that he had had 'some offers of marriage since, having only a few years (quite probably a few days) to live, and my widow would be well provided for'. He added: 'But I have had enough of marriage and I am quite happy alone. I inherit from my mother a great capacity for solitude in my own company.'

He told her, too—what we have seen him confiding to other friends—that Charlotte's death was 'an unspeakable relief'.

Ten months later, he had Molly proposing to leave America to come and live with him. As we have seen at this terrifying prospect he at once became his own trenchant self.

At this advanced age, Shaw had, at long last, given up his long-cherished ideas of his personal attractiveness. Constantly he spoke of himself as a half-dead, and ghostly spectre, unfit to be seen. Constantly now he told friends of both sexes that he could no longer be of use or interest to them, and urged them to drop his acquaintance and seek younger friends. Yet he never refused to be photographed and would send copies to his feminine friends even at ninety-three.

Old habits die hard. He who had been an inveterate philanderer in his thirties remained something of the male amorist—but only on paper—as a nonagenarian. He was wise to keep it on paper, for any approach to a reality would have been too horrible for endurance—and he knew it!

IX

If Bernard Shaw were to be brought to judgment—and he would have acquiesced in that, for he believed that all men's lives and selves ought to be judged as fervently as any fundamentalist Christian contemplating the Last Day for the Quick and the Dead —the Indictment brought against him would contain a far heavier charge against him in relation to womanhood. What would he plead to the Indictment in the case of the Life Force versus George Bernard Shaw?

Guilty or Not Guilty? So far as is known, Shaw never entered a plea of guilty, and therefore perhaps a plea of Not Guilty should be entered on the record. The charge is one of high—the highest possible—treason: treason against no earthly state or monarch, but treason against the governor of the whole universe, against his worshipped Life Force itself.

For nothing is more certain than this truth: that the main purpose of Life is to create life and yet more life: to ensure the continuance of every living species. Who, of his contemporaries, saw that more clearly, knew it better, proclaimed it more constantly and emphatically—in words—than Bernard Shaw? And he claimed and doubtless claimed sincerely that he had been a good and faithful servant of the divinity within him, that he deserved the accolade, 'Well done', and that he had never buried 'that one talent which is death to hide' in the napkin, but that he had used it in the unremitting service of his fellow-men for World-Betterment?

But the Devil's Advocate, prosecuting him in the name of the Life-Force, might assert that his marriage was a blasphemy, a mockery of the real thing, and reproach him and his Charlotte with the unborn. That indeed is the gravamen of the charge here: the deliberate and wilful denial of parentage-in-action by one who consistently preached production as the first essential duty of mankind.

Professor Henderson has an arresting phrase of extenuation in this connection. His chapter, *Joey and Stella* in one of his books,

George Bernard Shaw: Man of the Century, speaks of Shaw's 'anguished regret for the enforced sacrifice of parenthood'. But where is any evidence whatever of that anguished regret? Nowhere, so far as my search goes, in any of Shaw's published writings. It may be (though Henderson nowhere says so) that G.B.S. expressed himself verbally to that effect to his biographer and friend. But so far as is known, during its continuance, Shaw defended his barren marriage-which-was-no-marriage, and only publicly recognized its unreal character after Charlotte's death, probably out of a cowardly but understandable consideration for her feelings.

Hesketh Pearson, one of his two later-day Boswells, the other being Stephen Winsten, tells us that on the question of possible parentage, Shaw said: 'If we had had children, Charlotte would certainly have quarrelled with me over them and would have been jealous. Besides, she would never have allowed anything like that.'

This was not the only occasion when Shaw expressed this view. On the very day that his wife died, Eleanor O'Connell had asked him whether he was not sorry now that he had no children.

He blamed Charlotte, who always set her face against that, and went on:

'She had a feeling against children, but sometimes I have been sorry that I was not more insistent on the point . . .' It was then that he went on to say, 'I don't think I ought ever to have been married: I am not the marrying sort.'

But these fleeting and casual recognitions of the error of a supine acquiescence in a repudiation of physical reproduction are a very different thing from any 'anguished regret for the enforced sacrifice of parenthood', of which Professor Henderson speaks.

Impartial critics of the Shaw nullity of marriage will reflect that ninety-nine husbands in a hundred would have overcome Charlotte's resistance in the initial stage of the union, that Shaw, capable of sexual intercourse, as he boasted himself of being with other and perhaps more attractive women, must have been entirely destitute of physical desire where this particular woman was concerned. That is a phenomenon not unknown in suits for nullity in the Divorce Courts.

Nor is it possible to avoid the reflection that if Mrs. Patrick Campbell at the time of Shaw's infatuation for her had genuinely shared that infatuation and had demanded marriage as the price of the surrender, the Shaw marriage might have crashed in a divorce-decree of nullity on the ground of non-consummation.

But who would not agree with Milton that the spiritual side of marriage, the mutual help and comfort, is more important than the physical side—especially in later life? That part of the Shaw marriage was, by general testimony, ideal.

To the tragedy of the Shaws' barren marriage, the inevitable comedic anti-climax, which haunted Shaw's father and Shaw himself, came after the great man's death. Never was bathos more absurd.

Eleven years or so after Shaw's death, certain newspapers were 'featuring' the alleged claims of a woman to 'Immaculate Conception' of a babe-Messiah, on the classic lines of the familiar gospel story. She had given herself a 'spiritual divorce' from her earthly husband and had become the 'spiritual bride' of the dead G.B.S., who was said to be the father of the expected infant. There had been an Angel of the Annunciation to foretell this miraculous babe. He told it's expectant mother that 'she would bear a son who was coming to stop the world from blowing its top'. The child was to be called Jayser.

This parody of the Christian nativity, which to Christians might appear both blasphemous and shocking, went further. Patricia was both a clairvoyant and clairaudient. The dead Shaw was not only producing a child by her, he was also dictating plays to her, one of them 'undoubtedly the best drama Shaw has ever written'.

In addition, Shakespeare was coming through—by the help of Shaw—and fresh dramas by him were being written down by this remarkable medium.

Apparently this spiritual bride did not claim to be a virgin, since she had three other children already, and her husband remained with her and, according to the newspaper reports, accepted her claims.

Quite seriously and factually this strange rubbish was reported in the newspapers at considerable length. Of course, it made no impact on the public mind whatever, for it died its death at the end of the day like so many journalistic sensations, and it lies happily buried and forgotten in the newspaper files.

If George Bernard Shaw could return from the undiscovered country from whose bourne no traveller returns—in spite of countless asseverations to the contrary and of the Ghost in Hamlet, Shakespeare's words still hold good—he might smile at this *post mortem* instance of the Shavian comedic anti-climax that so persistently and wryly haunted his father and himself on their earthly pilgrimage.

THE END

INDEX

❋❋❋❋❋❋❋❋❋❋❋❋❋❋❋❋❋❋❋❋❋❋❋❋❋❋❋❋❋❋❋❋❋❋❋❋